SPEAKING TO THE STARS

SPEAKING TO THE STARS

An Introduction to Astrosophy

*A New Star Wisdom developed by Willi Sucher
from the insights of Rudolf Steiner*

Jonathan Hilton

2023
Lindisfarne Books
SteinerBooks / Anthroposophic Press, Inc.
834 Main Street, PO Box 358
Spencertown, New York 12165
www.steinerbooks.org

Copyright © 2023 by Jonathan Hilton. All rights reserved. No part of this publication may be reproduced, stored in a retrieval system, or transmitted, in any form or by any means, electronic, mechanical, photocopying, recording, or otherwise, without the prior written permission of the publisher.

The text is adapted from edited transcripts of a video course given by Jonathan Hilton in 2019–20
(available at astrosophy.com)

Book design: by W. M. Jensen

Library of Congress Control Number: 2023931006

ISBN: 978-1-58420-885-3 (paperback)
ISBN: 978-1-58420-886-0 (eBook)

Contents

	About this Book	vii
	Biography of Willi Sucher	x
	Introduction to Astrosophy	xxv
1.	Cosmic Intelligences and the Three Fundamentals	1
2.	The Zodiac	7
3.	The Planetary Spheres	34
4.	Christ and the Stars	76
5.	Charts Construction	107
6.	Heliocentric Astrosophy	142
7.	The Future Lemniscate Perspective	166
	Appendix I: Selected Quotations by Rudolf Steiner on the Stars	181
	Appendix II: Suggested Reading by Rudolf Steiner	235
	Appendix III: Willi Sucher's Books Indexed by Subject	240
	Appendix IV: Willi Sucher's Books Indexed by Title	255
	Appendix V: Books by Willi Sucher	267

This book is dedicated to the pioneers
of a new star wisdom out of anthroposophy:

Dr. Elisabeth Vreede and Willi Sucher
with his colleagues
Hazel Straker and Veronica Moyer

Special Thanks to Darlys Turner of the Astrosophy
Research Center for her decades of devotion
to preserving and publishing the
work of Willi Sucher

About this Book

This book is composed of the transcripts from an online video course given by Jonathan Hilton in 2019 and 2020. The text has been edited to adapt it from the spoken word to written form for better reading. Little has been changed so that readers may also follow the book with the video course. For this reason, the video sessions corresponding to sections of the book are indicated in the text. Other astrosophy resources are also included in the book in the introduction and the appendices.

About Jonathan Hilton

When I met Willi Sucher and began to study his work, it was clear I had come across a profound area of research out of anthroposophy, which was his life task. Over the years, I began to see that this great work was perhaps in danger of being lost and forgotten in its true purity and integrity. Out of this, I made an inner vow to Willi, then deceased, to insure that his work would be preserved and made available and accessible to those incarnating souls who seek it. I tried to maintain his work through study and teaching and serving on the Board of the Astrosophy Research Center, which published his work until my retirement in 2016, which then allowed me time to establish my website and social media platforms to make his work available in a more active way. The video course arose out of questions from those who encountered his work but were challenged in how to navigate the books in some sequential way to aid their understanding. The course began with a requested zoom course in November 2018 on how to construct a birth chart through astrosophy. From that beginning, the complete current video course arose in order to lay the foundations for how to understand the stars in a new way, as well as to offer a basic study overview of Willi Sucher's work.

I am especially grateful to Darlys Turner, who helped to establish the Astrosophy Research Center after his death in 1985 in Meadow Vista, CA where Willi lived. Willi had approved and supported the formation of the Center before his death. Darlys offered her home as a place for research and a Center for publishing Willi's work and to hold all of his archives. Over the years, her work has made possible the availability of his research through the Center's publication of his articles, lectures and other writings in various books (see list of publications at the end of this book).

◊

I would like to share with you a little bit of the story of my encounter with Willi Sucher, who was the pioneer of this new star wisdom founded and developed from the research and profound insights of Rudolf Steiner. About 42 years ago, when I was in my twenties in the late 1970s, I had been reading Steiner's works for a few years when I met Willi Sucher. I was at a weekend workshop in California, in which he presented amazing pictures of the new relationship of the human being to the stars. Willi was already in his seventies by then and had been developing this work for many, many years. Although I had no interest or background in astrology, wasn't really much of a scientist or interested in astronomy, the pictures he presented concerning the nature of the human being and our relationship to the cosmos of the stars really grabbed hold of something inside of me, and I wanted to know more. So, I wrote Willi a letter and requested the opportunity to come and study with him personally, and he accepted. The following summer, 1978, I went to California and to his home, and for one month we worked every day, all day, except Sundays, with him teaching me about this new star wisdom, astrosophy, and the work he had developed.

At night, I was in my room doing long hand calculations. This was the late seventies, long before internet technology, so all the calculations around the birth charts and historical charts had to be worked out in detail, and his rule was always do the math once and then do it again to double check, because the mathematical accuracy is key to getting a true picture.

This was a profound experience of my life and I've carried this star wisdom ever since that time. Willi and I stayed in touch and communicated by letter often, or I would come, when I could, to conferences he continued to give until his death in 1985.

Biography of Willi Sucher

For those readers new to the work of Willi Sucher (1902–1985), we begin with a short biography as an introduction to the life and work of this pioneer in the spiritual science of astrosophy. The content of the books assumes a familiarity with the work of Rudolf Steiner, for it is entirely on the foundation of Anthroposophy that Sucher's research is based. Therefore, a study of the basic works of Steiner is recommended in order to fully enter into the content presented here.

At the beginning of this century, Rudolf Steiner (1861–1925) began to speak of a new way of knowing spiritual realities, which he called Anthroposophy, wisdom reborn through the human being. Until his death, he brought to humanity the means for renewal through the cultivation of a modern spiritual science applied to a wide range of practical spheres of life, including education, medicine, agriculture, the arts, and social forms. Behind these areas of applied Anthroposophy stands an all-embracing wisdom of the relation of the human being to the cosmic world in the past, present, and future. Many individuals experienced Rudolf Steiner and were inspired to take up one area to develop as a life task.

One of these individuals was Willi Sucher, who as a young man heard Steiner speak. Sucher was especially inspired by Steiner's Vision of the new growing relationship of the human being to the cosmic world, that of co-creator with the divine beings. Steiner called for this relationship to become more and more of a reality, and Sucher picked up the challenge and devoted his life to the task of developing a new wisdom of the stars, astrosophy, that would recognize this new role of the human being in Earth evolution.

Biography of Willi Sucher

Willi Sucher was born on August 21, 1902, in the southern German town of Karlsruhe to a young bookkeeper and his wife. His earliest memories were of the death of his mother when he was four. This great loss marked the beginning of a childhood in which he experienced himself as the unwanted stepchild. His father soon remarried, and Sucher's new stepmother was, as he would later describe her, "just fiercely against my very existence." He was rejected and mistreated during these years, until at age thirteen he was sent to live with his uncle's family when his father was called up to serve in the military during World War I. Though his uncle, Karl Sucher, was kind, Willi Sucher was an extra mouth to feed in a large family that was suffering under the economic hardships of the war, and so after a year he was sent to live with relatives of his mother on a small farm in a nearby town. Life there was very strenuous. The family worked late into the night in the fields, so Sucher was responsible for tending the house and cooking for the others after a full day at school. He would later characterize his childhood as always being "just one too many," but he saw in this a positive force in his life that served to build inner strength and perseverance in the face of hardship.

In 1918, at the age of sixteen, Sucher decided to make himself independent. He saw that his original hope of becoming an architect was impossible due to his financial circumstances, so he applied to become an apprentice in a bank. He was accepted and began the two-and-a-half-year training. He did not like it, but he would continue in this profession for twenty-one years. He often pointed out how through this work he learned rigorous attention to details and accuracy in calculation. This mathematical training would serve him well later in his real life's work. In 1919, Sucher came into contact with the ideas of Rudolf Steiner. His uncle Karl, with whom he had kept in touch, had heard Steiner lecture and spoke to him about him. He recognized immediately that these ideas would become his path in life and soon applied for membership in the Anthroposophical Society, However, he was told he must wait another year until he was eighteen. His uncle Karl also spoke with him about astrology, expressing his concern about its unsuitability for modern humanity. Sucher recalled one such conversation in which his uncle spoke of how important it would be that someday an anthroposophist would bring new light to the entire field of astrology through the insights of spiritual science. His response was, "Why should we wait? Can't we do it ourselves?" He was eighteen years old, the time of his first Moon node return. He then began to read the literature on astrology in an effort to understand it, only to turn away from it time and again, repelled by its determinism, which he felt degraded the true dignity of the human being.

He continued also his study of Anthroposophy, attending lectures when possible and reading. In 1922, he became inspired by Steiner's ideas on the Threefold Social Order and moved to Stuttgart to join a small bank, Bankhaus Der Kommende Tag, which was connected with several businesses trying to put these ideas into practice. On one occasion Rudolf Steiner visited the bank and was introduced to all who were working there. Willi Sucher was deeply impressed by this personal encounter and with the way Steiner so fully entered their situation. It was typical of him that, when asked whether he had ever requested a private interview with Steiner, he replied that he had never felt his personal questions should take up the precious time of such a busy man. However, due to the increasing economic difficulties of those times, the bank was forced to close. Sucher then took a position in a bank in Bruchsal, Germany.

Through a friend Willi Sucher met his future wife, Helen, who lived with her parents in Stuttgart and was also attending the lectures of Rudolf Steiner. They both joined the newly formed Christian Community and were married in 1927 by Dr. Friedrich Rittelmeyer, the founder of The Christian Community and a leading Lutheran theologian in Germany at the time. Sucher was working and living in Bruchsal with some anthroposophists, and Helen was living with her parents in Stuttgart, so he would visit her on weekends by train. They were soon able to get their own place and, in 1927, moved into a small two-room apartment with a kitchen but no bathroom. Sucher would return home from his work at the bank and put in two hours of study in the evenings. On weekends, for recreation, they would hike in the Black Forest.

The year 1927 was a significant year in Willi Sucher's life, not only due to his marriage, but for another reason as well. He came across the report of a lecture given by Dr. Elisabeth Vreede, the head of the Mathematical-Astronomical Section of the School for Spiritual Science at the Goetheanum in Dornach, Switzerland, where the Anthroposophical Society was centered. (Dr. Vreede had first met Rudolf Steiner in 1903, when she was a member of the Theosophical Society. She became one among the groups of individuals who worked with Steiner in developing the Anthroposophical Society, moving with him from Berlin to Dornach in 1917 to help build the first Goetheanum. She was an original member of the Vorstand of the Society and was appointed head of the Mathematical-Astronomical Section by Steiner.) In this lecture, Dr. Vreede refers to remarks by Steiner about the configurations of the heavens at the time of the passing over of a human being into the spiritual world at death. Looking back at this moment forty-two years later, Willi Sucher wrote:

> This picture struck home like lightning. Here arose a perspective that no longer depicted the human being as a helpless object of the rhythms and movements of the stars. It was the soul of man that meant something for the stars; they were even waiting for what he had to bring them as the fruits of his Earth-experiences. A ray of hope that seemed to shed light on man's quest for spiritual freedom fell on the complex of astrology. Subsequent researches—just on the basis of the mathematics of planetary rhythms—fully confirmed that hope. Indeed, the biographical rhythms of a great number of historic personalities proved to coincide perfectly with the configurations of the heavens at the moment of their passing over. The experience that man was not only a creature but was on the road to becoming a cooperator even with the cosmos shaped itself increasingly. This gave hope that similar constructive views might eventually be found with regard to man's association with the stars at the moment of his incarnation. Later discoveries proved that this was no vain hope.

Now his studies took on an ever-deepening intensity. At that time he was studying the biography of Tolstoy. He worked out the configurations of the heavens at the time of Tolstoy's death and after careful deliberations sent this star picture, along with some very tentative suggestions, to Dr. Vreede in Dornach. She responded, as Willi Sucher would later say, "very positively" and invited him to Dornach the week after Easter 1928. Sucher was then twenty-five years old. Dr. Vreede, as part of her task as leader of the Mathematical-Astronomical Section at that time, was giving lectures and courses, and between 1927 and 1930, she published forty-two letters on the theme "Astronomy and Anthroposophy" (revised and published in book form in 1980 by the Philosophisch-Anthroposophischer Verlag at the Goetheanum). Her research found an eager pupil in Sucher, and this became the starting point for a working relationship that would develop over the next ten years, during which Dr. Vreede gave him encouragement and challenges to further develop the work she had begun. He often described how Dr. Vreede would send him a statement by Steiner on something about the relation of the human being to the cosmos with the command, "I cannot do it. You must do it!" Sucher would then work out astronomically-mathematically his understanding of these indications and send them back to Dornach. As he later wrote, "It was Dr. Elisabeth Vreede who suggested that I investigate the connections of the human being with the prenatal star events—i.e., during the embryonic development. She advised me to employ for this purpose the ancient Hermetic Rule—originating in Ancient Egypt."

Willi Sucher often traveled to Dornach during these years and in 1931, at 29 years of age, he was invited to lecture at the Goetheanum and later at the Anthroposophical Clinic in Arlesheim. In 1934–35, Dr. Vreede, on behalf of the Mathematical-Astronomical Section, published a series of Astrologische Betrachtungen ("Astrological Studies"), written by Sucher, except for the first one, in which she wrote:

> The following studies are meant to inform the reader about the investigations of our coworker Willi Sucher, as he has developed them in conjunction with the Mathematical-Astronomical Section for some years now. Willi Sucher's point of departure has not

been traditional astrology—which was known to him—but Rudolf Steiner's spiritual science, especially Rudolf Steiner's suggestions concerning the realm of astrology.

As Willi Sucher's work continued, conditions in Germany were becoming increasingly difficult with Hitler's rise to power. He and his wife realized they would not be able to continue their work in this environment. His correspondence with Dr. Vreede had been intercepted, and astrologers in Germany were being arrested. Anthroposophists had to meet secretly in small groups. Sucher later spoke of the need for secrecy during these times and described how he and Helen would go into the kitchen, fill the sink, and place a pot over the drain, in order to speak about things that should not be overheard by neighbors who might report them. In 1936, Sucher was again in Dornach visiting Dr. Vreede, after her expulsion from the Vorstand along with her colleague Ita Wegman and other original members. It was through her efforts after this visit that he was invited in 1937 to lecture in Holland and then in England at the Rudolf Steiner House in London, where George Adams translated his lectures. During this visit to England, Willi and Helen Sucher actively looked for opportunities to leave Germany. He spoke with his friend Eugen Kolisko, who introduced him to Fried Geuter, the co-founder of Sunfield Home, an anthroposophic home for handicapped children in Clent. Geuter said, "Mr. Sucher, come to us and I shall build you an observatory!" So on their return to Germany, the application process for a visa was begun. Their intention to emigrate had to remain a secret, except for a few close friends within the Anthroposophical Society. After several months, just after Easter 1938, the necessary papers were obtained, and the Suchers left their homeland for England on what was officially considered a "visit," with only twenty Marks and a few personal belongings. They would not return to live in Germany again. Willi Sucher was thirty-five years old.

After twenty years of working in banks, Sucher was plunged into working in a nursery with severely handicapped children, while Helen worked in the kitchen. The language was also new. Fried Geuter exhorted his teacher there in the nursery, "Teach him in English, but scold him in German!" Here Sucher gathered the clinical experience that he would later unite with Steiner's indications—to develop the idea that a dedicated staff, working with a deep knowledge of a child's star configuration, could effect healing. In describing such work, he said, "Often we would work deep into the night, and the next day the child was a different being." Of this time he also said, "So you see, it really was an 'observatory'...of the cosmic influences on human destiny!"

In 1938, Willi Sucher was able to meet once again with Dr. Vreede at a conference held in Bangor, Wales, near Penmaenmawr. He described how he and Dr. Vreede climbed a hill behind Penmaenmawr to two Druid stone circles: "So we took leave of one another at least for the time being, in the proximity of witnesses to an age-old star wisdom and with a deep feeling of responsibility for its future." This was the last time Sucher saw Dr. Vreede. Her last years were lonely ones. On account of the war she was cut off from her friends in Holland, England, and Germany. The death of Ita Wegman, her close friend and colleague, in 1943 came as a great shock. Just two months later she fell ill and moved to southern Switzerland in the hope that the warmer climate there would help improve her condition. But this was to no avail, and at 4:45 p.m. on the afternoon of August 31, 1943, she breathed her last breath, having lived a rich life dedicated to Rudolf Steiner and Anthroposophy.

Due to the war there was much concern in Great Britain that there were enemy informers among the many refugees. Thus, all German and Austrian men and some women were rounded up as "enemy aliens" to be interned in detention camps around the British Isles until their motives could be investigated. Anticipating this, Willi Sucher packed a small case with his most precious tables for working out star positions and other aids he needed to carry on his research. In those days modern ephemeredes, computers, and calculators were not available; all had to be worked out using special tables that were not easily obtainable. Thus when the police came for him and some others working at the home, he was fully prepared. Before they were taken away, all of the coworkers stood in a big circle and sang a song that had become a leading motif for the aim of their work with the children, "In the Quest of the Holy Grail," to bid them farewell. They were first taken to a kind of clearing house at a military barracks at Worcester, then on to a place near Liverpool. While his personal belongings were being searched for possible subversive material, the first man in their group told the inspectors that they had come from a home for children that had had an outbreak of scarlet fever, which was true. Because of this, their group was taken to an isolation unit, and their belongings were sent with them without being inspected. Thus Willi Sucher's research materials were spared. The group was later transferred to a camp on the Isle of Man, in the Irish Sea, formerly a holiday resort with various hotels that had been taken over and surrounded with barbed wire. Here several anthroposophists found themselves interned together—Dr. Ernst Lehrs and Dr. Karl König, the founder of Camphill, among others. Sucher would later describe this time as a most fruitful period of research. For 18 months, these individuals were given time to hold a kind of "super college," as he called it. They had long conversations about their studies and research and practiced giving talks to each other. All of their material needs were provided, and they were left free to organize their daily lives within the compound. They could go out and work on farms, which Sucher tried but found too strenuous.

Since he was a medical doctor, Dr. König was released first in January 1942, and he secured Willi Sucher's release by inviting him to come to work at his home for children in Aberdeen, Scotland. Sucher was joined by Helen, who had remained at Sunfield, and he carried on his researches while helping to care for the children. He also started to write a "Monthly Letter" for a number of subscribers and also to give lectures. It was at one of these lectures, given on a return visit to Sunfield Home in Clent, that Hazel Straker first met him. She describes this meeting in the following way:

> I have very vivid memories of him coming to lecture at Sunfield where I had come to work just after his internment. I remember this modest man, immaculately dressed, walking up and down in front of us, telling in a sure but quiet and pictorial way about his researches into the gestures of the stars during the three years that

Christ worked on Earth. It was about the gestures of Mercury, its meetings with the Sun, and their relationship to the seven signs or miracles described in the Gospel of St John. The pictures he painted in the air have remained with me, growing as a reality that means much to me still, having become intimately related to daily life. On another occasion he spoke of the cycle of the year, and from that I carry the certainty of the "living being of the Sun." The depth of his disciplined research work shone through, radiating confidence, which left one totally free.

Later, in 1944, when Willi and Helen Sucher returned to Sunfield, Hazel Straker came to work more and more closely with him and his research. In 1946, at the request of Eleanor Merry and Maria Schindler, Willi and Helen moved to London for a short time and taught evening classes. In 1947, Dr. Alfred Heidenreich, the founder of the Christian Community in Britain, instigated an invitation to Garvald, a curative home in Scotland, where Willi Sucher became the director for a short time. Here Hazel Straker joined them as a coworker. At Garvald, Willi came into conflict with one of the coworkers on account of his "astrological" work with the children, so they left when Dr. Heidenreich invited them to work at Albrighton Hall, a center for Christian Community conferences, near Shrewsbury.

This time, Sucher wrote, "was one of the most positive and creative periods of my life. Dr. Heidenreich gave me absolute freedom to develop my work." Here the English manuscript of *Isis Sophia*, published in 1951, was prepared (it had already been published in Germany), as well as *Man and the Stars*, the second Isis Sophia series, published in 1952. Also during these years the "family" of coworkers was formed. Willi and Helen Sucher had no children, but coworkers came who would give lifelong support to the work. They joined together in research and practical life. In addition to Hazel Straker, Helen Veronica Moyer and her sister, the artist Maria Schindler, came together in this work. They cared for the conference house and assisted in the star work, allowing Sucher time for research besides lecturing at conferences there and traveling to meet increasing requests to speak to other groups in England, Scotland, and Holland. During this time the work on the starry background of the Greek, Norse, and Celtic mythologies was done, much research into historic periods and personalities was conducted, and the very new areas of heliocentric and lemniscatory views of the universe were explored.

In 1953, the conference house closed for financial reasons, and the group moved to Larkfield Hall, a curative home in Kent, England, where they were able to build a small house through the help of a devoted friend. Because of his lecturing commitments, Willi Sucher did not have time to work with the children, but his coworkers did, and they would sit together with Sucher and work over the children's incarnation charts. This work was described by Hazel Straker:

> This was not just a horoscope, the stars at the moment of birth, but a picture of the gestures of the stars during the nine months' preparation for birth, the embryonic development. Dr. Vreede had introduced this, and following her request, Willi had done much further research. This meticulous, painstaking work that he had carried out over the last years showed rich fruits as he led us through the starry events to the great imaginations behind, which were able to inspire us in a very helpful way for our further work with the individual children. Here too the recurrences of gestures connected with the deeds of Christ during the three years that He worked on Earth were an integral part of our considerations. Although I had already committed myself to this work, it became ever clearer that here was a great potential for true healing.

In 1955, Willi Sucher was invited to America to lecture at the Threefold Farm anthroposophical community in Spring Valley, New York. During this first trip to the U.S., he gave 70 lectures or workshops in his 19 week stay, which included a visit to Los Angeles to teach a course in the teacher training program at the Highland Hall Waldorf School. This California connection would play a significant role in his later destiny. On returning to England, Sucher began to work on the book *Drama of the Universe*. The two previous books, *Isis Sophia* and *Man and the Stars*, had been written from the geocentric (Earth-centered) perspective. Now his researches into the heliocentric perspective had progressed to the stage of putting them into this book.

It was a big task, with much of the work of preparing it for publication being done by Hazel Straker and Veronica Moyer. It was published in 1958, and to celebrate they all decided to take a holiday. Helen had always wanted to see palm trees, so they decided to make a journey to Egypt. But as plans were being finalized, Sucher suggested, "Why go east, why not go west to America?" So the family of coworkers journeyed across America, from Montreal to Denver, through Salt Lake City, on to Los Angeles. Here Helen saw her palm trees, and it was here that she decided they would stay. The persistent requests to come and join the work at the Highland Hall School and to begin a much-needed school for curative education were another reason to move to California, so they decided to immigrate. They returned to England, sold their home, and in 1961—through the generosity of a friend—this group of four founded the Landvidi Center for Exceptional Children in Los Angeles, which operated under their guidance for seven years.

During these years Sucher gave many lectures and courses in other parts of the States, as well as returning to Europe to lecture in England, Holland, Switzerland, and Germany. With the closing of the school in 1968, the Sucher's searched for an area in which to retire. Many places were considered, including some in England and Canada, but eventually their choice was Meadow Vista, a small town on the lower slopes of the Sierra Mountains not far from Sacramento. Now there was more time to devote to writing and research. Willi Sucher also continued his traveling lecture activities, besides holding courses and study groups in his home. During this time an increasing stream of individuals came seeking help in their lives, and his work with the profound pictures given in the birth and prenatal asterograms brought light onto the destiny path of those who sought him out. It was during this time that Cosmic Christianity (1970) and The Changing Countenance of Cosmology (1971) were published. Both of these books, of which this volume is composed, are the content of a series of parallel morning and evening workshops taught by Willi in August 1969 at Hawkwood College in England, which he later wrote down for publication. He later wrote about the research published in Cosmic Christianity:

Finally, I must mention the research work that I did about the Christ Events. I came more and more to the impression that these cosmic perspectives of the Christ Events are a foundation for the experience of the workings of the Christ Impulse in times after the so-called Mystery of Golgotha. It turned out that whenever one of the cosmic events during Christ's ministry repeats itself, then there is offered the opportunity to understand and even to realize in an inner spiritual sense the significance of the corresponding Deed of Christ. As I said, these possibilities are "offered" to the human being. He can freely accept them and identify eventually with them.

He also continued to write the monthly *Star Journal* (1965–75) to subscribers. In the November 1970 letter, he wrote of his life work since first reading the article by Dr. Vreede:

It is now forty-two years since this lightning storm happened, and ever since I have been enabled to carry on this research. Sometimes external circumstances were difficult, but there seemed always to be a helping hand in the background, which often arranged things forcefully in order to facilitate the work. As I said before, the road was never easy; suspicion and distrust acted as forceful breaks. One can fully understand this if one views the grave dangers that beset the road right and left toward a new, constructive astrology. Human egotism is all too easily inclined to misuse this knowledge in ignorance and dilettantism. All throughout the years the shining beacon of Rudolf Steiner's wisdom was an unceasing encouragement and also consolation when distrust led to direct attack. There is, particularly, one passage in Rudolf Steiner's lecture cycle *Christ and the Spiritual World* [Dec. 28, 1913 to Jan. 2, 1914] that I would like to quote: "It became clearer and clearer to me, as the outcome of many years of research, that in our epoch there is really something like a resurrection of the astrology of the third epoch [the Egypto-Chaldean civilizations], but permeated with the Christ Impulse. Today we must search among the stars in a way different from the old ways, but the stellar script must once more become something that speaks to us" [lecture 5, Jan. 1, 1914].

On such foundations the work was carried forward. Eventually other friends joined in as best they could. The guiding beacon was an unceasing sense of responsibility to lay the groundwork for an astrology that clearly and scientifically recognized man's connection with the stars and yet fully respected the domain of his spiritual freedom and dignity. Thus things gradually shaped themselves.

In 1972, at seventy years of age, Sucher was invited by a group of young people to lecture at the International Youth Conference at the Goetheanum in Dornach, where he had given his very first lecture forty-one years earlier at the encouragement of Dr. Vreede. Though the lecture invitations increased and the breadth and depth of Sucher's work grew, it was a great sorrow to him that so few people actively took up the development of astrosophy. He saw the great need to draw from the potentials it contained for humanity to face the oncoming trials at the turn of the century in a positive and constructive way. It was this concern for the future of his fellow human beings that enabled him to overcome his natural reserve and speak out of his convictions. He always said that, for himself, living only in the world of research would have been sufficiently satisfying. In the following years, publication would be limited to the ongoing "Monthly Letters" to subscribers. A portion of these letters (1972–74) would be published as Willi Sucher's final book, *Practical Approach toward a New Astrosophy*. It is in this work that he brought forth his many years of research—first indicated in *Drama of the Universe*—on a spiritual approach to a heliocentric astrology.

This was a revolutionary incision into the world of astrology, which opened the way for a spiritual-scientific understanding of the heliocentric Copernican perspective of the universe. The development of this work was a monumental addition to our understanding of the relation of the human being, and indeed of all of Earth evolution, to the heliocentric universe. As he later wrote concerning this:

> Another perspective that I was able to work out in great detail over the years was the connection of the human being with the world of the stars from the heliocentric astronomical viewpoint. Some people are still strongly opposed to the heliocentric approach. However, Rudolf Steiner pointed out in the lecture cycle *The Relationship of Earthly Man to the Sun*, lecture 4, Jan. 11, 1924, that this

perspective is correct, although it has come to be a reality through a great mistake or failure in evolution. In the research that I undertook in this direction, it turned out that the heliocentric approach does not cut out the geocentric completely. Rather it proved to be a kind of complementary relationship. The study of the very slow movements of the so-called "elements" of the planetary orbits—i.e., nodes and apsides (perihelion and aphelion)—turned out to be extremely helpful in historic research and also in the relationship of the individual to the world of the stars.

In 1973, Hazel Straker was called back to England to tend to her mother, bringing to a close the twenty-five years of working together with the "family" of colleagues. For a time publishing activities were no longer possible, but distribution of the books by mail was maintained by Veronica Helen Moyer, the fourth member of the little group who emigrated to America with the Suchers. Two years later, Willi Sucher's wife died quite suddenly. In spite of this, he carried through a lecturing commitment in the East shortly thereafter. He then gradually curtailed his travels and focused on teaching closer to home. Veronica cared for the house and continued helping with the star work. Now, toward the end of his life, he came to accept that his work had not been in vain but that he had managed to lay firm foundations, which would be built on in the future. For the next ten years, Willi Sucher's home became a center of activity. He was encouraged as people separately and in study groups came to learn of the work. Countless individuals seeking guidance streamed to his home. Quietly listening to each one, he never addressed the tangled web of personal crisis, but rather lifted one's gaze to the cosmos, gently offering pictures of the great, objective Christ Events to shine like rays of light on the path of destiny.

During his workshops at this time, Sucher repeatedly referred to Steiner's lecture of October 10, 1919, "Cosmogony, Freedom, and Altruism," in which Steiner outlined the tasks for different parts of the world and pointed to the imperative need for a new cosmogony to arise in America. Sucher recognized the importance of this work for Americans to awaken, in a realistic way, to their citizenship in the cosmos. Fittingly, he gave his last lecture, at eighty-two, just two months before his death, to the American Studies class at Rudolf Steiner College in Fair Oaks, California, where he often taught. It was on the Christ Events in relation to the founding of America in 1776.

Willi Sucher died peacefully in his sleep on May 21, 1985, receiving visitors until that night. Before his death, together with a small group of friends, he established the Astrosophy Research Center in Meadow Vista, to care for his publications, personal papers, and library after his death. Space was promised in a nearby house where, as of this publishing, this material is being cared for and is available to anyone wishing to conduct research. Obviously, all personal charts were returned or destroyed, but there is much historical material, medical research, and notes on many other aspects of his far-reaching work. As one of his students later wrote:

> Willi Sucher brought a powerful new impulse toward restoring our knowledge of the stars to a level of mystery wisdom. Most important of all, he opened up the way to a new moral consciousness—one that acknowledges the significance of Christ—in what concerns the profound relationships prevailing between the cosmos, the Earth, and humanity.

Today, scattered here and there around the world, a small but dedicated group of people has devoted themselves to cultivating Sucher's work, to helping astrosophy live as a spiritual impulse in our time.

Late in his life, he wrote:

> Thus, I can finally only say that I was given by destiny great opportunities of discovering and working out new creative perspectives of the human being's connection with the stars [i.e., a new "astrosophy"]. I am most grateful for these opportunities. However, the great question for me was always, how can I bring this wisdom to the knowledge of humanity? The answer to this question was never easy, all during my fifty-two years of working in this field. But there is hope that this work will be carried into the future and find more and more possibilities of practical and spiritual application in civilization.

Introduction to Astrosophy

Astrosophy, or Star (*Astro*) Wisdom (*Sophia*), is the spiritual-scientific understanding of our new and enhanced relationship to the world of the stars. Rudolf Steiner spoke of the visible stars as the physical manifestation of a complex and exalted world of spiritual beings who, in the past, helped to shape and guide humanity in its evolution. In ancient times, we were far more conscious of these spiritual beings and their guidance as can be seen in the pantheon of gods described in many ancient religions. As part of the greater divine plan for humanity, this awareness of the guiding beings was gradually lost as we became more conscious of the material world of the senses and less aware of the world of spiritual beings. As is described in an image from Norse Mythology, the "Bifrost Bridge" was destroyed; thus the direct bridge to the spiritual world that humans at one time "crossed" in their earlier awareness was no longer there. Our path to becoming human required that our gaze be turned more toward the Earth as our primary focus in order to fully develop Self-consciousness and Self-determination.

During this gradual descent into earthly consciousness, human beings were not left totally without guidance. Mystery schools and temples were maintained in which select pupils were specially trained and led on a path of initiation. Some of these mystery traditions can be seen in the ancient cultures of Persia, Egypt, and Greece, for example. In very early times, the "Kings" were all also initiates and therefore were able to lead their people out of a knowledge of the world of the gods. These initiates were able to understand the heavenly beings who revealed themselves through the movements of the stars in order to guide them. Thus they had a knowledge of the time-rhythms of the planetary spheres within the fixed stars, as the "speech," so to speak, of the heavenly beings guiding humanity. This knowledge extended not only to matters concerning daily life, but also to the greater processes of ages of time. With this understanding, the initiates could know the timing of important future happenings. For example the three Magi (or Kings) who went to Bethlehem were such Initiates who knew that the child born there was the incarnation of a great initiate who would also become the bearer of the Christ.

This once direct and grand star wisdom (astrosophy) was gradually replaced with a more mathematical and mechanical star knowledge, bereft of direct vision, which became what we know as astrology (*astro*=star, *logy*=logic). As human individuality become more ego-centric, star knowledge shifted from awareness of the larger forces at work in the world and the guidance of humanity to a more personal focus on the individual destiny. Out of this, the personal astrology chart came into being. The ability to reach "behind" the angular relationships and planetary rhythms to the beings that these reflected was lost as humanity descended further toward a purely sense-bound science. The use of the personal asterogram as a tool to forecast personal destiny contained only a dim memory of the great truths behind the relation of the stars to human destiny.

Yet the great paradox is that the loss of direct spiritual perception of the gods was necessary in evolution so that human beings could fulfill their great task in world evolution. According to Rudolf Steiner, this task is that we become beings of freedom and of love that is born out of that freedom. This means that the experience of separation from the divine, unique to humanity among all beings, has the possibility, not the predetermination, to establish something new in the cosmos: a rank of beings who freely choose to participate with the divine plan out of the love born from that freedom. To learn this, humanity must traverse a long evolutionary path that descends into isolation and separation from the world of the spirit and then they must struggle to find their own way back, in freedom, to a relationship with the gods. Like the great stories of heroes, such as the tale of Parsival, each human being must leave "home" (the world of union with the gods), become lost and adrift, and out of their own striving find again a new relationship to the world of spirit. The great words of John the Baptist in the New Testament, rightly translated, express this human condition already experienced by some at the time of Christ: "I am the voice of one crying in the aloneness [spiritual wilderness]."

The core of what was revealed by Rudolf Steiner is knowledge of the turning point in world evolution that would give human beings the power to find their own renewed, free relationship to the divine world and, in this freedom, learn the true meaning of love. This turning point was the world-changing event of the deed of Christ: His death and resurrection. In that deed, Christ united with the Earth and with humanity, imparting the power to find our way back to the divine world. Within this context, Steiner addressed the need for a new "Christianized" cosmology. What does this mean? During the time that Christ walked on the Earth, He performed many deeds of which we only begin to glimpse the full meaning. These deeds were not only earthly "miracles," but they were also archetypal deeds that brought new meaning to the cosmological rhythms, thus giving birth to a new relationship of the human being to the cosmos. This relationship is new because humanity will then not be children led by a "father" but will, rather, be conscious partners with the gods. Christ came to be the brother of humanity, and through His deeds each human being is capable of becoming a brother/sister to the gods. This new relationship to the divine is not one ruled from above by the law, but one that has come through truth and grace. Therefore the new astrology is not one that seeks answers and guidance from the stars for what we should do; but rather it is one in which we learn to give back to the world of the stars the gifts that humanity has to offer in order to create the new cosmos, the "New Jerusalem" described in the book of Revelation in the New Testament. Christ's deeds, as seen in relation to the starry movements, serve as models for us. The ground-breaking work of Willi Sucher, in his life's work of building the understanding of the deeds of Christ in relation to the movements of the stars, can serve as a foundation for the greater work of creating a new Astrosophy: a star wisdom in which "we" speak to the stars, uniting consciously with the Christ Will at work in the cosmos in order to fulfill our evolutionary task as independent, self-transformed, self-conscious individuals.

Based on our own karma from the past, as we descend through the planetary spheres to a new Earth life, we gather into our being all that we will need in a new life, which includes all of the challenges and obstacles we must face in order to grow. Once here on Earth, though external events may seem to compel us, we can inwardly choose how we meet those events as spiritual human beings in order to use them fruitfully for our own higher calling and for the greater human community. We also have the freedom to go our own way and not listen to the inner voice guiding us through the wilderness.

Steiner's researches into the spiritual world have been the basis for many scientists, artists, and scholars of all kinds to take up their work in a new way. Willi Sucher (1902–1985) was just a young man of seventeen when he asked his uncle about the value of astrology, to which his uncle replied, "Oh, we'll have to wait for something to come out of this anthroposophy." "Why wait?" asked Sucher, who then immediately devoted himself to the study of astronomy and anthroposophy.

He became friends with Dr. Elizabeth Vreede (1879–1943), whom Steiner chose to be the first leader of the Mathematical-Astronomical Section of the School for Spiritual Science in Dornach, Switzerland, at the Goetheanum. She recognized the quality of Sucher's researches and invited him to speak there; and in her later years, asked him to continue with her monthly articles. In time, Sucher developed a comprehensive astrosophy, which has as its foundation the archetypes implanted in the rhythms of the planetary spheres in their movements through the zodiac by the life and resurrection of Christ Jesus.

Using his vast reservoir of knowledge, gained from both anthroposophy and his spiritual research into both ancient and modern star events, Willi Sucher developed a new astrosophy. As a deep student of the Bible, of history, of philosophy, and of the biographies of historical individuals, he conducted research into the star configurations for the birth, life, and death of many individuals: What were their gifts? What did they contribute to the stars? What can we learn from them? During his life, Sucher gave countless lectures and wrote a number of books and monthly letters that were later collected into books. He did this to help all of us; knowing that if we choose, we can respond fruitfully in our individual way to impulses from the cosmos.

In order to serve this new Astrosophy, all of Willi Sucher's published materials are available as free downloads on this website: astrosophy.com.

Stars once spoke to humanity
It is world destiny that they are silent now
To be aware of this silence can be pain for
earthly humanity
But in the deepening silence
There grows and ripens what humans speak
to the stars
To become aware of this speaking
Can become strength for Atman (Spirit Man)

—Rudolf Steiner

I

Cosmic Intelligences and the Three Fundamentals

Cosmic Intelligence[*]

One could go into this verse in depth over a long period of time, but I think you get the idea of this picture of the evolution of consciousness when we—and I say "we" because "we" existed then also—were at one time in a kind of union with the beings of the world of the stars. Our consciousness was such that we participated with the consciousness of the cosmos. The gods and beings who were captured in the great mythologies and sagas were reality to us in those times, because we had not yet lost touch with this primeval relationship with the world of the gods.

This period of time, which is captured by this verse, is also captured in the ancient Indian cultural wisdom, in the Vedas, and in their description of the great time periods called the Yugas. The Yuga we have just come out of was called the Kali Yuga, which began in 3101 BC and ended 5,000 years later, in 1899.

We will go into that a little bit later, but now we'll just get an overview feeling for the change of consciousness. We can look back to around 3000 BC as really the beginning of the kind of consciousness that began to calculate the movements of the stars. The Chaldeans and Babylonians began to measure time, began to create systems, writing began, tablets were used to record things. Beginning in about 3000 BC, this is the progression of humanity's descent of consciousness into a particular kind of relationship to the physical material world.

---
[*] See video: Introducing Astrosophy: Session 2.

This has continued through these many thousands of years (we won't go into the whole time frame or the various cultures that evolved), but the idea is that this was a time, as well as earlier, when stars "spoke to humanity." Humanity was childlike in a way, in that it was guided by the wisdom of the stars in everything from planting and sowing to how to measure, how to have festivals, all aspects of human life. Over time, as the verse says, the stars became silent. This was a time when humanity began to hear the gods less and less with instinctual clairvoyance and, more and more, to calculate the planetary bodies we see in space—seeing the stars and planets as objects, though still infused with spiritual being. Different systems were developed that were more focused on the physical appearance of the stars and the planets, and the wisdom of what was behind these stars and planets gradually faded away.

For those who are sensitive to that, as the verse says, this silence "can be pain for Earth humanity." Human beings experience a sense of alienation, or disconnection, from the greater universe. But then the verse goes on to state that "in the deepening silence there grows and ripens what we now speak to the stars." This is the source from which astrosophy arises, because we are at a time in our evolution (with the end of Kali Yuga) when the materialistic view of the planets and the stars and the zodiac should now come to an end. Rudolf Steiner once spoke about how, at the end of Kali Yuga, we entered a new light age, and that a tidal wave of spiritual light and knowledge is now available to us.

So, a new star wisdom is addressing where we are now, when it's time for us to become conscious again—not as earlier humanity was conscious, not in the way of myths or a kind of passive receptivity to the stars, but through active thinking. This means that, through the conscious development of new faculties of consciousness, we can begin to perceive and see through the veil of matter and, once again, reach an awareness of the beings behind what we now know only in an astronomical and mathematical way.

Let us think about consciousness. You know, in everyday life—I think most people would agree, and it's even been shown scientifically—that we are limited in our ability to hear the full spectrum of sound; we are limited in our ability to see the full spectrum of light; we are limited in our capacity to perceive the full spectrum of color. We are aware on many levels that there are experiences and perceptions that remain beyond the capability of our senses. So, we can also think in terms of consciousness. Our present consciousness—which is governed by our sense experience and the thinking associated with it—is bound, so to speak, but there are also other levels of consciousness, for which we must develop our capacity to access.

Now, when we speak of consciousness, we must speak of *being*, because only "beings" have consciousness. So, when we speak of beings and consciousness, we are referring to "intelligences." In fact, the gods were once called the Cosmic Intelligences.

I will not quote much from Rudolf Steiner, because I think it's better just to share what I've experienced and learned, as well as what Willi Sucher has presented. But I would like, in this introductory chapter, to offer some quotations form Steiner that I think are helpful in our understanding of the new star wisdom. This can be a way for us, in a conscious, ego-present way, to begin with our expanded intelligence to communicate with the beings of the stars and planets, the cosmic intelligences.

> For these ancients knew that the Gods alone knew the secrets of the stellar world: the Gods, or as they were called later, the Cosmic Intelligences. The Cosmic Intelligences know the secret of the stellar world, and they alone can tell it. Therefore, the student had to follow the path of cognition that leads to an understanding intercourse with the Cosmic Intelligences. The real true Astrology depended upon a human attaining this possibility of understanding the Cosmic Intelligences.... Everything that in ancient times was Astrology was the result of intercourse with the Cosmic Intelligences.
>
> What is Intelligence? These abstract generalizations do not of course exist in reality. "Intelligence" means the mutual relationships of conduct among the higher Hierarchies. What they do, how they relate themselves to one another, what they are to one another— this is the Cosmic Intelligence. (Rudolf Steiner, *Mystery Centres*, lect. 13; *Karmic Relationships,* vol. 3, lect. 11)

When we begin in this course to look at the beings of the constellations, and particularly the beings of the planetary realms that include the movements, the interrelationships of the planets, one could say we are engaging with the Cosmic Intelligences. The intelligences of these planetary spheres, all representing different levels of consciousness, commune, communicate, relate to each other. The true astrosophy, of which we are only at the very beginning, would be when the human being is able to join in that communication, to know the communication of these planetary beings.

From Willi Sucher:

> Rudolf Steiner speaks frequently about how the path of spiritual cognition/knowledge begins with wonder and reverence. To approach astrosophy, one must cultivate this sense of reverence. But what is reverence? One cannot really revere a planet or sign. Why? Because these are not the complete story. They are only representations of something behind which is more real and more complete. And that something behind is "being." For one can really only revere or have reverence for a being. So, when we begin a study of astrosophy...we also begin a path of knowledge to know beings, the beings who stand behind and are the reality of the symbols and objects we can perceive.

Three Fundamentals*

We began with the understanding of Cosmic Intelligences. When in 2018 I did the first astrosophy online course, I reached out to people who had been reading my articles on Facebook and asked, "What do you want to learn in a course?" Many people were interested and involved in astrology and trying to find a new way into a deeper, more meaningful astrology. In my own biography, when I first came to this star wisdom, I actually had no background in astrology, nor an interest in astrology, no interest in astronomy, so in a funny way at that time it seemed odd that this would take hold of me as an area of study. I did not come to this work from an astrological background

---

* Video, Introducing Astrosophy: Session 3.

(I had, of course, familiarized myself with it through years of study), though many people come to astrosophy through questions surrounding astrology and how it can be renewed in some way.

So, the question to which most people wanted an answer was: "How do I do charts through astrosophy?" I was reluctant at first to start out with the complex work of charts, because, as you can see from this introduction, it's not just a matter of doing calculations and reading the aspects. It's also a matter of getting to know the beings, the intelligences of the planetary realms and stars. Then, through that path of knowledge, gaining an understanding of the chart or understanding an event, or how communication with the intelligences can, perhaps, be achieved.

One must be clear that the study of astrosophy is also a path of knowledge, or cognition. Following is one quote to make this point a little clearer. It speaks of something that I find personally very moving, and I think anyone who has a meditative practice might be familiar with this experience.

> One must never speculate about the spiritual world in research, never invent anything, but only make the preparations for enabling something to reveal itself from the spiritual world. Anyone who believes he can force the spiritual world to reveal this or that to him will be very greatly mistaken; nothing but errors will come of it. Preparation must be made for what one may hope to receive out of the spiritual world more or less by grace. (Rudolf Steiner, *Karmic Relationships,* vol. 8, lect. 7)

So, for astrosophy we have these very fundamental points that are necessary. One is about the evolution of human consciousness and the other about the path of knowledge, or spiritual cognition, in order to get to know the beings who stand behind the so-called physical bodies.

There is also an additional, third element that is integral to a new star wisdom: understanding karma and reincarnation. This is because, when we look at an incarnation chart and when we study the relationship of the human being to the stars, we will look into the journey of the human being—not just the moment of incarnation on the Earth, but also the long journey preceding birth when, as Wordsworth describes it, "We descend trailing clouds of glory from where we have come." One must understand this long process before the moment of birth, as well as the process after death, of the soul and spirit expanding and returning to these worlds of being. What this all entails and how we relate to these planetary spheres and the world of the stars is the great work of understanding the stars and the complete human biography.

There is one other area that we will go into more as we get into the section on constructing the chart. I think many of those who understand astrology and work with astrology are already familiar with the fact that *aspects* are central to astrological interpretation. Aspects represent the angular relationships among planets. There's the sextile, the square, the quintile, the opposition, the conjunction, and so on. They show varying angular degrees that have a certain meanings. In these angular relationships, you can visualize a kind of spatial picture of the angles between bodies in space. But in astrosophy, because we are living with planetary spheres instead of only bodies in space, we look more at the cycles of time and rhythms among the planets, and we will go into this in great detail. We will come to see that it's really these planetary rhythms, in the realm of time, that reveal the life of the planetary spheres, opening the door for us to more fully understand the consciousness or being of these realms.

So, we will begin with the zodiac, or better to say, the zodiacs.

2

The Zodiac

THE TROPICAL ZODIAC AND THE VERNAL POINT*

Let's look at the zodiac, or actually the zodiacs, plural. Perhaps most people are aware of their Sun sign. Everyone talks about it—"I'm an Aries" "I'm a Taurus" "I'm a Scorpio." This is based on traditional astrology, in which most people note that their Sun is in a particular sign of the zodiac. But what does this mean?

Let's look first at what is used in most traditional astrology. Of course, there are now many different approaches in astrology, particularly sidereal astrology, which have other perspectives. We will get into that, but I would like to preface this by saying that our perspective comes out of a Western star-wisdom tradition and history beginning around 3000 BC. There are, of course, many ancient star maps, for example from the Chinese and from the Vedic Indian astrology. These mythologies and zodiacs are really from a time prior to the kind of conscious development of humanity that began in Chaldea, from which our own astrology arose. So, we won't address the ancient Eastern perspectives, since they belong to a quite different consciousness and tradition.

Let's begin with the traditional zodiac of astrology, which is called the "tropical" zodiac. This great circle of the twelve begins with the sign of Aries at the start of spring and moves on to Taurus, Gemini, Cancer, Leo, Virgo, Libra, Scorpio, Sagittarius, Capricorn, and Aquarius, culminating in Pisces.

Our world of space, the biosphere in which we live, is defined, one could say, by the number four—the four elements, the four compass

---

* Video: Introducing Astrosophy: Session 4.

points, etc. The twelvefold zodiac, one could say, consists of four trinitized, or three times four, and it has this element of space on a higher level. The fixed stars of the zodiac always remain in the same relationship to one another. They do move, but very, very gradually and not enough for us to notice that movement. So, this kind of holding presence of the twelve, the zodiac, is a kind of spiritualized space.

The tropical zodiac is not really determined by the actual stars. This touches on the whole evolution of consciousness, which we talked about elsewhere and will explore again later. The tropical zodiac is "tropical," meaning related to the tropics that determine our seasons, thus it is related to the movement of the Sun and its journey through the year in relation to the Earth. The tropical zodiac is determined by the seasons. The sign of Aries begins with the Sun crossing the spring Equinox point on March 21st. From there, the signs are measured 30° each around the Sun's path, with autumn Equinox being 180° opposite, marking the start of the sign of Libra. The tropical zodiac is really not related to the stars themselves. It is simply a division—30° for each sign—based on the vernal equinox as starting point. However, there was a time when the tropical zodiac was related to the stars. This was when this tropical zodiac received its definition and names, which was during ancient Greek times. In those Greek times, this zodiac was defined by the spring point, the vernal equinox, and had a relationship to the stars. Yet now it does not have that relationship to the stars, the actual stars of the twelve constellations of the zodiac. What does that mean?

This vernal equinox point is an intersection point in the heavens. It's an actual calculable point defined by the Earth. It is the point where two planes, two cosmic planes, intersect each other. We all know that the Earth tilts at an angle. The line of the North pole and South pole is angled. We are not perpendicular to the zodiac but we tilt at a 23° angle. So, because of that, you can imagine this great circle of the zodiac around and the Earth in the middle, at least from the way that we're looking at it geocentrically (we can't go into Copernicanism here). From this perspective of astrology, the Earth is in the center of this great belt of the zodiac that is the apparent path of the Sun. It is the road that the Sun travels in one year. This belt has as center the tilted Earth. The Earth also has a belt, which is our equator and which is tilted to the plane of the zodiac, which is called the ecliptic plane. The equator of the Earth, if you would extend that plane out, would cross the zodiac in two points, one in spring and one in fall. So, this extended equator is called the celestial equator and it intersects the ecliptic plane of the Sun's path at these two points.

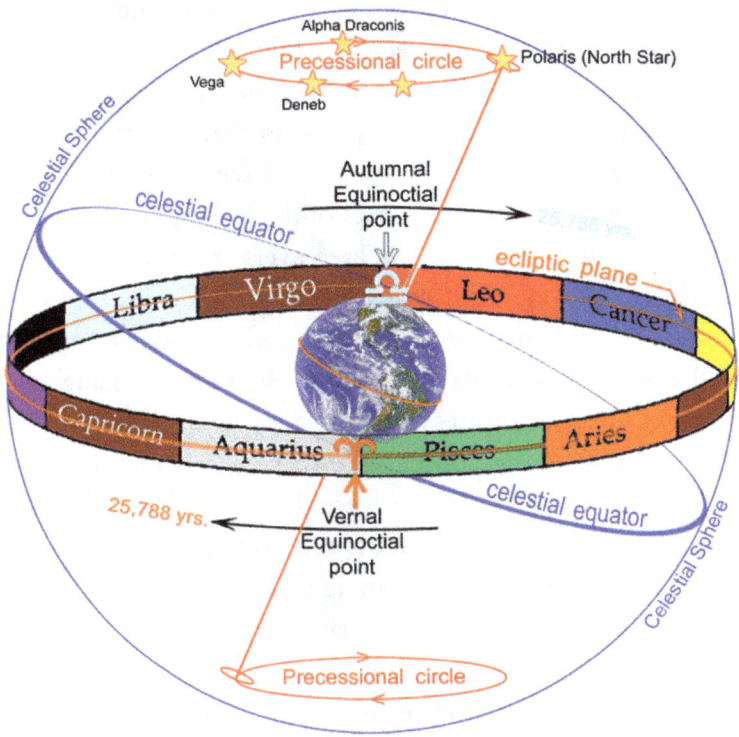

During the ancient Greek period, the spring point, this intersection point of the celestial equator and the ecliptic plane, was at the beginning of the stars of Aries, the Ram. But this point, which we might know from high school astronomy (or maybe grammar school today), doesn't remain in one position but moves. You can imagine it if you were to picture the spin of a top and notice how the spinning top begins to slow down and you can see the wobble of the top. So, on a cosmic scale the pole of our Earth is also making this wobble, once around a full circle, creating a kind of little cone in the North, in the sky. This wobble causes the whole intersection point of the equator and the Sun path to shift. This intersection point of the vernal equinox then moves slowly backward along the ecliptic plane, so that the spring point moves in relationship to the actual twelve stars of the zodiac, which do not move. It moves at a rate of 1 degree every 72 years. Now this is all wonderful when you get into numbers and there's a relationship between this 72-year movement of the vernal point and the human lifespan, as well as the human heartbeat, which averages 72 beats per minute. These are great cosmic relationships between the human being and the macrocosm of the cosmos (but that's for another time). Thus, this vernal point moves backward 1 degree every 72 years, so that in reality, when your Sun is in the sign of Aries today, you would see behind the Sun in the sky not the stars of Aries but the stars of the Fishes, Pisces.

This vernal point, moving 1 degree every 72 years, can be multiplied by the 30° in one sign, which gives us 2,160 years for the vernal point to move through each constellation. This is essentially the time of a cultural epoch. Part of Rudolf Steiner's amazing work on the evolution of consciousness and the ages of cultures that evolved on the Earth shows how you can see these changing ages and their relation to the movement of the vernal point through the stars of the zodiac, from the Ancient Indian age, to the Chaldean and Egyptian age into the Greek and Roman age, into our modern age and of course the next age, the age of Aquarius.

This means that this vernal point at the time of Ancient India was in the Crab, in Ancient Persia in the Twins, in Egypt and Chaldea it was in the Bull; at the time of the Greeks and the Romans it passed through the stars of the Ram; in our time, this so called modern age, it's passing through the stars of the Fishes, and it will move into the stars of the Waterman, Aquarius, in the future.

This relationship of the vernal point to the constellations is deeply significant for a kind of major evolutionary, cultural time frame, during which humanity has a certain task directed from this region of the constellations. Once we get into the meaning of the constellations, we will be able to make some sense of what the age of Pisces or the age of Aquarius really means.

So, that's just a brief explanation of the distinction between the tropical zodiac, the traditional zodiac of astrology, and the actual stars of the zodiac. I know you will probably be terribly disappointed to find out that you are really a Pisces and not an Aries, but we have to let go of the superficial and dive into the deep. We will get into that a bit later. I think you'll find it much more exciting to explore all of this in a more complex way.

The Sidereal Zodiacs and the Houses*

We have the tropical zodiac, which you could say is a seasonal zodiac. It's basically defined by the relationship between the Sun and the Earth, this weaving relationship of life through the seasons.

The tropical zodiac from one perspective you could say is really the life zodiac. This other zodiac of the constellations, the twelve groups of fixed stars that don't move, don't wobble, don't have any change, are the world of what Rudolf Steiner described as "duration," or eternity. Those stars would comprise what is called the sidereal (or star) zodiac.

We can then look at a little variation with this sidereal zodiac. I bring this up because there is a whole movement in sidereal astrology now, which has to do with working with the constellations. There is a sidereal astrology and sidereal zodiac in which the constellations are also equal to 30°. This has its origins in the Babylonian times, the Chaldean and Babylonian times, when the early days of astronomy and astrology evolved. This equal sidereal zodiac is created from what was observed and understood by the Babylonians.

Now, again, let's return to the concept of the evolution of consciousness. It wasn't that everyone was out there calculating, with everyone looking up and seeing the stars and figuring things out. Rather, there were the so-called mystery schools—temples in which pupils were trained in secret and put through a particular kind of training that would lead them to a kind of initiation, a kind of awakening of their spiritual capacities.

---

*   Video: Introducing Astrosophy: Session 5.

It was those initiates who were the guides of humanity. In ancient times, the kings were all initiates and the priests were initiates, and in those times initiates were the ones who could read the stars. So, these stars, out of which the zodiac was determined, weren't solely a mathematical observational calculation, but arose out of a deep understanding of the nature of the zodiac from a spiritual perspective.

This zodiac was based on four of the brighter stars in the heavens that we can all see. These stars were called the four "Royal Stars," the "gatekeepers of the sky," or the "guardians of the sky."

There was Aldebaran, which is the star called the "Bull's eye," the "eye of Taurus," the "eye of the Bull." This star marked the vernal point during the Chaldean times. Aldebaran was the watcher of the East, the spring. And over in the constellation of the Lion was the star Regulus, which was the gatekeeper of the North, the summer point. And opposite Aldebaran was the star Antares, the heart of the Scorpion and gatekeeper of the West. And the star opposite Regulus—Fomalhaut—is a fish receiving into its mouth the water being poured out of an urn by the waterman, Aquarius.

These four stars were the foundation. Here again, you have the four in space, the basis for the Babylonian zodiac. Each sign, then, was defined as 15° on either side of these four Royal Stars, and the sidereal zodiac was marked off in that way. So, they remained 30 equal degrees, based on these four cardinal stars.

We now have the tropical zodiac based on the vernal point. We have the sidereal zodiac from Babylon/Chaldea, based on the four cardinal stars. However, we also have the astrology of the constellations that form the modern zodiac, which astronomy recognizes and is called the unequal sidereal zodiac, or the astronomical zodiac, because by actually observing the constellations we can see that they are not all the same size.

Now we move through this evolution of consciousness to modern science, which is now based purely on scientific observation; looking up at the stars demarcates those configurations that were defined originally by the ancients—the Lion (Leo), Virgo (the Virgin), and so on—and calculates the size of these constellations. This was formalized

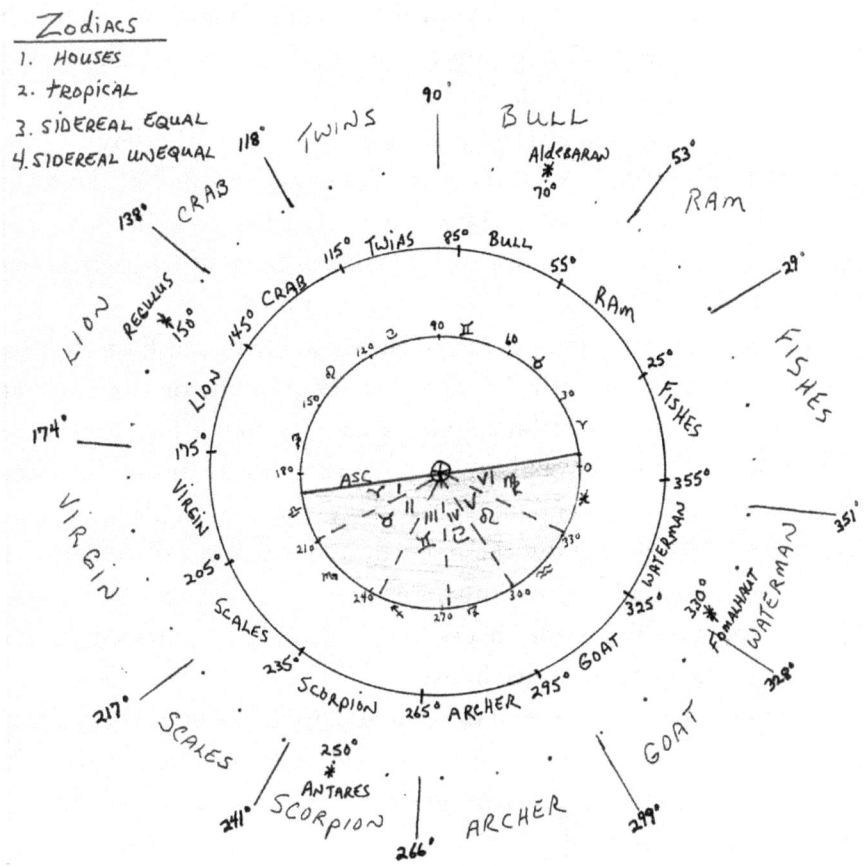

in 1928 by the International Astronomers Union (IAU) as the sizes of the constellations. So, these unequal sidereal constellations are really the actual constellations that we would perceive in our modern way of defining them.

Willi Sucher and Elizabeth Vreede worked with these unequal constellations. It was his belief and his experience that, if we are truly going to break through the materialism of the modern age and the thinking of the modern age into a true spiritual perspective, we can't ignore what the scientific community has represented with the constellations, but must look through and go beyond that.

We have three zodiacs: the tropical zodiac and the Babylonian equal sidereal zodiac, as well as the unequal modern astronomical sidereal zodiac, which forms the basis of astrosophy as developed by Willi Sucher.

We also have a fourth zodiac, which I will only mention here but not go into in detail. This is, you could say, the zodiac of the houses. Although the houses are designated by numbers—the first, second, third houses and on around to the twelfth house, they also have a kind of relationship to the zodiac. The first house is the house of the Ram, Aries, the second house is the Taurus house, and so on. This zodiac is not based on the seasons or on the stars, but is based on the Earth, the physical Earth, and defined by the moment of birth.

This is so because the house zodiac begins with the Eastern horizon at the moment of birth. Thus, if we were standing on the Earth at the moment of someone's birth and looked out to the East along the plane of the horizon, we could see the stars coming up at that moment, which is called the Ascendant in astrology and astrosophy, and this marks the first house. Now there are different schools of thought in houses, but essentially the Ascendant is the indicator for the first house of the Ram, and then it goes below the horizon and up around, creating the segments of the twelve houses.

So here we have a picture of the four zodiacs. The work that we'll be doing here will focus more on the unequal sidereal zodiac, and will touch somewhat on the tropical zodiac. But when we think of the descent of birth through the stars, the heavens, and the movements of the planets in relation to the zodiac, we will work with this unequal sidereal zodiac.

The Zodiac Symbols: Aries – Gemini[*]

We will now add some meaning to some of the things we dealt with in the Charts Course, which was basically technical sessions on how to construct a chart. Of course, there was also an introduction to astrosophy and we went a bit into the meaning, some of the deeper spiritual questions around astrosophy and around the various charts we explored.[**] However, we did not really go into the meaning of the planets and the zodiac as a process of beginning to help us in eventually interpreting what the events in the chart mean. For example,

---

[*] Video: Course 1: The Zodiacs, Session 1.
[**] Video: Course 4: Charts Course

what does it mean when Jupiter stands in Scorpio? What does it mean with Mars in Aries the Ram?

I would like to begin by exploring the zodiac from different perspectives. We'll start from the periphery, the zodiac, and then further along we will look more closely at the planetary spheres.

Let's begin very simply by looking at the enigmatic symbols that represent the twelve signs of the zodiac. Everyone has seen them in astrology—little figures that, over the centuries, have been passed down as symbols for the twelve signs of the zodiac. Some make sense, perhaps, by just looking at them. Others are more mysterious. As I have said before, the whole work of astrosophy is to go behind the image, behind the material body, behind the letter, so to speak, to the meaning behind the letter. We begin with looking at the zodiac in terms of the traditional symbols used for the twelve signs.

First of all, just imagine a sphere—a kind of primordial pre-beginning: the sphere. Then imagine that an event occurs, and this sphere is broken into. There is a direction, a gesture of coming in, of entering the sphere in order to initiate activity, to initiate a beginning. This we could say is what the symbol of the Ram, or Aries, represents. In fact, if you look at the drawing and see this sphere, it's as if this sphere itself dives inward, toward its center, to create this initiation, this act of beginning.

Now some might say that this symbol is connected to the horns of the ram. Very true, but you can also imagine this symbol in the brow line of the human head and down the middle of the nose. This curve and arc in the face is also a picture of the symbol for Aries the Ram. Aries is the first sign, the beginning of the zodiac. It's also very much connected with thought and with the "I am," because it is the "I Am" that initiates a beginning.

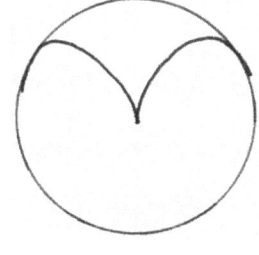

As we move on, we have the symbol of the Bull, Taurus. As you can see on the diagram, it's a smaller circle with two long horns coming up from the smaller circle. It could be seen as a kind of imagination of the bull's horns. In fact, in the fixed stars of the constellation of Taurus you can see these two points like the two horns of the bull going out into the sky.

Perhaps there is another way to look at these symbols in the sense of an evolution of the sphere, or evolution of an environment. We can also imagine this small circle with the two curves going up from it and you could continue those curves around to form another circle on top of the small circle. This is a picture for the stage after the initiation of Aries, after the beginning, or the breaking into the unity of the one sphere. Here there is a beginning of a separation out, and the smaller sphere, like a separate cell, begins to form outside of the large sphere that is above it, but attached. So, you have a kind of connection still to the large sphere of unity or, you could say, to the divine world, the divine unity, but the beginning of a separating out in the small sphere.

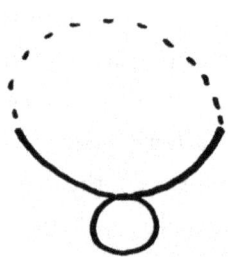

Then we move on with the symbols and come to the symbol for Gemini. What is this symbol? There a kind of column, and then the two curved arches on either end of the column. Once again, if we take these small curves and continue them on, we can imagine a sphere on the top and another sphere on the bottom, joined by the column.

A further evolution of separation takes place. Before, the worlds were beginning to separate, the independent unit was beginning to form out of the whole. In the Gemini symbol we already have the separation of the two, but still bound together, still connected. In fact, you can imagine the middle column as a kind of bridge connecting this higher world above and the lower world below. The constellation of the Twins and the twins themselves represent a kind of polarity. When we look at the myth of Castor and Pollux, we learn that one of them had to remain below, who is of mortal nature, and one remained above, who is of divine nature. Yet the one sacrificed his divine nature in order to rescue his brother the mortal twin. We can also look back at Norse mythology to the story of the Bifrost bridge, which was the bridge that connected Asgard with Midgard, the world of the gods to the world of humans. So, in the Twins we have, just in the symbol itself, a picture of an above and below, of a hierarchy, the world above in the one sphere and the world below, but still connected.

Then, when we move on to Cancer, the Crab, something changes.

Zodiac Symbols: Cancer – Scorpio*

When we progress on to Cancer, the Crab, something changes. There is a radical change in the symbology. You have this kind of curve in one direction and a curve out in the other direction and a gap in the middle. The two arcs, or vortexes, do not connect. One can imagine that in this image is a picture of the condition of when the bridge is broken. There is chaos and separation. The two spheres are no longer connected but have come apart with this gap in the middle of Cancer. It also has a bit of the Yin/Yang symbolism, but in thinking of this evolution of the one unity, the one sphere—the 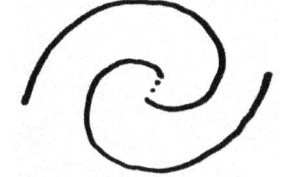 initiation, the beginning of separation, the bridge—we now come to the breaking apart.

If we then move on with this theme of the evolving sphere, we come to the symbol for Leo, which looks, you could say, a little bit like a heart. It's a small circle with this tail that curves and winds out to the periphery, like the flowing blood from the center.

In this imagination of the evolution of the entity from the whole sphere, we can imagine now that we have come to this break of Cancer, when the spheres of the above and below, the divine and the earthly, separate. Out of that separation, the entity comes to itself in the center with the small sphere and this tail that curves out. We can imagine that the end of the tail is connected to a broader circle around it, to the periphery. We now have the possibility of the center that has this harmonious, flowing relationship to the periphery, to the greater circle.

---

* Video: Course 1: The Zodiacs: Session 2.

It is no longer attached to the greater sphere, no longer above or below it, but has a kind of breathing relationship to it, just like the heart and the lungs, with which Leo is connected in the human organism. We can see this breathing relationship in the image of the new center with the curve out to the periphery.

Now, of course, one can also see a duality in this, which one often finds with Leo. This entity has come into the center of the self, and yet it can get stuck in this center, and there is no flow out to the periphery, no connection to the periphery, the greater whole. Here there can be a kind of egotism, or self-centeredness that is inflexible that gets stuck in the center. The other option in this picture is that one has the sense of community in the greater circle, a sense of relatedness to the greater all. This healthy relationship of a flowing connection to the all is one of recognizing the "I Am" in the community around me, one that shapes and forms me, both the spiritual greater circle as well as the human greater community, and yet I can also return to my own center. This is the gesture of Leo, the ideal gesture of Leo, which carries with it a flowing polarity between recognition of the greater community, or periphery, and the center.

When we move on to the Virgin, we leave this spherical evolution.

With Leo we have now come into the center of self and the self now begins a path. The traditional symbol for the Virgin is kind of like an M with a curling form (see image). Willi Sucher developed these new zodiac symbols as a way to help understand the meaning of the constellations. He has modified or enhanced this symbol of Virgo. Now the M becomes the three gates of initiation through which one passes to encounter the serpent of wisdom. This is then the initiation into the mysteries of wisdom, of life, in the Virgin. In fact, the Virgin, and one could talk a lot about the Virgin, is itself a representation of the divine Queen of Heaven, the Sophia, the great

Isis from Egypt, the Demeter Earth Mother—all of the great divine representations of this feminine element of the world of living wisdom.

We move onto Libra, the sign of the Scales and now we cross a threshold. The traditional symbol of Libra is a little bit like a symbol for the scales. Willi Sucher has evolved it and suggests, perhaps, simply a straight line passing  through the middle of a circle or sphere. This represents that a transition takes place. It is an important transition from the higher world to the lower world; from the mysteries of wisdom into the Scorpion, which we will go to next. But the symbol of the Scales significantly represents a kind of border, or boundary, or threshold between two worlds; a picture of the human journey of descent in evolution. This is of course the sign that occurs at the autumn equinox, which is also a threshold or boundary where the Sun crosses from above the celestial equator to below the  celestial equator into the dark portion of the zodiac.

If we can take these pictures and expand them more into pictures of soul experiences, of the nature of the being, then one approaches the qualities that come from these constellations. So, as we had the three gates to the mysteries of wisdom in the Virgin and crossing the threshold in Libra, we come then to the Scorpion. This symbol is  again traditionally a kind of an M figure but with a little arrow coming down (see image). We could also take this symbol and enhance it.

Then we come again to the M form as three gates of initiation, but now into the mysteries of death. So, after the gates we place the cross. This represents not only the mysteries of death, but, since the event of Golgotha, also the mysteries of resurrection. Scorpion carries this profound

encounter with death, as well as the challenge of breaking through to resurrection—the encounter with the death perspective in life from which the resurrection force can be found.

In ancient times this constellation was once regarded as an eagle. One can think of the eagle as this magnificent creature of the sky, used symbolically in a lot of cultures, which hovers above the world and sees all. This is an image of an old clairvoyance, of a time when human consciousness hovered above the world and could see through spiritual vision. Then the eagle fell, as this consciousness waned, and became the scorpion with its sting of death. Death became a separation, something to fear. This is a picture of the journey of the human being's descent into separation and freedom but also the loss of the former natural clairvoyance.

Willi Sucher suggests that the new symbol for Scorpion is not a return to the eagle, because we have gone through the stage of change into egohood. He suggests a new kind of bird, when Scorpio is transformed, in the new image of the dove. For those of you who know biblical stories, the dove is symbolic in many ways, one as the bird that hovered above the being of Jesus when he was baptized in the Jordan. It represents the Holy Spirit.

Well, that takes us into what is the Holy Spirit? But one can imagine the dove is a representation of what becomes of the human soul once the death forces are transformed and resurrected. What is the spiritual nature of the human being once the forces of death are transformed? So, the dove is a new kind of bird representing a different stage of vision, of knowing. The Scorpion is also connected with the Phoenix, the bird that gets consumed by the fire and rises again out of the ashes, which again is a resurrection image.

Zodiac Symbols: Sagittarius – Pisces*

As we move along, now we've crossed through the Scales and down into the three gates to the mysteries of death and resurrection. We move on to the constellation of the Archer, or Sagittarius.

---

* Video: Course 1: The Zodiacs: Session 3.

Here we can return to this spherical image. Having gone through this mystery journey, the human being, in a certain way, takes up an outward direction, to move forward into the world, to realize its true humanness. We move into the lower human, the realm of the will and the connection to the Earth. We have in the Archer a symbol that is like a bow and arrow. It's a straight line with the arrow pointing, and a kind of curve across the 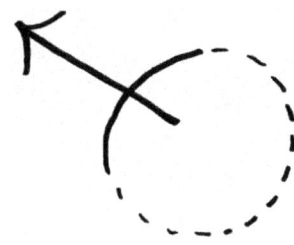 arrow as if it's the arrow being shot out of the bow. This is the symbol for the constellation of Sagittarius or the Archer.

However, we can also imagine this curve of the bow continuing on into the formation of a sphere. So, we had this kind of past history of the human being coming into self—the breaking up of the sphere. Now we have more the sphere of Earth, from which human beings direct their self toward the future.

In fact, this mythological symbol of the Archer is a magnificent picture. It is really a kind of archetype of the human being. We have in this picture of the Archer the bottom half as a horse upon which the human being is the upper half, forming the Centaur, but the human being has a bow and arrow aimed toward a future goal. We have the threefold element of the human being arising from the lower nature into the human being and then aiming toward the future, or higher spiritual goals.

In Sagittarius, we also find a kind of polarity, a relationship with its opposite constellation, the Twins. However, the polarity in Sagittarius is a more internal duality, of the human being working out in itself the above and below. With the Twins we have the duality more as a kind of historical event—the above and below of the worlds out of which we descended and our past hierarchical relationship to the divine.

We move on to Capricorn. In Capricorn and Aquarius, we get a bit into the mystery of the unknown in a certain way, even into the future of the path of initiation. In Capricorn, there are various similar symbols used. Some look a bit like a sharp edge with a little spiral curlicue at the bottom. Perhaps this is a kind of abstract version of what one might call the Goat-Fish, which is the mythological image of Capricorn. In the Goat-Fish we have a hardening and a fluid element. If we take just the symbol, as you see it in the diagram, of this curve up to the horn and a squiggle down, we can also form a sphere. It's a picture of the continuing evolution of the human entity's relationship to this spherical world, you could even say both the earthly and the spiritual world. There is a kind of movement and flexibility, an adaptability, to how we relate to this world.

If we move on now to Aquarius, to the Waterman, the symbol contains what is traditionally seen as these waves of water of the Waterbearer. Willi Sucher has slightly modified it to represent the wave and again, hovering above the wave, the sphere. It is an image of the condition of hovering over the waters of life, a kind of mastery of the life forces, which points us into the future human condition. This sphere now has gone through a certain metamorphosis, arising out of the lower to the true human, developing an ability to be flexible in relationship to the spheres of the spiritually upper realm and the earthly; and then a kind of hovering above in the life element, the waters.

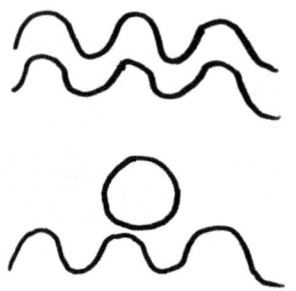

Finally, we come to Pisces, the Fishes. The symbol here is basically two curves, as you can see, with a bar or line connecting them. Again, it's not too difficult to imagine these two curves continuing on to form two spheres that are connected. This presents an interesting metamorphosis to consider. In the Twins we also had two spheres with a connection, but that was an above and below connection. You could see it as a hierarchical connection—the gods above directing the humans below.

In the Fishes we've come full circle. Now we stand side-by-side. The world of the human and the world of the divine, as brothers/sisters. The Fishes, the stars of our current age, in this symbol of the two spheres connected side-by-side, carry the goal of brother/sisterhood of human to human, of human to the world of Nature, and of human to the world of the divine—a side-by-side relationship, not as children, but ultimately as friends and co-creators.

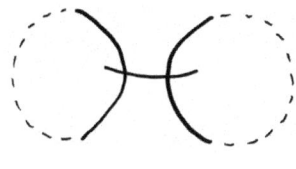

The Zodiac and Historical Ages*

In looking at the zodiac from the perspective of these symbols or glyphs and bringing some imagination into them, what do these forms suggest? What are they really a picture of? What do they tell us about the nature of the constellations themselves and the forces that stream down from the beings, the creative beings of these twelve constellations?

Let us return to this but look at it from the perspective of the various cultural ages, which I mentioned in a previous session. Here we move in the opposite direction through the signs. We spoke about the vernal point and the movement of the vernal point falling back along the zodiac one degree every 72 years. Thus, if we have roughly 30° per zodiac constellation and multiply 30° times 72 years, we come to 2,160 years, about the length of each great cultural era.

Let us go back and think about the vernal point. In the previous session I spoke about the vernal point being in the Bull during the Chaldean/Egyptian age. Let's go back to the first cultural age of our greater historical epoch, which is called the first post-Atlantean epoch. That first age is the time known as the ancient Indian culture. This was a culture of immense wisdom, of which we have only an echo now in the Vedas and the Bhagavad Gita. This lofty "knowing" of the spiritual world gave the feeling of being at home with the divine world, the gods. But as that era progressed there grew a greater longing for this union as a result of a dimming and waning of that sense of union. There was an experience of the loss of the relationship that was once so clear.

---

*   Video: Course 1: The Zodiacs, Session 4.

The vernal point during the ancient Indian era was in the constellation of the Crab, Cancer. So, if we go back to look at this image, we spoke earlier about the two spheres that broke apart. It's a picture, in a way, of the experience of the ancient Indian culture. This breaking apart of the unity, this loss of the bridge, of the connection, that they once experienced.

In fact, when we go into the Spiritual Nativity in Chart Construction, one will see that in the twelve philosophies of the zodiac, Cancer has a relationship to the philosophy of materialism and the evolution of materialism in the world. It is also connected to the coming into embodiment in matter.

The era after the ancient Indian era was when the vernal point moved on into the stars of the Twins. Remember that the vernal point is going backward along the zodiac. So far, we have followed the images and the glyphs in a forward direction, but now we are moving in a different direction.

During the great Persian era, following the Indian era (this is not the time of Babylon and Chaldea, but the Persian era before that), we had then a kind of recognition of the two worlds, and a working together of the two worlds. It was during that time that the great Sun initiate Zarathustra spoke about these two beings: the Sun being, Ahura Mazda, and the being of darkness bound to the Earth called Ahriman.

During this time, spiritual knowledge of the relationship between the Sun and the Earth arose, as well as the need to bring these worlds together in some way, because they were apart, one above the other below. So, that culture was one of spiritually recognizing the separation, but also recognizing the connection between these two worlds. This is the theme of that culture. Agriculture began with this culture. What is agriculture but a system of breaking into the darkness of the Earth so that the light can come in and grow the plants. It is a cultivation of the interpenetration of Sun and Earth for life.

The vernal point continues on, as we spoke about in other sessions, into the stars of the Bull. Here you have a picture of the next stage of human consciousness, as humanity's connection to the Earth grows greater. The Bull has this heaviness, this weight, standing on the Earth.

It was in this culture, actually, that the mysteries of the Mithras cult of slaying the bull originated. But also, just look at the temple architecture of this period. You have these great pyramids in Egypt and in Chaldea, the step pyramids. Such a representation of, on the one hand, this strong base connection to the Earth but at the pinnacle is an orientation to the stars, the divine guidance from above. These are the temples through which people were guided as they descended into the development of working with matter. It is during this time that you had the start of writing, of observational astronomy, of systems of measurement and calculation. All of this reflects taking up the Earth relationship when the vernal point was in the Bull.

Then the vernal point moved on into the Ram during the Greek and Roman period. Here we have the picture in the Ram of the head, even the brain. The initiating of thought in a new way as well as the awakening of the "I" is the theme in the Greek and Roman culture. We have the great philosophers, the thinking of Plato, Aristotle, Socrates, Pythagoras, the Buddha. We had the concept of "citizen" in Rome for the first time, as the concept of the "self" or the "I," not as a tribal folk but as an individual. Of course, it is in this era that the Christ, the true "I Am" incarnated. The entire age is an expression of these forces described by the gesture of the symbol of the Ram, of the "I Am" and the development of thought, as well as a new beginning.

Now we move into our present modern age with the vernal point crossing into the Fishes. In this era human beings are learning what it means to be brothers and sisters with the world. As hard as it may seem, this coming into a brotherly relationship with our fellow human beings, as well as to the Earth and the divine world, is part of the task of this age. As Rudolf Steiner described it, in the age of Pisces, humanity learns to "stand on its own two feet."

So, these are just some thoughts for you to take in and consider, as ways to go a little more deeply into the meaning of these constellations. How do these symbols become letters of an alphabet that speak and tell us more about what lives behind these symbols?

The Zodiac and the Human Form*

In this session we will continue with our exploration of the zodiac from another perspective in an effort to learn the mysteries of these twelve constellations.

To get started, I ask that you just stand for a moment and think about your body, your human form. Think about the roundness of the form of your head, resting on top of your body. Think about your uprightness along your spine. Think about your left and right sides and the symmetry between the two. Think about the trunk, the chest cavity and all of the activity that occurs inside.

Think about your hips, this major region of the pelvis in relation to our movement and balance. Think about your upper arms and your thighs and your joints, elbows and knees. Think about the forearms and the calves, and particularly think about the hands and feet. These all make up something we share in common as human beings, varied as we are, as our unique human form.

When we go into the prenatal epoch in the course on chart construction, I will share a quote by Steiner about the spiritual germ of the physical body. It is this spiritual germ of the physical body that is deeply related to our human form, the form that makes us human. I won't go into this in detail in this course, but Rudolf Steiner builds a marvelous understanding of how this human form is in essence the expression of the ego. This form, as the one thing we all share in common, originates in the zodiac. The periphery becomes the spirit germ as the forming forces of the twelve.

Now let's work through this, one constellation at a time, so we can reach an understanding of not only the human form, but also what comes from each of the twelve directions in creating that form. This will be another key to understanding the mystery of the nature of these constellations and the activity they generate.

We will present this in a diagram I'll build up for you (see video). Then, in the end, we'll have a complete picture of the human form in symbols. Again, as in the previous session, we start with the sphere

---
* Video: Course 1: The Zodiacs, Session 5.

and imagine our head as that sphere, the beginning. And again we start with the sign of the Ram, the first sign. It forms a gesture of the brow line down through the nose. The Ram has a connection to the head in this brow gesture, but underlying this physical manifestation the forces of the Ram represent in the human form the orientation to uprightness. Think about a child's desire to stand, the experience of becoming upright, the joy children experience when they first stand up. This is really the beginning of one's "I Am" experience. It's truly the activity of the ego in the human being that pushes a child to this orientation of uprightness, unlike any other creature. Only human beings have this as a natural orientation to the Earth. Thus, in the Ram we first have this picture of the brow line and the head when we want to build the human form, and the head's relation to our upright orientation and the "I Am" initiates that uprightness.

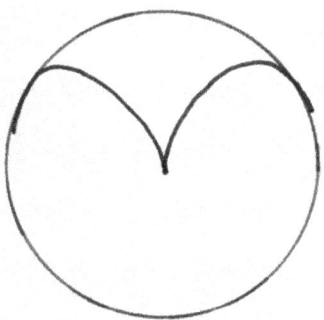

If we continue with our drawing, we have the round head and we find now the sphere of Taurus in the throat. The two "horns" of the sign of Taurus go up, you could say, into the ear canals (image). In Taurus, we have the orientation to self-expression, or speech.

One important point to remember is that in all of these descriptions I will be talking about a dynamic forming power, which over time becomes manifest in our physical material body. So, though I will link the form to a physical material part of the body, or the physicalized aspect of the form, one should remember that it is an expression of an archetypal form, not matter. It is a creative, formative dynamic out of which the human form comes into being, which is an activity of the loftiest of spiritual beings of the zodiac.

For example, in Taurus we have a connection to the larynx, the physical organ of speech, but in Taurus altogether we have the orientation to self-expression, our orientation toward the word, not only as we speak of the word, but also the Word as creative force of self-expression. The fact that the horns go up into the ear canals is connected with the fact that our hearing and our speech are naturally intertwined.

We move now to the Twins. Here we have the two curves and the vertical column in the middle. We can draw it in our form in an elongated way and we have this long middle column with the curve below along the hips and the curve above in the shoulder blades (see image). Here we can see a kind of spine form, a long middle line to our uprightness. This is the activity of Gemini that carries the orientation toward symmetry. We have left and right created by this line down the middle. The orientation to symmetry is carried by the forces from Gemini.

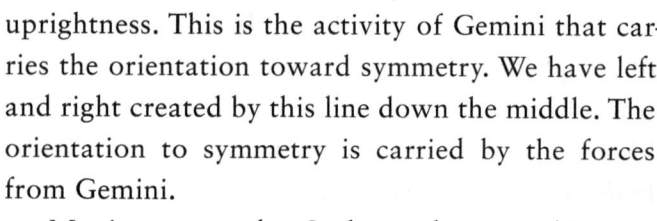

Moving on to the Crab, we have in this symbol a gesture of the two lines curling inward. In the Crab we have the orientation toward enclosure within. This orientation toward enclosure within manifests in the physical form as the chest cavity, or one could say the "house" of the inner organs of a human being. Cancer is the form of the rib cage, this enclosing form like a shell, that contains and protects the mysteries of the organs within, the life within. So, in Cancer we have the orientation to enclosure within.

Moving on to the Lion, we could say that within this house of Cancer, which you can see in the drawing in the image of the Crab form, there is this center that spirals out and spirals back again. This is a real image of the heart, or the entire rhythmical system of blood and breath, of heart and lungs.

In the forces from the Lion we have that orientation toward a breathing in-and-out relationship with the world. It's the orientation that connects us both inwardly and outwardly, which we talked about in the last session. This is the region of what Steiner calls, "the active inner organs," which means those organs that are inner organs but are really dependent on and deeply related to the external world in their activity and function. In the lungs, of course, we take the air in from the environment. We inhale oxygen for life and exhale carbon dioxide into the environment. The blood is really kept alive and dependent on this relationship with the breathing. So, this flowing active, inner world is what arises out of the forces from the constellation of the Lion.

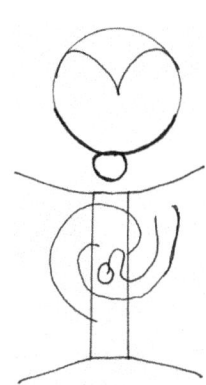

We continue to the Virgin.* You can see in the diagram that we have the house (Cancer) and the heart (Leo), and below that we have the symbol of the Virgin. This brings us to that in the human form called "the true inside." We have already mentioned Virgo and the mysteries of wisdom. Now we can think about the true inside, the true inwardness, brought into our human form by the stars of the Virgin. Of course, it is in this region that we have the physical organs of transformation, particularly the digestive system and intestines, those curling, serpentine forms. Here also takes place this most mysterious of events, the transubstantiation of matter into life. Here we find the true mysteries of wisdom and life, our true inside.

After the Virgin, we come to the Scales. The Scales are manifest in the physical body as the pelvis, this great hip socket, which in our body gives us balance. Think of this region in relation to upper and lower body and how we bend front, back, left, right. So again, we have the image of a real threshold, but now in the physical form. Libra is, in this form, that which separates the

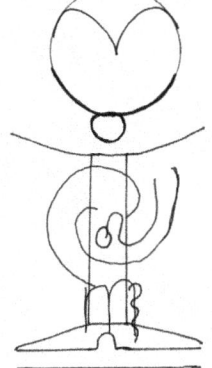

---

* Video: Course 1: The Zodiacs, Session 6.

mysteries of the true inside from the turning outward into expression in the earthly world, the threshold of transition.

When we move on from Libra, we go into quite a different direction and realm of experience. You can imagine now, following this drawing of the form, that in the upper part from the Lion on up to Aries, we have that which is really oriented to the outer world: our orientation to uprightness, symmetry, self-expression, the active inner organs. These are all continually moving more inward to Virgo. Then with the Scales, the balance in the human form, we begin to move out again, down toward the Earth.

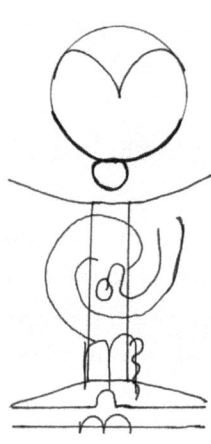

Next we come to the stars of the Scorpion, which are connected to the forces of reproduction, the creative force to procreate, to recreate outside of ourselves. It's also connected to the Bull, which is opposite. Here, we can see the connection between the Bull and speech and the Scorpion and sexual development. Just consider puberty and the change of voice that occurs in males along with sexual maturity. Similarly, in the Scorpion we have in the human form the orientation toward reproduction, and though we will not go into it now, this carries profound connections with the fallen forces of creativity and the relationship to sexuality.

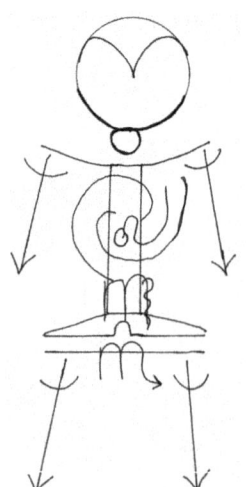

We move on to the stars of the Archer. In the Archer we have the orientation toward moving outward into the world. This is manifest in the physical body in the thighs and in the upper arms. These are the limbs that express the will, the initiation of forward movement into the world, this moving out from the thigh and the upper arm.

We continue on into Capricorn. Capricorn is connected, which we spoke about a little bit in the earlier sessions, to meeting the environment with flexibility, which manifests physically in the elbows and in the knees in the limbs. You can imagine what our will activity would be if we didn't have joints! How would it be moving around in the world if our limbs did not bend with flexibility?

In the joints we have a physical expression of the dynamic that comes out of Capricorn, which is the capacity for flexibility in meeting the environment. In the Archer we have moving out into the environment, the orientation toward forward movement. In Capricorn, we have the orientation toward meeting the environment with flexibility. There's also a tendency in Capricorn that can become rigidity—not flexibly meeting the environment.

We move on then to Aquarius. In Aquarius, as we discussed in the previous session, we have the meeting with the periphery. Just think of that as a dynamic. The capacity, the orientation to meet the periphery, whatever that periphery may mean either materially or dynamically. This dynamic of the human form physiologically is expressed in the forearms and in the calves. If you think about it, the forearms and the calves are the parts of the body where the blood comes closest to the skin, or you can say where the blood meets the periphery of the body, the skin. I don't know if it's done anymore, but in the 1950s women used to check the temperature of the milk bottle on their forearms where it's very sensitive to temperature. Thus, in Aquarius we have the meeting with the periphery, the physical manifestation here in the forearms and in the calves.

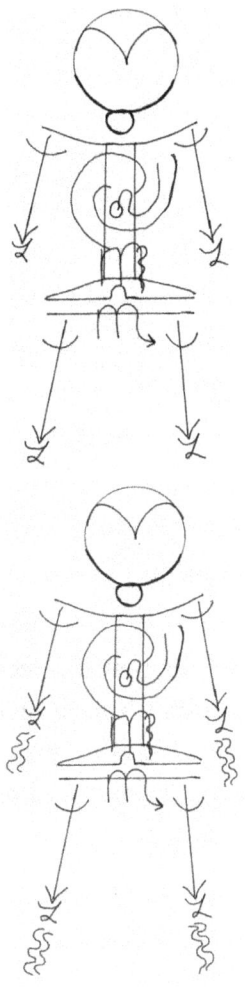

Finally, we come to the conclusion of the twelve in the Fishes. We come to these two great aspects of the human form that are possibly the most "human" of all, the hands and the feet. In the human form, both of them as a dynamic carry the orientation to taking up or working with the periphery. This differs from Aquarius in meeting the periphery. Now we take up the periphery as humans. The truly the human is distinguished from the animal in the differing functions of hands and feet. In our hands and the feet we have a whole special category. The hands themselves are a remarkable life study. What a miraculous thing the hands are! It is with the hands that we shape, take up, mold, and create in the world. It is with the feet that we live out and walk the path of our destiny. Through our feet, we meet the world differently. They take us to places where we make choices, encounter our destiny, we go in directions, we meet our karma. So, the culmination of this human form in the hands and the feet is really this taking hold or taking up or engaging with the world. In Aquarius, it is meeting the periphery, and in Pisces we take up the periphery—take up the environment and transform it.

You see in the diagram how this amazing human form is constructed. It's a kind of zodiac "stick figure." It's a somewhat dry image, but our discussion is meant to "flesh it out." Hopefully, looking at it you can see the miracle represented by the zodiac and what we have here in the form of our body, which has taken on matter to serve its own evolution in this time. However, the creative archetype of this form resides in the twelve constellations as a true reflection of the microcosm in the macrocosm.

All that I have presented here comes almost directly out of the work of Rudolf Steiner. In his lecture cycle *Man in the Light of Occultism, Theosophy and Philosophy* (CW 137) he develops this twelvefold human form and speaks at length about it, also going into the threefold human form and how intimately they are interrelated.

The Zodiac

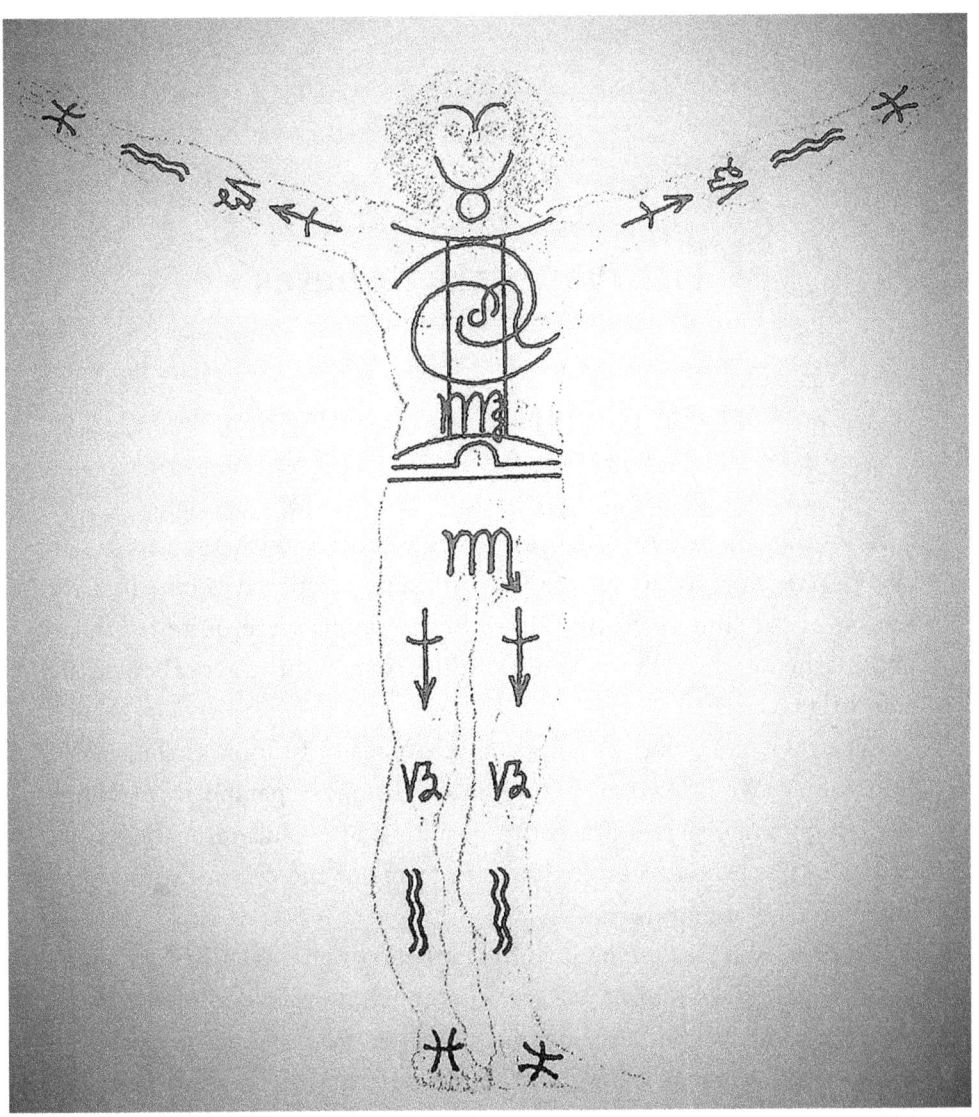

3

The Planetary Spheres

The True Nature of the Planets[*]

We began this introduction to Astrosophy with the chart construction section and a few different perspectives on the incarnation of the human being. Those first sessions were quite technical and mathematical and really about the process of the actual construction of a chart.[**]

Then we had some sessions where we began to look at the twelve-fold zodiac. We looked at it from an evolutionary perspective on how the symbols themselves present to us a kind of evolution of the nature of the zodiac. We also looked at it in terms of the relationship of the zodiac to the human form.

In these sessions we go into the planetary spheres. When we move into the planetary realms, we move from what are called "fixed stars," which Rudolf Steiner describes as the realm of duration, into what the ancients called the wandering stars. These are the stars that moved as they were observed in the heavens and were not fixed on this celestial sphere, but moved in relation to the other stars on this sphere. These stars at times even appeared to turn and move backward against the background of the celestial sphere and then move forward again.

We also began these courses with a verse by Rudolf Steiner, in which he speaks, in this verse form, about the whole evolution of

---

[*] Video: Course 2: The Planetary Spheres, Session 1.
[**] This refers to the Charts Construction videos, which were recorded first, but come later in the online video course.

the consciousness of humanity in relationship to the stars. He speaks about a time when the stars once spoke to humanity; about that time when they became silent; and about this time, out of which a new astrosophy is born, when the human being must now begin to speak to the stars.

This whole process of the evolution of human consciousness is a central theme in the work of Rudolf Steiner. It presents us with a profound understanding of the whole evolutionary change that humanity has gone through, particularly in relationship to the spiritual-divine element.

To begin, I include a quotation from Steiner, which will affect how we now understand the nature of the planetary spheres in the context of human evolution from the past.

> Humanity confronts a world that was once entirely divine-spiritual in nature, a world to which we belonged as an integral part. The world of this belonging was then divine-spiritual. But at a subsequent evolutionary stage this was no longer the case; the world was a cosmic revelation of the divine-spiritual, its essential being hovering behind the revelation. But that being lived, nevertheless, and was active in the revelation. The starry world was already in existence, with the divine-spiritual living and active as revelation in its shining out and its movement. It would be accurate to say that in the way a star stood or moved was a direct demonstration of the activity of the divine-spiritual. Other times came. The starry world ceased to be a direct, immediate revelation of divine-spiritual activity. Rather did it live and move in continuation of such activity as had earlier been engendered in it. The divine-spiritual no longer lived in the cosmos as revelation, but only as ongoing effect. A definite split had appeared between divine-spiritual being and the universe; they were now separated. (*Karmic Relationships*, vol. 3)

To truly understand this evolutionary change in the nature of our relationship to the stars would require a far more in-depth study than this introduction to astrosophy can take up. For those who would like to understand more of this evolution as it progressed through the human relationship to the cosmos of stars, I hope to develop a few separate courses that will take up Steiner's ideas on the evolution of human consciousness. For this session, we will continue on and delve into the world of the planets. Taking up this idea of the change in human consciousness in relationship to the stars, we arrive now in our time, which is what we can describe as object consciousness. We experience the world, we learn about the world, almost completely through our sense perceptions—what can be measured, counted, and weighed. So, we tend to look at the bodies of the planets in space as if they are the planets, but in reality we must learn to understand the planets in a different way.

Rudolf Steiner describes how the planetary bodies are the least spiritual aspect of the planetary realms. They are similar to the hands of a clock. They are indicators for our modern consciousness of the activities of the entire sphere of planetary beings. This sphere of planetary beings—looking at it in terms of our spatial understanding—is defined by the orbits of those planets. Thus, within the entire orbit of Jupiter, for example, the sphere created by its orbit, is the activity, or workshop, so to speak, and the revelation of the divine spiritual beings of that planetary sphere.

How can we come to understand the nature of the planets if we think about them in terms of these spheres of activity that interpenetrate each other? In an earlier session, we spoke about the nature of cosmic intelligence. The planetary realms, or the interactions among the planetary spheres, are a kind of communication between the cosmic intelligences. Thus, the first step in reaching a deeper understanding of the planetary spheres is to begin to understand them in terms of time. It is their movements and the rhythms of their movements that reveal their nature. We view the planet body in space and the movements it makes over time to reach the time configuration. We then come to a revelation, so to speak, of the nature and meaning of that planetary sphere.

THE MERCURY SPHERE*

With this beginning sense of coming to know the planets as expressions in time, let's begin with the planet Mercury and work our way out from the Sun. Mercury, in astronomy, is the planet that is closest to the Sun. It moves rapidly around the Sun. It has a sidereal orbit of 88 days. Recall that *sidereal* means from star to star.

For Mercury to make one complete revolution around the Sun—from a star point back to that same star point—requires 88 days. However, Mercury also has another rhythm that is called the synodic rhythm. This synodic rhythm is based on the planet's conjunctions with the Sun. The rhythm is 116 days. The synodic cycle of Mercury is the time it takes for Mercury to go from one "superior conjunction" with the Sun, around the Sun to another superior conjunction with the Sun. Superior conjunctions are the conjunctions with the Sun as seen from the Earth looking to the Sun, where Mercury would be, in a line from us, behind the Sun.**

There is another conjunction of Mercury with the Sun in which it moves around and comes in front of the Sun as seen from the Earth; this is called an "inferior conjunction." The synodic cycle of Mercury is from one superior conjunction to another superior conjunction, but when we look at it from the Earth's perspective, we see that Mercury appears to move forward and then reverse direction and then move forward again. It appears as a kind of loop as it circles around the Sun.

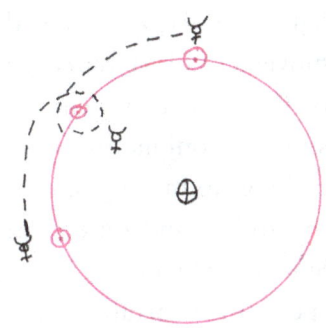

If you look at the diagram you will see this one synodic cycle of Mercury drawn, from the superior conjunction around into the loop

---

*   Video: Course 2: The Planetary Spheres, Session 2.

** This is not an exact line, such as would be called an occultation, but behind the Sun, which is the celestial longitude, though above or below the Sun, due to the angle of the planetary orbit. Of course, Mercury and Venus are blocked by the Sun as they go behind it.

where there is an inferior conjunction and back around again to a superior conjunction.

In about one Earth year, actually 348 days, but within one of our solar years, Mercury makes three loops plus a bit more. These three loops of Mercury going around the Sun create a form in the heavens. If you look at the diagram you can see the completed looping of Mercury in relationship to the Sun.

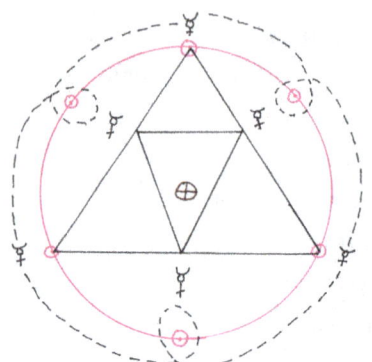

You can see this weaving, with the Earth in the center and Mercury moving around the Sun, creating the loops. You can see that if you connect the inferior conjunctions there is an equilateral triangle, and between the superior conjunctions, if you draw the lines, there is another larger equilateral triangle with its point at the top in this drawing, and the small one with its point at the bottom.

So, what is this gesture in the movement of Mercury? You know in mythology Mercury is called the messenger of the gods. He, in many figures in art, has winged sandals or a winged helmet. This weaving movement of Mercury through the year is an expression of the nature of this planetary being. In a certain way, you could say that, at the superior conjunction when Mercury is behind the Sun, it is, so to speak, picking up messages, or picking up substance from the cosmos, from the zodiac and outer planets. Then it swings around in front of the Sun and when it comes into an inferior conjunction it hands off, so to speak, the substance that is picked up for humanity.

Then it swings around again and picks up substance, moving the whole time through different constellations of the zodiac. So, in a certain way Mercury is the communicator, the messenger, the coordinator of the relationship between cosmic intelligence and the Earth, bringing it into Earth and converting it, so to speak, in action or in realization into earthly intelligence. This is the goal of Mercury.

As you see in the drawing, the form that Mercury creates is the six-pointed star. This six-pointed star actually rotates on the background of the constellations. It takes about 20 years for the whole six-pointed star to make one full rotation through the twelve constellations. So, when we think about the six-pointed star and what it says to us, or what Mercury reveals to us through this form, we could look at it in another way.

Again, if you look at the diagram, we begin with the two triangles, one below with the point up and one above with the point down. There is then a gradual coming together until they are one six-pointed unit or the double triangle.

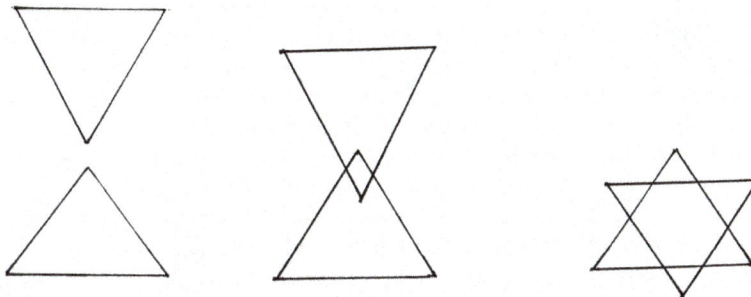

This six-pointed star of Mercury is the basis in astrology for the sextile aspect. If you divide 360° by 6 you get the 60° angle of the sextile. There is another picture we can put up that shows this relationship between Mercury and the higher world of the cosmic intelligence.

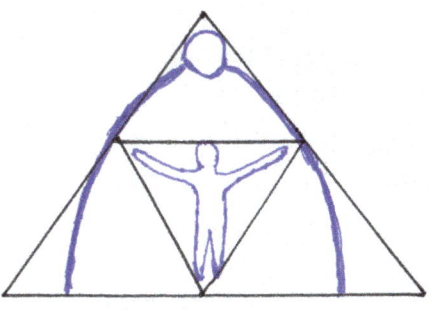

If you look at this picture again you have the two triangles, the one with the point at the top and the smaller triangle inside. One can imagine that in the smaller triangle you have the human form, with the arms up in receptivity, or in offering, to this form of a higher being, in a certain way enveloping, holding the smaller being.

This gives us an essential context for how we begin to understand the nature of Mercury. Below is a quote by Steiner about the nature of Mercury:

We come next to Mercury. In contrast to the other planets, Mercury is not interested in things of a physical, material nature as such, but in whatever is capable of coordination. Mercury is the domain of the Masters of coordinative thinking; Jupiter, the habitation of the Masters of wisdom-filled thinking. When a human being comes down from pre-earthly life into earthly existence, it is the Moon impulse that provides the forces for his physical existence. Venus provides the forces for the basic qualities of heart and temperament. But Mercury provides the forces for capacities of intellect and reason, especially the intellect. The Masters of the forces of coordinative knowledge and mental activity have their habitation on Mercury. (*Initiation Science*, lect. 1)

The Venus Sphere*

Let's move on to Venus. Venus of course is the next planet out from the Sun astronomically, between the Earth and the Sun, so likewise Venus also has this kind of weaving pattern of superior conjunction behind the Sun and inferior conjunction between the Sun and the Earth.

The sidereal orbit of Venus, meaning from star to star, is 225 days. The synodic year for Venus, which means from superior conjunction behind the Sun to superior conjunction again, is 584 days. So, let's just try to understand the nature of the beings of this spheres, get to know them, so that we can understand what they mean and how they work into the human being.

If you look at the diagram you can see that these loops of Venus, from superior to inferior, over a four-year period create five points equidistant. The first point is a superior then Venus goes almost completely around the zodiac and then comes into an inferior conjunction, and then goes back around. Venus stays very close to the rhythm of the Sun. So, we have this period where Venus is catching up slowly to the Sun and comes into superior conjunction. Then it passes beyond the Sun slowly, and then it wants to turn back toward the Sun, which is the gesture of the orbit of Venus going around the Sun and coming into inferior conjunction. This is the loop formation.

---

* Video: Course 2: The Planetary Spheres, Session 3.

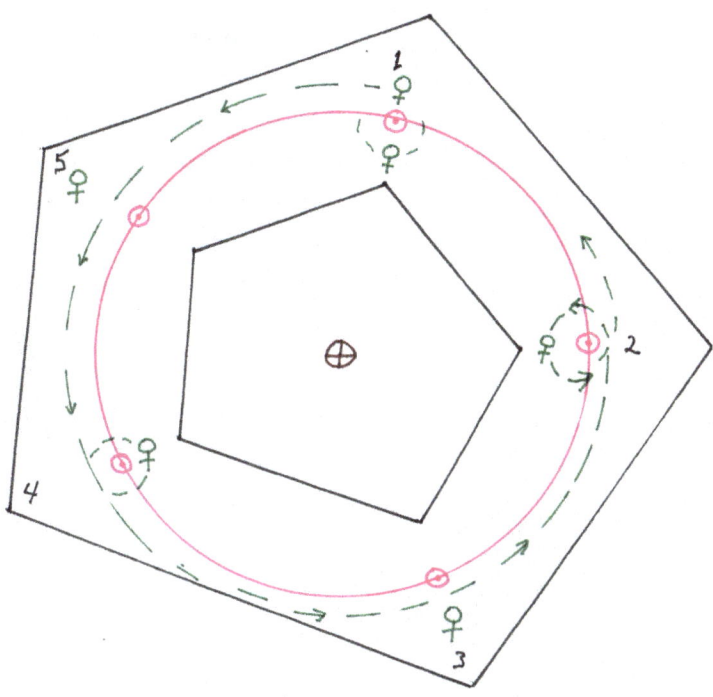

So, it takes about four years for these alternating five points, as you can see in the diagram, to create this equidistant five-pointed star or pentagon. Then after another four years a double five-pointed star or a double pentagon is formed, because the point where Venus originally made a superior conjunction with the Sun, after the five points have been completed, comes back to that same point, but this time in inferior conjunction. It then alternates in reverse as how it did over the four years preceding, so that what was superior before becomes an inferior. Thus, you have created this amazing double five-pointed star, or double pentagon, in the eight-year biography cycle of the planet Venus.

The following living geometric form in time creates a double pentagram, an exact double pentagram, with each point equidistant. This star stays intact, it doesn't alter, except that it rotates backward in its form about 3° every year. That would be about 30° every 100 years, and in 1,200 years this perfect five-pointed star makes a complete rotation through the zodiac. This means you can follow this five-pointed star through history, to where the points returned. This is a beautiful expression, so to speak, of the nature of the Venus sphere. It is a sphere of harmony, a sphere of integration, of balance and beauty. This is the basis in astrology for the quintile, the 72° angle. If you divide the 360° by five you get the 72° angle that this five-pointed star creates. We will come back to these much later when we go into more depth as to what these points and loops mean, in a deeper context.

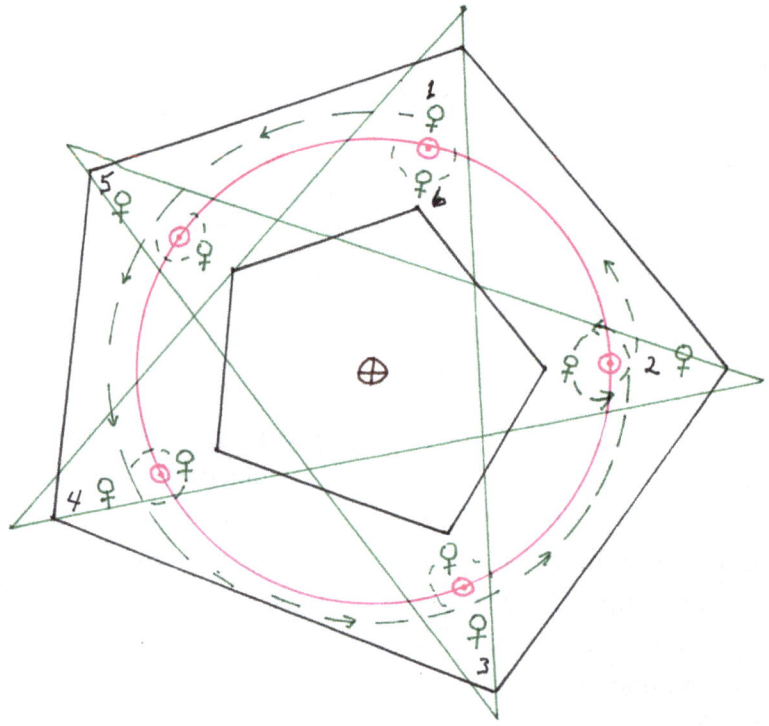

But before we go on to Mars, I will mention one other aspect about this planet Venus. Venus is the planet that is called the morning star and the evening star. It's the morning star when it is approaching and beginning to go around behind the Sun, so it comes up in the morning before the Sun rises. It's the evening star after it has passed behind the Sun, as seen from the Earth, and is beginning to come around again between the Earth and the Sun, so as the Sun sets Venus is still in the sky. Venus is famous, of course, for its brilliance in the sky when it's the morning and as the evening star. Its brilliance leads us to another aspect of Venus, whereby it has this relationship to the being we call Lucifer. The name Lucifer means the light bearer. It is often said that Venus wants to compete with the Sun in its radiance.

Also, if we think about the pentagram, the image of the pentagram, the number five is the number for the human being, but the higher human becoming spiritual. Five is 4 + 1. Four is the number of space, of this object realm in which we exist and from which we form our earthly self, or ego. The 4 + the 1 brings the added higher dimension with the higher self. One way to imagine this is to draw the square. Then place the trinity or triangle on top and you will see the five-pointed form. This trinity on top can be seen as the three higher members of the transformed human being, manas, budhi, atman, which then make, out of the fourfold human, the spiritualized human. Of course, one can take this further, but for another course, in that Venus makes a double pentragram, so the full completed form is related then to the number 10. This then is the fully spiritual human, the five fulfilled as spiritual.

We will go into this further when we go into the relationship of the Christ events to the Venus pentagon. Historically Venus has been the planetary sphere that is deeply associated with what one could call the religious life of humanity, or what in ancient times was called the Temple Wisdom or the Mystery Centers, out of which humanity received illumination from the spiritual world. So, Venus has a long history with the mysteries, which, in a certain way, reintegrated the human being with the divine. In evolutionary history, as the human being lost its connection with the divine, these mystery centers or temples were there to take in pupils who could still be trained to have access to the divine in order to help guide human beings, yet they too fell into decline by the time of the coming of the Christ. So, this sphere of Venus has a relationship with the being of Lucifer, that being who is also a bearer of light and wisdom, but we shall see how this Venus sphere was transformed during the time of Christ. So let us go on to Mars.

The Mars Sphere*

In traditional mythology, we are familiar with the polarity of Mars and Venus. Venus is often depicted as a beautiful woman, the bearer of love. Mars is usually depicted as a warrior, an aggressive male. There is some truth in this. But let us look at Mars in relation to its form—this weaving, living pattern that Mars creates in the heavens, which is different from what Venus weaves in the heavens.

Mars is on the other side of the Earth from the Sun. It has a much longer orbit than Mercury and Venus. Its sidereal orbit from star back to the same star is about 687 days, and its synodic orbit is about 25 to 26 months. The Sun and Mars come into a conjunction about every two years, and they come into opposition, meaning Mars is opposite the Sun as seen from the Earth, about every two years.

The interesting thing about Mars is that the conjunctions occur in about the same place that the oppositions occur. There are 8 conjunctions of Mars with the Sun in about 15 or 16 years, and there are 8 oppositions of Mars with the Sun in about 15 or 16 years. Then they start the pattern again, in about the same place. So, what form does Mars create? What's interesting about Mars versus Venus, is that we saw how Venus creates this perfect five-pointed star, this double pentagram, which stays intact in this perfect harmony as it moves and rotates around us. Mars, on the other hand, is a bit rougher. It creates another form, but the form isn't exact and the form it creates, if you see the diagram, is two squares, or an octagon. However, they are not exact squares. They are sort of off angle a bit. So, we have, even in its form in the heavens, the pentagram versus the square. What can that tell us about Mars?

The square is the image of our object-consciousness world, the spatial world of north, south, east, and west; the four elements. This is an expression of the nature of Mars. Now as we go further into these sessions we will hear about how Rudolf Steiner writes quite extensively about Mars, the sphere of Mars, and the nature of the Mars sphere, and how it has gone through a change, or evolution.

---

*   Video: Course 2: The Planetary Spheres, Session 4.

Willi Sucher writes that Mars is that sphere in the cosmos, in the life between death and rebirth, which facilitates for the human being the ability to meet the objective world, to confront the world of objects.

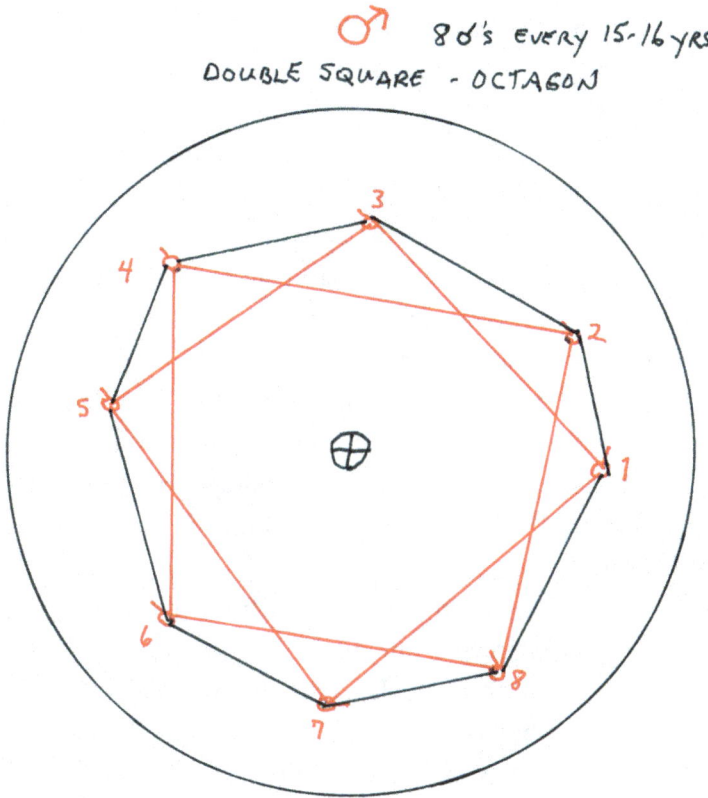

We are living now in the Mars consciousness, which is that consciousness out of which we can say "I am not that." In other words, the ability to separate and confront is what helps us to define ourselves as "not" everything else in the world. This is the journey of the young child who begins to say "no" and to experience its own self as not merged with the parent self. This means that Mars helps us not to merge with the world, not to be in union with everything, as an infant is, but begin banging our head on the table to wake up to the distinction between "I" and "that." Mars has been instrumental in this confrontational aspect, and in the fact that it carries, so to speak, the archetypes of the physical object world, helping us come to a kind of ego self-consciousness, which is separate from the world. Venus, on the other hand, is a kind of future (and a past) consciousness, which wants to find a way back to identifying ourselves with what is around us in the world.

So, with Mars and these double squares we have what in astrology is called the "aspect of the square"—the 90° and 45° angles, square and semi square. If we look at this, even in the form and gesture of Mars and Venus, on either side of the Earth, we have in Mars the relationship to space, to the object world, the number 4, the path to self as a separate individual.

Mars is also connected with the capacity for speech, with the voice, naming things. Speech is needed to name and identify what is outside of us as well as to express our inner world to an outer world. Mars, therefore, in this separating out, is deeply connected with our journey toward freedom and recognizing our own selves as independent and able to act upon the outer world. Therefore, we can see in Mars a relationship to the material sciences, to technology, to industrialism...to all that has brought us to mastery and to knowledge of the external world of the senses.

Venus, as we move into the future, is the four-plus-one—the human plus the spiritual, resurrected human. This is the path to the new mysteries, the transformation of the I, so that humans come to realize not only "I," but "not I but the divine in me." It leads us to a conscious reunion with the divine world, the so-called new mysteries.

THE GOLDEN TRIANGLE[*]

Before we go on to Jupiter and Saturn, I will just point out that Rudolf Steiner lectured and wrote a tremendous amount about the human being's relationship to the starry realm, and the hierarchical beings in relationship to the stars and the planets.

On the website astrosophy.com, and at the end of this book, you'll find a bibliography of references to the works in which he focuses on these aspects of the human being and Earth evolution, as well as a selection of numerous quotes from his lectures. You certainly can go

---

[*] Video: Course 2: The Planetary Spheres, Session 5.

into great depth in understanding astrosophy by delving into some of Steiner's works and, of course, Willi Sucher has written several books and articles. Those are all available for free download on the website. So, there is an abundance of material for further research.

This introductory course is just to begin to give us stepping stones to enter into the depth of meaning that lies in these starry realms, so that when we look at interpreting a chart we realize what a vast amount of wisdom underlies the movements of these planets and their coming into a particular constellation at the moment of birth.

If we move now to Jupiter and Saturn, we are moving out in the solar system further into what are called the classical planets. Jupiter's orbit is 12 years, so there is this wonderful movement of Jupiter in which it takes about one year for Jupiter to move through one constellation of the zodiac. Here is expressed a wonderful relationship and harmony with the Sun and Jupiter, and as we go deeper into Jupiter we can maybe understand a bit more about this harmony with the Sun. Our Sun goes through one sign of the zodiac in one month during the twelve months of one year, and Jupiter goes through one sign of the zodiac in one year in its twelve-year cycle.

Saturn, the farthermost classical planet from Earth, takes exactly 29.458 years for a single sidereal orbit around the Earth. So those who are somewhat familiar with astrology or with biographical rhythms might recognize this 29½ years as the so-called Saturn return, meaning the point in the human biography when Saturn returns after nearly 30 years to where it was at one's birth.

This has a meaning that we will go into in future sessions, but I think maybe everyone has had a bit of an experience at around age 30 of this question: "What am I doing with my life? Am I really living out what I had intended to live out? Am I fulfilling the intentions that I thought I had wanted to accomplish?" This is deeply related to the sphere of Saturn. We'll go into it a little bit later.

But now we come to the rhythm of these two planets and their form in the heavens. Jupiter makes a certain rhythm with its 12-year cycle, as does Saturn with its much longer cycle, but the important form that we find with Jupiter and Saturn also reflects the relationship of these two "great beings" that envelop us in the cosmos. The form that Jupiter and Saturn create together is another living geometric form. They conjunct each other every 20 years or so in a certain location in the zodiac. Over a period of 60 years, they meet in three different locations, one every 20 years, and they create in these conjunctions an equilateral triangle in the heavens.

You can see this in the image below. After 60 years the conjunction returns again to the first point, and then returns again to the second point, so that these 20-year conjunction cycles, creating this equilateral triangle, also retain their form. The form rotates about 8° to 10° forward with each cycle of 60 years. The whole triangular form takes 2,500 years to make one complete great rotation. This great equilateral triangle is a significant esoteric symbol. You can actually see it on the U.S. dollar bill, the top of the pyramid. It was also called "the star of Zoroaster"—"zoro aster," meaning golden star.

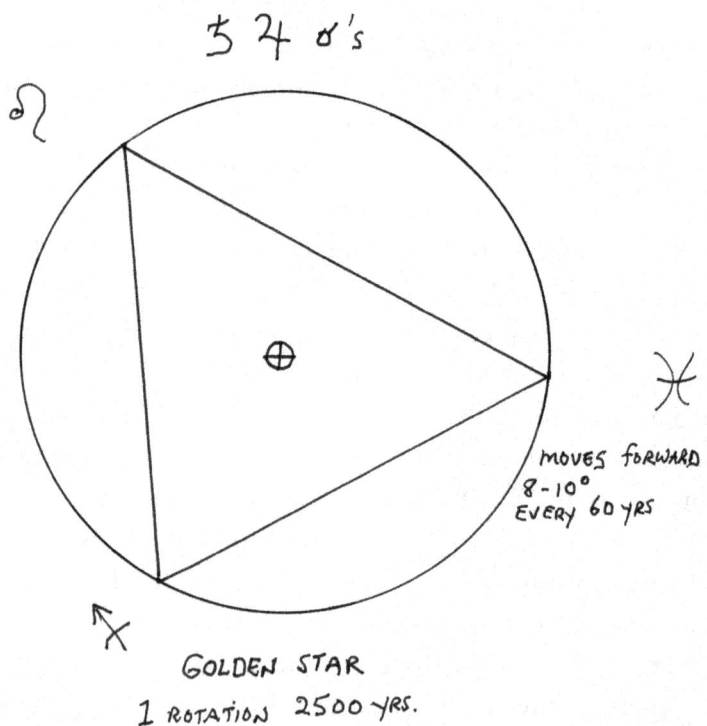

This is the Golden Triangle, or Golden Star, and it is deeply related to the entire influence of the great Sun initiate Zarathustra, the founder of the very ancient Persian cultural epoch, who has incarnated since in various individualities. It is deeply connected to what is described in the Gospels as the Star of Bethlehem, but we will go into that later when we go more deeply into the meaning of these stars in relation to the Christ events.

The profound historical context of the rotation of this golden triangle is expressed in its 2,500-year rotation, which in Eastern tradition is called a *Kalachakra,* each of which lasts 2,500 years. One Yuga is two rotations over a period of 5,000 years.

Kali, in Hinduism, is The Guardian of the Threshold. She is described as terrible and wonderful and stands holding a sword on the prostate form of Shiva, her spouse. If we look back in evolution, say to 3100 BC, this was the beginning of what is called the Kali Yuga, which is the Dark Age. That Dark Age lasted for 5,000 years and ended in AD 1899. So, if we think of 3100 BC as a kind of starting point for this Kalachakra and move it through one 2,500-year cycle, we come to 600 BC, around the time of the birth of Gautama Buddha. If we go another 2,500 years forward, we reach the end of Kali Yuga in 1899. If we then go another 2,500 years into the future, we come to AD 4400, which is the time of the next Buddha, the Maitreya Buddha.

So, you can see a glimpse here of the profound significance of the rotation of this golden triangle. In his research, Willi Sucher traced this triangle back to the time of the incarnation of the Christ into the Earth. He found that the dates of those three great conjunctions are also related to three great events within that incarnation, or rather just before the beginning of Jesus' life, during His life, and shortly after Christ's resurrection—all tied significantly to the great impulse of this being. We'll go into that also as we look at these planetary spheres in relation to this cosmic event in the Earth at the turning point of time in the next chapter.

The Spheres of Jupiter and Saturn[*]

The Greeks called Saturn *Kronos,* or *Chronos* (chronology), Father Time. Rudolf Steiner speaks about the sphere of Saturn as this "sphere of all cosmic memory." Saturn records everything that happens in the world and keeps the memory of all history. It is oriented to the past. This means that Saturn is the sphere that wants to ensure that the divine evolutionary plan, from the very beginnings, is maintained—the law, the plan of evolution, originally conceived by the Godhead. Saturn's task is to ensure that this divine plan is carried out. It remembers and records the past. So, in this sense Saturn is deeply related to karma, not only world karma, but individual karma. That's why it is often depicted as an old man with the sickle of death, the old Father Time as grim reaper, who insures that we reap what we sow.

Steiner goes deeply into the nature of Saturn in his description of the great evolutionary cycles, which would be far too much to go into here. But in general, to understand the realm of Saturn, the realm of Jupiter, and the realm of Mars, one will want to go deeply into the esoteric foundations of these planetary spheres by reading Steiner's book *An Outline of Esoteric Science* (the various translations have different titles). There he goes into these planetary stages of the Earth prior to Earth evolution, which can provide a deeper understanding of these three planets, with Saturn holding the memory of Ancient Saturn, Jupiter carrying the memory of Ancient Sun and Mars carrying the memory of Ancient Moon.

So, Saturn is always there to remind us of our origins, of our intentions, of our alignment with our karma and with the divine plan, so to speak, of the Father. It is also connected to the skeleton, the bony form in the human being; the forces of contraction, of hardening.

Jupiter is its counterpart. Jupiter was the Greek Zeus, and in Rome was called Jupiter, or Jove, which is where we get the word jovial from. Whereas Saturn carries this weight of the past, the memory of the past, the laws of karma, Jupiter carries the intention to expand into the future. It's connected with idealism, with a deep living, creative

---

[*] Video: Course 2: The Planetary Spheres, Session 6.

wisdom, with levity vs. gravity. It wants to unfold into the future, in an expansive way, with the vision for what is to become. Thus, it is also connected to our ideals. In fact, in Rudolf Steiner's description of the great evolutionary cycles of our cosmos, the next evolutionary period after Earth evolution is called Future Jupiter. Jupiter carries the memory of the evolutionary cycle of Ancient Sun, when life and light unfolded. In this cycle we see the primary working of the Kyriotetes, the Spirits of Wisdom.

We have then in the conjunctions of Saturn and Jupiter, a kind of great conference between the forces that carry the divine plan of evolution from the past and the forces that want to take the plan and develop it into a future. So, these conjunctions are significant moments in human evolution, reflecting the progress and movement of our evolution. The conjunctions carry a new impulse out of each of the three corners that evolves with humanity and are colored by the constellations in which they occur, each carrying a different kind of stream.

Following are a few quotations about Jupiter and Saturn from Rudolf Steiner and Willi Sucher:

> Jupiter is the thinker in our planetary system, and the thinking is the activity cultivated by all the beings in his cosmic domain. Creative thoughts received from the universe radiate to us from Jupiter. Jupiter contains, in the form of thoughts, all the formative forces for the different orders of cosmic beings. Whereas Saturn tells us of the past, Jupiter gives a living portrayal of what is connected with him in the cosmic present. But what Jupiter reveals to the eye of spirit must be grasped with thoughtful intelligence. If a man does not himself make efforts to develop his capacities of thinking, he cannot, even if he is clairvoyant, approach the mysteries of Jupiter, for they are revealed in the form of thoughts and can be approached only through a genuine activity of thinking. Jupiter is the thinker in our universe. (Rudolf Steiner, *Initiation Science*, lect. 1)

> Jupiter is in essence weaving wisdom.... And now imagine that you are looking, not upon weaving clouds of water vapor but upon weaving wisdom itself, weaving thought-images that are actually

beings. Then you will have an impression of Jupiter. (Rudolf Steiner, *Karmic Relationships,* vol. 2)

What the Saturn beings behold as a vista of past ages of evolution unites with a vista of the past evolution of all beings belonging to the entire planetary system. The consciousness of the Saturn beings may therefore be characterized by saying that they gaze back upon the memory, if I may so express it, of all the beings of the whole planetary system. Everything is inscribed in this faculty of cosmic remembrance, cosmic memory, of the Saturn beings. If the vista of the weaving life realities of existence in the Saturn sphere is a shattering experience for the initiated observer, it is even more shattering for him to perceive how the effects of a previous incarnation are carried down into a new earthly life by individualities whose karma, determined by their particular experiences, was shaped and given configuration in the Saturn sphere. (Rudolf Steiner, *Karmic Relationships,* vol. 7)

The soul finds itself confronted in this sphere with the real spiritual background of life manifestations, which originally came into the world by the great sacrifice of the Spirits of Wisdom or Kyriotetes. Thus the sphere of Jupiter is the expression of this hierarchy.... This immeasurable wisdom of creative life, which knows the beginning and the end of all existing life manifestations, is the deed and heritage of the Spirits of Wisdom in the sphere of Jupiter..... The wisdom acquired here is not intellectual knowledge that can only analyze, but a creative wisdom able to consider simultaneously all the stages and consequences of any creative deed, working as do the life forces of the plant. (Willi Sucher, *Isis Sophia II*)

Out of the innate qualities of the sphere and planet of present Saturn, these forces act as guarantors of the will of the divine Father world. The spiritual beings, who are connected with it, have assisted and witnessed all evolution since the very first beginnings. On account of being the oldest, who have taken part in everything, they take care in the solar world that the original intentions of the Gods are never deviated from or forgotten. Thus, this planet is, in the highest sense, the memory of the whole solar organism and the physiological foundation of memory and conscience within the human being. This is also the reason why Saturn is connected very deeply with the manifestations and the laws of destiny (karma) and reincarnation. Saturn holds, as it were, the threads of evolution leading from the past to the present. (ibid.)

Here we have just a first attempt to understand the planets through the forms woven in the cosmos by their relationships to the Sun and Earth and, in the case of Saturn and Jupiter, with each other as a kind of life-body of each planet. In a certain way, one can say that the woven form in time *is* the planet, not the mineral body, which is just the indicator that we see in materialistic astronomy.

These classical planets are built into the human organism. In the next section we will look at the outer planets, Uranus, Neptune and Pluto and their relationship to the so-called classical planetary system.

THE OUTER PLANETS*

Now we come to the so-called outer planets or the new planets of the solar cosmos. We have gone through the so-called classical planets Saturn, Jupiter, Mars, Sun, Venus, Mercury. Now we come to these mysterious new planets and explore what they mean out of this new approach to a star wisdom, based on the work of Rudolf Steiner.

Steiner did speak about Uranus and Neptune, but not very much. Pluto, which was discovered in 1930, after Steiner's death, thus he never would have spoken directly about this planet. Willi Sucher has done a great deal of research and work in taking up what Steiner had to say. He has developed a perspective on all three of these outer planets out of anthroposophy.

Let us go into these three outer planets and look at what can be called their trinitarian aspect, a threefoldness on many different levels, as a way of understanding them. To begin with, we start with a couple of quotations from Rudolf Steiner about the outer planets. I have a larger selection of them that are included in the appendix.

---

*   Video: Course 2: The Planetary Spheres: The Outer Planets: Uranus, Neptune and Pluto Planetary Spheres, Session 7.

It is to be noted that the two outermost planets now reckoned as belonging to our solar system by physical astronomy—Uranus and Neptune—did not originally belong to our Solar System; they came much later into the sphere of attraction of our system: they then joined company and remained with it. They cannot therefore be reckoned in the same sense as the other planets as belonging to our system from Saturn onward, for they, so to speak, belonged to it from the beginning. (Rudolf Steiner: *Spiritual Beings in the Heavenly Bodies and the Kingdoms of Nature*, lect. 10)

As antiquity did not discover Uranus and Neptune, Saturn was taken to be the outermost planet and it is still justifiable today to go as far as Saturn. Astrologers still have an inkling of these things for they connect Uranus and Neptune only with those human qualities that transcend the personal and make a man a genius go beyond the individual personal element—where he is concerned with things that no longer have to do with his personal development. All astrological statements are to this effect. Uranus and Neptune come into play only when a man becomes a genius or strives to transcend the human element, when his organization has the tendency to expand or decay too strongly. (Rudolf Steiner, *Understanding Healing*, lect. 11)

Remember the comments about transcending the human element, transcending the personal or decaying too strongly. This will help inform us as we move forward into these three outer planets. Let us begin with the astronomical information to familiarize ourselves with these planets from an astronomical and then from a historical perspective. Below are the traditional symbols for these three planets and some information about their discovery and their orbits.

Uranus

84 year sidereal orbit
Discovered March 13 1781 in stars of Taurus

Sir William Herschel observed Uranus from the garden of his house in Somerset, England. He initially reported it as a comet. "I don't know what to call it. It is as likely to be a regular planet moving in an orbit nearly circular to the Sun as a Comet moving in a very eccentric ellipsis. I have not yet seen any coma or tail to it."

Neptune

164.8 year sidereal orbit
Discovered September 23, 1846, conjunct Saturn at border of Capricorn into Aquarius

First discovered mathematically by Urbain Le Verrier before it was directly observed. The only planet in the Solar System found by mathematical prediction rather than by empirical observation.

Pluto

247.68 year orbit
Discovered February 18, 1930 (one orbit of Uranus, 84 years, after discovery of Neptune in 1846)

Discovered in America (only planet discovered in America) by Clyde Tombaugh. Discovered in stars of Gemini opposite the constellation where it is now, so has only completed half an orbit since its discovery.

Threefold Great Opposition July 1930; Jan. 1931; June, 1931 (Jupiter was near conjunct Pluto in Twins, opposite Saturn in Archer.) Connection to 2020! Pluto conjunct Jupiter and Saturn in Archer.

You can see that Uranus has an 84-year sidereal orbit and was discovered in 1781. Each of these planets was discovered one in each century: Uranus in the 18th century, Neptune in the 19th century, and Pluto in the 20th century. As indicated in the insert, Uranus was discovered by Sir William Herschel and it was observed from his garden in Somerset, England. At first, he thought it was a comet until he could study it further and realized that this was not a comet, but it had a regularity to it that was more like a planet.

Neptune was discovered by Urbain Le Verrier in 1846 and has a 164.8-year sidereal orbit. It made one complete orbit (turning 1 year old since its discovery in cosmic terms) in 2011. It is interesting to note that Neptune was discovered before it was directly observed. So,

Neptune is the only one of these three planets that was discovered by pure calculation, which is relevant to its spiritual quality as we will see going forward.

Pluto was discovered in February of 1930, and has a 247.68-year orbit. You can just imagine the length of time of that orbit. We have yet to see one full orbit of Pluto since its discovery. Not until 2178 will it have completed one full orbit around the Sun. Pluto was discovered in America by Clyde Tombaugh. It is the only planet that was discovered in America, which is another significant qualitative factor to contemplate as we move forward.

One interesting fact about these three planets is that all three of them were discovered when they had a special relationship with the planet Saturn. Uranus was opposite Saturn. Neptune was conjunct Saturn, and Pluto was just about opposite Saturn. If you recall, we spoke earlier about Saturn as the sphere that carries world karma and the evolutionary plan for humanity. It holds world destiny as we move through evolutionary consciousness. So, the fact that these were discovered when in this special relationship with Saturn speaks to these discoveries as moments in the karma of humanity when something new enters.

On the one hand, we can look back historically and trace the movements of these outer planets: Saturn, Uranus, Neptune, and Pluto. One can do historical research on their conjunctions and oppositions. Willi Sucher has done a great deal of that research, looking at what happened in early history when these planets came into certain relationships with each other. But from my perspective there is an important distinction to consider, which is that something changed in the nature of our relationship to these planets when they entered human consciousness. There is a different relationship. In fact, it is a relationship that indicates in world karma that now humanity is able and called on to take up the qualities of these planets in a conscious way. We became "aware" of them. We were ripe in our consciousness, through the consciousness soul, to take upon ourselves both the challenges and potentialities of these planets. One could say that when each of these planets was discovered, humanity was potentially "ready" for it.

The Planetary Spheres

Let us now explore the deeper meanings of these planetary spheres. Here is an image of a human form standing on the plane of the Earth; Earth below, the heavens above. We can imagine how the classical planets are contained within this human form; they are built into our physical body. So, where then are these three outer planets? How do they relate to the human being?

We can add to this image and imagine three spheres around the human being. One elliptical sphere that goes above the head and below the feet of the human into the interior subterranean levels of the Earth. A second sphere higher and lower and a third sphere even higher and lower into the subterranean element of the Earth.

Willi Sucher has related these three spheres (we will go into them in detail) to those outer planets. This first, inner sphere around the human being is connected with the sphere of Uranus; the next sphere around the human being relates to Neptune; the outer sphere connects with Pluto. They enter the "aura" around the human being—an aura of consciousness. If we just begin with this image as an idea, we can explore further how this applies to the trinitarian aspect or threefold aspect of these three planets.

We will begin with a quotation by Steiner to give us one picture. He does not name the planets here, but Sucher draws a correlation among these three realms surrounding the human being, above and below, and the three outer planets newly entering human consciousness and human capacities.

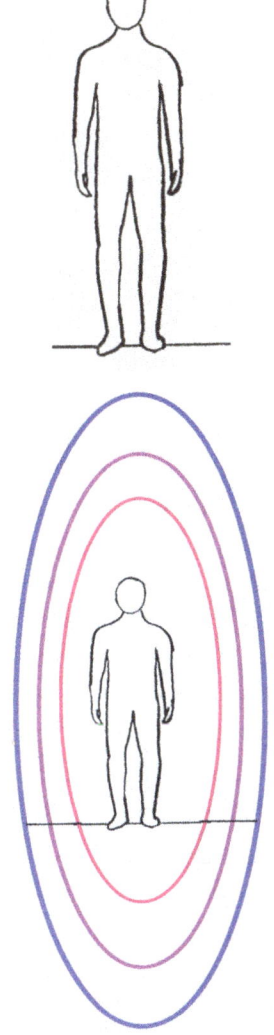

We have the physical world, the astral world, the Lower Devachan and the Higher Devachan. If the body is thrust down lower even than the physical world, it comes into the sub physical world, the lower astral world, the lower or evil Lower Devachan and the lower or evil Higher Devachan. The evil astral world is the province of Lucifer. The evil Lower Devachan is the province of Ahriman, and the evil Higher Devachan is the province of the Asuras. When chemical action is driven below the physical plane—into the evil Devachanic world—magnetism arises. When light is thrust down into the sub-material—that is to say, a stage deeper than the material world—electricity arises. If what lives in the Harmony of the Spheres is thrust still further down, into the province of the Asuras, an even more terrible force [which will not be possible to keep hidden very much longer] is generated. It can be only hoped that when this force comes to be known—a force we must conceive as being far, far stronger than the most violent electrical discharge—it can only be hoped that, before some discoverer gives this force into the hands of humankind, men will no longer have anything immoral left in them. (Rudolf Steiner: *Esoteric Christianity*, "The Etherization of the Blood," Q&A session)

This is quite a powerful statement by Steiner about the nature of the Asuras and what he calls this third force. So here he relates the first lower realm to the realm of Lucifer and electricity, the second lower realm to the realm of Ahriman and magnetism and the deepest lower realm to the Asuras and what he calls the third force of incredible destruction.

This quote is continued with the image below, which Steiner then drew on the blackboard to illustrate what he said. You can see in this image the sub-earthly realms, but he also then connects them to the higher realms: the light ether falls to the sub realm of electricity, the chemical, or what's also called the tone ether, falls into the realm of magnetism, and the life ether falls into the realm of the terrible forces of destruction.

The Planetary Spheres

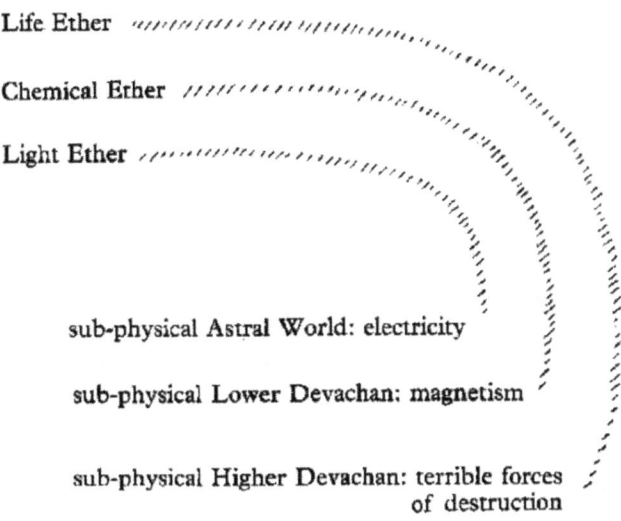

Let's add this to our image of the human form standing on the Earth with these three spheres around it (next page). As you can see in the diagram, the first lower realm is electricity, or Lucifer as fallen light; the second, magnetism, Ahriman, fallen tone or chemical; and the third, the Asuras, or fallen life ether. Above the human form is the higher elements of light, tone, and life.*

To further our understanding, take a look at what was happening in the world at the time these planets were discovered, which gives us a further clue to their meaning. As we can often see in the world, when certain cosmic events occur, there is a kind of reflection in human consciousness. What was unfolding in world events, science, and in human consciousness that might be related especially to awakening awareness of these three spheres?

As mentioned earlier, Uranus was discovered in 1781, during the fullness of the Age of Enlightenment, or the Age of Reason. In fact, it was exactly in 1781 that Immanuel Kant published his book *Critique of Pure Reason*. The year 1776 saw the establishment of the Illuminati, a religious order devoted to creating a kind of utopia on the Earth. Of course, the United States Declaration of Independence was

---

* Video: Course 2: The Planetary Spheres: The Outer Planets: Uranus, Neptune and Pluto Planetary Spheres, Session 8.

written in 1776 as a call for the freedom of the individual from the divine right of kings, a call to self-determination. And in 1781, the U.S. Constitution was ratified to spell out those freedoms.

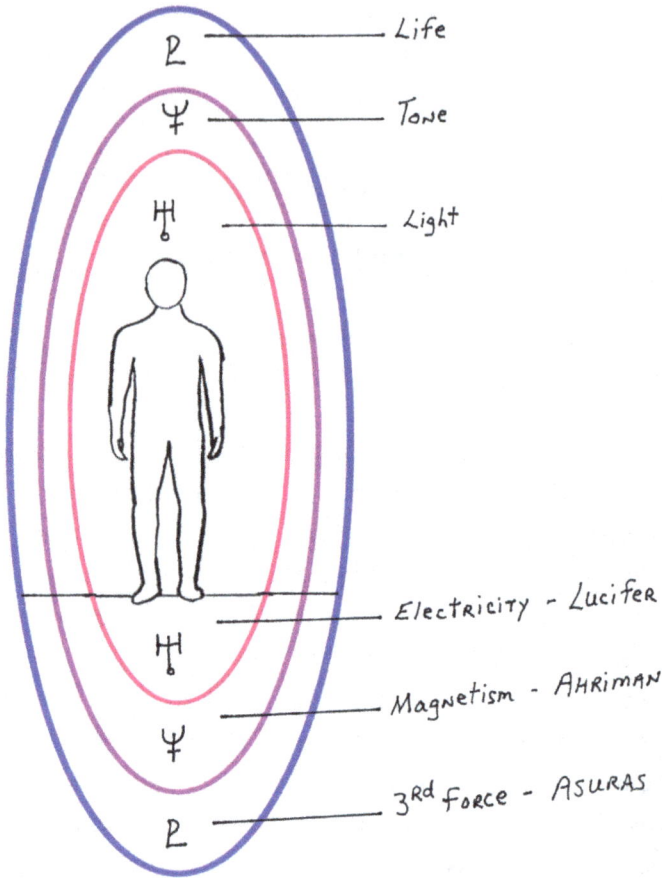

The time of the Uranus discovery also included the Industrial Revolution, which spans quite a period of time, with 1760 to around 1820 or 1840 covering the real fullness of the Industrial Revolution, which would have been impossible, of course, without electricity.

In regard to electricity, Benjamin Franklin conducted his famous experiment in 1752 with the kite and key during an electrical storm, which provided his aha discovery concerning electrical forces. In 1791 Luigi Galvani was able to demonstrate that it is electricity that allows neurons to pass signals to human muscles. This was the beginning of the awareness of the electrical forces that live in the human organism. Then, in 1800, Alessandro Volta (whose name gives us the word *volt*) invented the battery as a source of electrical energy.

Thus, you can see around this discovery of Uranus, various themes that we might associate with Lucifer and with electricity—ideas of enlightenment that called for the sovereignty of reason based on the evidence of the senses, awaking to the impulse of individual freedom and the revolution against the old forms of royal divine rights and class system and the rule of hierarchical authority, and, in science, discoveries related to electricity, or fallen light.

Uranus Discovery, 1781

Electricity

1752	Benjamin Franklin's experiment with a kite, a key, and a storm
1791	Luigi Galvani demonstrates electricity as the medium by which neurons pass signals to the muscles
1800	Alessandro Volta invented the battery as convenient source of electrical energy

Age of Enlightenment or Age of Reason

1781	Immanuel Kant published *Critique of Pure Reason*

History

1776	Founding of Illuminati
1776	U.S. Independence: freedom from "divine right of kings"
1781	U.S. Constitution ratified
1789–99	French Revolution: liberty, fraternity, equality
1760–1820	Industrial Revolution (as result of electricity)

Uranus

1. Electricity: fallen light
2. Enlightenment: sovereignty of reason based on evidence of the senses
3. Revolutions: Removal of divine rulership/assertion of self-determination

With the discovery of Neptune in 1846, we find activity around the whole development of electromagnetism, including the emergence of chemical industry, telegraphy, Morse code, hydroelectricity, and electromagnetism. In 1840, an American, Charles Grafton Page, conducted an experiment through which he discovered the ringing sound of magnets. In 1844, Manzetti first conceived of the idea of the telephone. In 1860, Johann Philip Reis made an electromagnetic device that could transmit musical tones, calling it the telefon.

Neptune Discovery, 1846

Electromagnetism: chemical industry, telegraphy, Morse code, hydroelectricity, and electromagnetism.

Science and Technology

1840	American Charles Grafton Page experiment discovers ringing sound of magnets
1844	Innocenzo Manzetti first conceives idea of a telephone
1860	Johann Philipp Reis makes a functioning electromagnetic device that can transmit musical notes. He called it a *telefon*.

Philosophy

1843	Karl Marx develops his theory of dialectical materialism
1848	*The Communist Manifesto* first published
1838	Darwin conceives his theory of natural selection
1859	Darwin's *On the Origin of Species* published
1860	Henry Huxley coins the term *Darwinism*
1836	The Transcendental Club founded
1840	In America, first flagship journal, *The Dial*
1841	Emerson publishes *Essays,* his second book
1841	Rudolf Steiner: start of the Great War in Heaven

Neptune

1. Electromagnetism
2. Dialectical materialism / Darwinism / Transcendentalism
3. War in Heaven

In human ideologies, in 1843, Karl Marx was developing his theory of dialectical materialism, publishing the "Communist Manifesto" in 1848. In 1838 Darwin conceived his theory of natural selection, which was developed over years into his 1859 book, *On the Origin of Species*. We also have the thinking of Ralph Waldo Emerson, who was developing his work in 1841 related to transcendentalism and publishing his second book, *Essays*.

This was also a significant time from a spiritual-scientific perspective. Rudolf Steiner identified 1841 as both a kind of peak of materialism and the year when the Great War in Heaven began between Michael and the Dragon forces, which culminated in 1879, when the dragon was cast down to Earth and entered human thinking.

So, we can see in history this relationship perhaps to the ahrimanic forces working in humanity—the idea coming through Darwin and developed further that the human being evolved from an animal; the ideas of Karl Marx, dialectical materialism; the scientific developments around electromagnetism; and then this picture of the War in Heaven that began in that year when Neptune was discovered.

PLUTO DISCOVERY, 1930

SCIENCE AND TECHNOLOGY

1927 Big Bang Theory first noted by Georges Lemaître
1932 First cyclotron ("atom smasher") invented by Ernest Lawrence
1934 Induced radioactivity created
1939 Albert Einstein writes letter to Franklin Roosevelt about building an atomic bomb

Philosophy—Existentialism: Humans are "condemned to be free" and have no essence, because there is no Creator (the term *existentialism* was coined in the 1940s by Gabriel Marcel)

1925 Gabriel-Honoré Marcel essay on existence and objectivity
1927 Marcel, *Metaphysical Journal* (metaphysical alienation)
1938 Jean Paul Sartre, novel *Nausea* (manifesto of existentialism)
1939 Jean Paul Sartre, *The Wall*

HISTORY

1924 Hitler writes *Mein Kampf*
1929 Great Depression
1933 January, Hitler becomes German Chancellor
1934 Stalin begins the Great Terror in Soviet Union
1933–35 Rudolf Steiner, the return of Christ in the etheric

PLUTO

1. The atom: nuclear destruction / radioactivity
2. Big Bang materialistic origin of the cosmos from atomic explosion
3. Existentialism: godless universe
4. Nazism
5. Christ in the etheric

Now let's move on to Pluto, discovered in 1930. (We will come back to this date a little later with regard to its significance in relation to the Great Conjunction of 2020.) What were the discoveries and the emerging thinking associated with Pluto? In 1927, the Big Bang model of the universe was first proffered by Georges Lemaître as the theory that our origin, our whole cosmos, was born through a huge atomic explosion.

In 1932, the first cyclotron, or atom smasher, was invented. In 1934 induced radioactivity was created. Here we have in science, though Steiner did not name it so, what many consider as the third force: atomic energy, nuclear power, radioactivity. It seems very possible that this is the third force, which Steiner described as more destructive than the greatest electrical discharge that one could imagine.

In 1924, *Mein Kampf* was written. In 1929, of course, there was the Great Depression. In 1933, Adolf Hitler became Chancellor of Germany. In 1936, the Great Terror (or Great Purge) of Joseph Stalin began in the Soviet Union. So here in world events, we can see world changing upheavals and destruction, which we will explore later. Significant in this is the great disaster wreaked by Nazism on Central Europe.

In philosophy, we have the unfolding of the philosophical perspective of Existentialism, which basically states that human beings are "condemned to be free," and that we essentially have no essence because there is no God, therefore we must find purpose and meaning out of nothing.

Most important, perhaps, Rudolf Steiner speaks about the years 1933–35 as the time of the event that he called the return of the Christ being in the etheric realm.

So, we can see in the world the new developments in science, the cataclysmic events in humanity and the philosophical perspective of Existentialism with its essential message that the human being has no creator and must find itself out of nothingness. We will go into this a little later, but I think this all points to the emerging activity of the Asuras. Though there is little written about them by Steiner, in what he does say we find a relationship of the Asuras to physical annihilation, the destruction of the body and with it the destruction of the ego of the human being, or one might say, the experience of nothingness out of which humanity descends into destruction or rises to a newfound relation to the force of the "I Am" to the new Christ experience.*

Let us continue building on this a little further, particularly in relation to Rudolf Steiner's picture of the sub-earthly realm. We can use this to elaborate on the threefold, or counter-trinity, perspective based on what Steiner spoke about in lectures he gave on the interior of the Earth. He speaks about the nine sub-layers of the Earth, going below the crust of the Earth and into the interior. He divides those layers into three sets of three: the first set is lower realm of three layers, with the being of Lucifer, mirroring the Third Hierarchy; the second three layers, with Ahriman, as a kind of sub-mirror of the Second Hierarchy; and the lowest three realms, seven, eight and nine, with the realm of the Asuras, as a kind of sub-mirror of the First Hierarchy.

Here we have Steiner developing this lower aspect of the three threefold realms, connecting them with three adversarial beings in the nine layers of the Earth's interior as a kind of shadow, or sub-mirror, of the nine realms of the hierarchies. If we consider this we can, from one perspective, consider the Third Hierarchy as an expression of the Holy Spirit's activity; the realm of the Second Hierarchy as an expression of the Son forces' activity; and the First Hierarchy, the highest of the three, as an expression of the Father.

Let us just hold this idea as we begin to build our complex picture of the human being with the three spheres around the body, with their higher and lower aspects connected to Uranus, Neptune and Pluto. From this, we can see the luciferic forces as anti-Holy Spirit, the ahrimanic forces as anti-Son forces, and the asuric forces as anti-Father forces, against the ground of the world, the formation of the physical body, and the beginning and foundation for all human evolution.

How do we now look at the counterbalance to these lower forces? This brings us to the relationship between the timing of the discovery of these realms and the time of the consciousness soul, when the human "I" can consciously begin to transform its being. This is an area

---
*   Video: Course 2: The Planetary Spheres: The Outer Planets: Uranus, Neptune and Pluto Planetary Spheres, Session 9.

that Willi Sucher developed for presenting these three spheres and their relationship not only to the obstacle forces in humanity, but also to the potentials within the human being in our time. These are the human potentials that Rudolf Steiner laid out in *How to Know Higher Worlds* and elsewhere regarding the development of new faculties in human consciousness that can transform our human nature.

So let us return to the image of the human form with the three sub realms of fallen light, fallen tone, and fallen life and the higher aspects of light, tone, and life, which we related to the spheres of Uranus, Neptune, and Pluto. Willi Sucher relates these three realms to the higher potentialities. First is the realm of Uranus in relation to Imagination, which Rudolf Steiner describes as the first stage of spiritual cognition. One can see how this realm of Imagination is connected to spiritual light, illumination, enlightenment; to the transformation of thinking. This realm of Imagination is a kind of spiritual seeing in living picture consciousness with the spirit-eye.

The sphere of Neptune and its relation to the tone ether, Sucher relates to the realm of Inspiration, the second level of spiritual cognition. One can think of Inspiration as a kind of spiritual hearing. Whereas Imagination is connected with sight and transformed thinking, Inspiration is connected with tone, a kind of spiritual hearing, and with the transformation of the feeling realm or middle realm.

Last, the outer sphere associated with Pluto and its relation to the life ether, Sucher associates with the third stage of higher cognition, which is the realm of Intuition. As Imagination is kind of spiritual sight, Inspiration a spiritual hearing, so Intuition is a kind of spiritual knowing, a union and direct knowing of divine being. It is connected to the transformation of the will.

So, we have this relationship to the Father, Son, and Spirit principles and the counter realms of the luciferic, ahrimanic, and asuric beings. One could view the destructive force of the Asuras as connected deeply with the will; the obstacle forces of Ahriman with a death in the middle realm, this coldness, this lack of feeling; and Lucifer with the fallen thinking, which expresses itself in the seduction of the senses, but also in the realm of illusion and fantasy, or spiritual thinking that takes us away from our real relationship to the Earth.

Now we can build this picture even further. We can take these three higher realms another stage higher. We can connect the first realm and the transformation of Lucifer and Imagination into what Rudolf Steiner describes as Manas or Spirit Self, which is the transformation of the astral nature. This is of course where the Fall took place in the human being out of Lucifer's activity in the astral body. The realm of Neptune where Ahriman works becomes transformed into Buddhi or Life Spirit, the transformation of the etheric nature of the human being, the life forces. The realm of Pluto where the asuric forces work becomes transformed into Atman, or Spirit Human. Here we come even to the transformation of the physical body of the human being as a kind of distant goal moving forward.

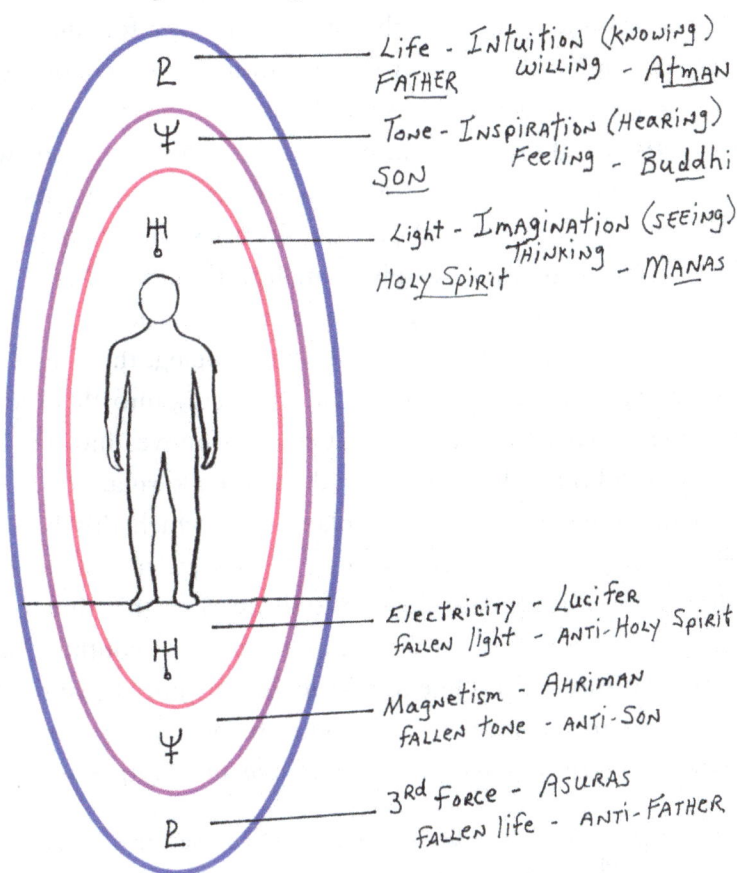

Thus, we have in these three spheres of Uranus, Neptune, and Pluto the obstacle forces, the opposition forces, that work against the transformation of the astral nature, the transformation of the etheric nature, and the ultimate transformation of the physical body out of the Ego.

If we are exploring these planets in for example a birth chart, let us come back to the earlier quote and remember what Rudolf Steiner said about them as related to the super personal or what goes beyond the personal individual element and excessive decay. So, of course, one will have these planets in their chart along with certain relationships to other planets. They certainly have a relationship to the karma and the destiny of the human being. But I think we can begin to see that this relationship to these outer planets is less about the individual human being and more about the greater forces within world karma, and the transformations and challenges that need to be met for humanity to move forward rather than fall into destruction. They are more related to our tasks, not so much for personal karma, but how we participate in human karma and the challenge of our times. This is how one would look at it in the chart, because you could say once we get outside the physical body and the classical planets into these higher realms and we talk about Imagination, Inspiration, Intuition, and Manas, Buddhi, and Atman, we are speaking then about the journey of the human being to unite itself with the universal human being, the Christ I Am, working to transform the individual human being into this representation of the universal human. In that sense, it moves into the super personal, beyond the individual ego and personal karma.

This video course on the outer planets, of which this book is a transcript, was given in March, 2021.* This section is related then to events of 2020/2021. We have gone through in this time quite a world dilemma, a world crisis, which may very well continue in new ways into the future. So, I'd like to take an opportunity because of this particular time, to speak about these outer planets, particularly Pluto, in relationship to these times, in order to give an example of how one

---

* Video: Course 2: The Planetary Spheres: The Outer Planets: Uranus, Neptune and Pluto Planetary Spheres, Session 10.

can see these planetary spheres working into Earth evolution and into human consciousness.

I spoke earlier about the discovery of Pluto in 1930. On the next page is a chart that lets you see it. With regard to the discovery of Pluto in 1930, we discussed world developments at that time, particularly the unfolding of Nazism, the development of nuclear forces, and the return of Christ in the etheric. You can see that Pluto now (2020) is opposite its position in 1930, when it had a relationship to Saturn and Jupiter, with which it also has a relationship today.

Within the inner circle (there are two circles, so it's clear—in orange is the movement of Jupiter in 1930–31. Jupiter was conjuncting Pluto in the Twins and opposite Saturn, which was in the Archer, which is also where Saturn is in 2020. Written on the image are the various dates when Jupiter came into direct opposition to Saturn and into conjunction with Pluto. However, you could say that, during that whole time period, there was this great opposition of Saturn and Jupiter in line with Pluto in this axis of Archer and Twins. (I have written articles about this, available at astrosophy.com.)

This axis of Archer and Twins is, you could say, the vertical egoic axis of our time. It is the axis of the summer and winter solstice. So, it represents the vertical axis of the great cross of the cosmos in our times, and is connected with the egoity of the human being, the awakening and development of the "I," with the great question, what is the human being?

In the Twins, there is a certain kind of development, and in the Archer another, but they each present a kind of dualistic picture. In the Twins, you have the hierarchical above and below. In the Archer, you have the animal half of the body with the human emerging from it and aiming an arrow toward spiritual goals for the future. This represents the duality of the human being, whose of the animal-nature forces wrestle with the higher goals for its spiritual becoming.

Thus, in this picture of 1930 we have a representation of what I think, from my own research, is the beginning of the work of asuric forces in the world in relation to this discovery of Pluto. This is revealed in the very particular way that Nazism created the Holocaust

SPEAKING TO THE STARS

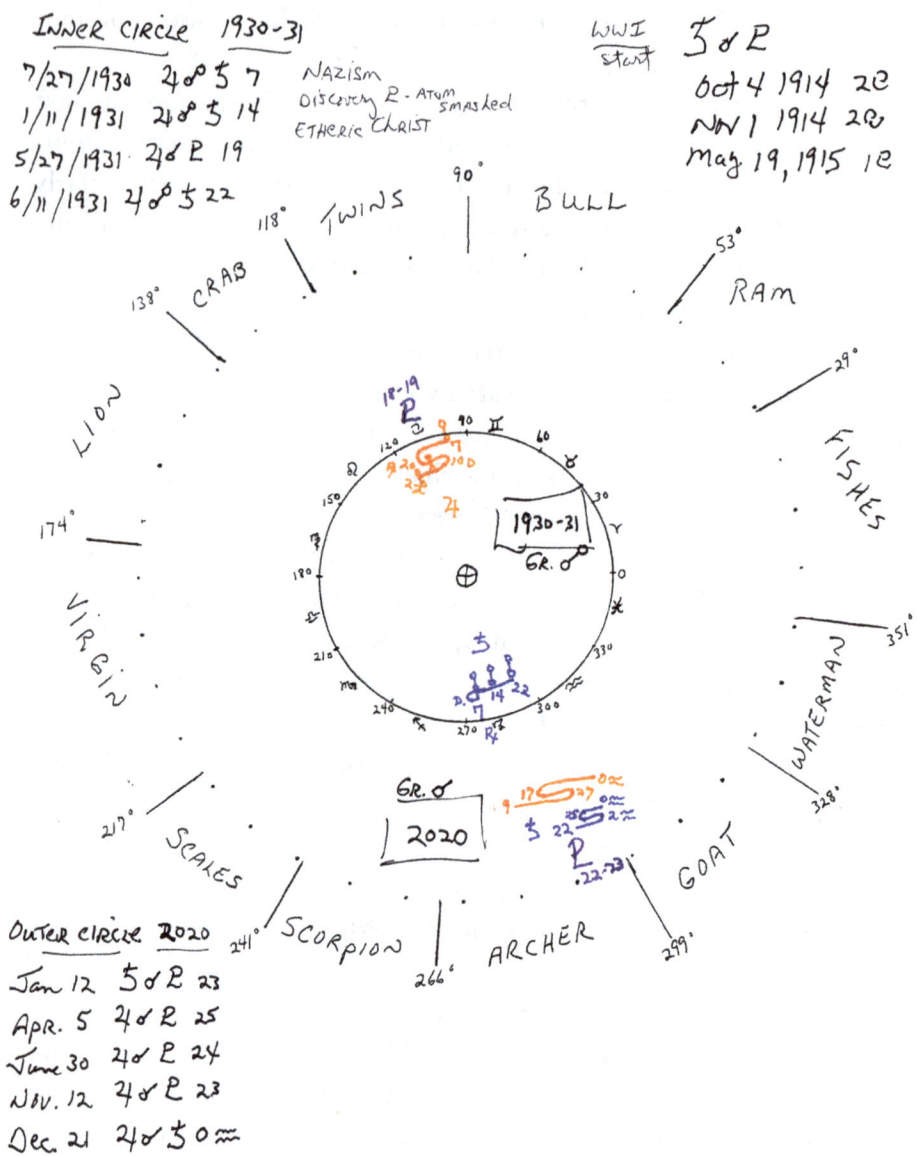

in humanity with the massacre of millions of people in a very calculated and mechanical way. One can also see it in the use of the atom bomb against Japan and in Stalin's massacres during the Great Terror. In these, a new relationship to killing on a mass scale emerges. We see in history in the rise of Nazism and the resulting War the attempt to block what Steiner predicted as the beginnings of the capacity to come to an awareness of the Return of the Christ in the etheric realm.

These activities in the 1930s are directly related to our times. How? Now we come, as you can see in the outer circle, to a conjunction of Saturn and Jupiter in the same line, and they also come into conjunctions with Pluto, leading up to their Great Conjunction during 2020. You can see the movements of Jupiter and Saturn over all of 2020, passing back and forth in conjunction with Pluto. The dates are on the bottom left of Jupiter conjunct Pluto three times, Saturn conjunct Pluto, and Jupiter eventually conjunct Saturn at winter Solstice, but now just stepping out of Sagittarius at the conjunction into the constellation of Capricorn. This occurs when Pluto has actually made half of its orbit.

Now, you might say, *Well, that's not half of 248 years,* but the odd thing about Pluto is that it has an extremely eccentric elliptical orbit. The shorter part of the orbit, the perihelion (which we will go into in the heliocentric course) is much shorter than the long, aphelion part of the eccentric ellipse of Pluto. So, let's "see" the parallel. Pluto is now (2020) essentially opposite its position in 1930, when it was discovered, and in conjunction with Saturn and Jupiter, whereas in 1930 it was in opposition, though in the same constellation axis as now when coming together with Saturn and Jupiter in conjunction. These great conjunctions have world karmic significance, and we have it happening all in the body, the animal part of the Archer. (For clarity, the meetings of Saturn, Jupiter, and Pluto are all in the body of Archer, but the Great Conjunction just steps into stars of Capricorn, but this will be left another level of discussion.) Research needs to continue, but I think this conjunction is deeply connected with the emergence of covid 19, the vaccines, and all that is happening not only in the medical realm, but also the implications for it in the economic realm, in the global social realm and in the political realm. What is beginning to awake? What is beginning to take place in humanity as a consequence of this situation that might be related to the asuric forces?

My own thinking is that we are now really witnessing the activity of the asuric forces in what is happening in the world today. I think we are seeing just the beginnings of its unfolding in the forms that are being set up out of the rationale behind the virus and the vaccination program, with broader impact not only on health, but on world economy, world social and government life and on human relationships. It is deeply related to the root activity of the asuric forces, which are anti-Father, anti-physical body, and anti-ego, and ego depends on the physical body for its further development on Earth.

I will add something a little later in which Rudolf Steiner speaks about this very intimate relationship between the ego of the human being and the body, the physical form, as the expression of the ego. In the whole progression of evolution, it's important that the human being unite with the body and transform the body spiritually. It is not a matter of leaving matter behind, leaving the body behind and ascending to a spiritual bliss. It is a process of the human "I Am," out of its spiritual faculties, taking up the body, the physical body, and transforming it for the next stage of evolution to be fulfilled. This is the fundamental work of the Christ activity in the Earth. The activity going on now is working against that possibility and, by so doing, against the proper evolution of the human being and the divine plan of the Father.

I include a few quotes from Steiner about the Asuras, just to bring this into the context of his work. I will say in advance that I only bring this in because it's a deeply disturbing time, and I think it's of utmost importance for humans who are capable to be very awake to the forces that are at work on a spiritual level. So, these are a call to awaken and be conscious about what is happening and not in any way to cause alarm or create sensationalism. Below are three consecutive quotes by Steiner. In anthroposophical circles, there's a lot of talk of Ahriman and Lucifer, but I think it's time we begin to awaken to the activity of the Asuras who are emerging in the world.

> In the course of the Earth-period man will cast away all the evil brought to him by the luciferic spirits together with the blessing of freedom. The evil brought by the ahrimanic spirits can be shed in the course of karma. But the evil brought by the asuric powers cannot be expunged in this way. Whereas the good Spirits instituted pain and suffering, illness and death in order that despite the possibility of evil, man's evolution may still advance,

whereas the good Spirits made possible the working of karma to the end that the ahrimanic powers might be resisted and the evil made good, it will not be so easy to counter the asuric powers as Earth existence takes its course. For these asuric spirits will prompt what has been seized hold of by them, namely the very core of man's being, the consciousness soul together with the "I," to unite with earthly materiality. Fragment after fragment will be torn out of the "I," and in the same measure in which the asuric Spirits establish themselves in the consciousness soul, man must leave parts of his existence behind on the Earth.

What thus becomes the prey of the asuric powers will be irretrievably lost. Not that the whole man need become their victim—but parts of his spirit will be torn away by the asuric powers. These asuric powers are heralded today by the prevailing tendency to live wholly in the material world and to be oblivious to the reality of spiritual beings and spiritual worlds. True, the asuric powers corrupt man today in a way that is more theoretical than actual. Today they deceive him by various means into thinking that his "I" is a product of the physical world only; they hue him to a kind of theoretic materialism.

But as time goes on, they will blind man's vision of the spiritual beings and spiritual powers. Man will know nothing nor desire to know anything of a spiritual world. More and more he will not only teach that the highest moral ideals of humanity are merely sublimations of animal impulses, that human thinking is but a transformation of a faculty also possessed by the animals, that man is akin to the animal in respect of his form and moreover in his whole being descends from the animal—but he will take this view in all earnestness and order his life in accordance with it. (Rudolf Steiner, *Disease, Karma, and Healing*, lect. 16)

This makes one wonder, what would Steiner say about technology and biotechnology today and the whole language in common usage around the human being as computer, needing an upgrade and downloading a new operating system. We have now this representation of the human being, not so much as an animal out of Darwinism, even though that's still present in humanity and taught, but rather more from the perspectives of artificial intelligence and transhumanism, in which humans are a kind of computer that can have parts exchanged and replaced with biotechnology. Eventually, according to many new thinkers, the human species as we know it will come to an end and a new hybrid of human-computer will take our place. What, then, are the spiritual beings associated with transhumanism?

> An economic life like the Anglo-American, which should end in world dominion—if the effort is not made to bring about its permeation by the independent spiritual life and the independent political life, it will flow into the third of the abysses of human life, into the third of these three. The first abyss is lies, the degeneration of humanity through Ahriman; the second is self-seeking, the degeneration of humanity through Lucifer; the third is, in the physical realm, illness and death; in the cultural realm, the illness and death of culture. The Anglo-American world may gain world dominion; but without the Threefold Social Order it will, through this dominion, pour out cultural death and cultural illness over the whole Earth; for these are just as much a gift of the Asuras as lies are a gift of Ahriman, and self-seeking of Lucifer. So the third, a worthy companion of the other two, is a gift of the asuric powers. (Rudolf Steiner, *Michael's Mission*, lects. 9–12)

Last, the quotation from Steiner is on this relationship of the human form to the ego. We have gone through this in our course on the Zodiac in speaking about the nature of the human form and the zodiac. This human form has been filled so to speak with matter over the course of evolution, but its true form is physical-non material.

> The one and only expression for our "I," it is the human form.... In other words, in all the vast realm of our experience there is one thing—the human form—which is the expression of the human being. It sounds a trivial thing to say, but it is in reality one of the most important utterances that can be made, and one upon which we do well to ponder and meditate. (Rudolf Steiner, *Man in the Light of Occultism, Theosophy, and Philosophy*)

So, with these outer planets, we have gone over all the planetary realms and their relationship to both the potentialities as well as the challenges and obstacles that humanity must begin to take up out of its own spiritual ego forces. Their discovery and emergence reflected in the unfolding of world events, world philosophies, science, are all a part of this freedom of the ego, which now stands at a pivotal point when the transition is required to awaken the spiritual faculties that are necessary to move humanity forward.

4

Christ and the Stars

The Sun and the Cosmic "I Am"*

We will now enter into the heart of a new star wisdom, which is at the same time the core of the work of Rudolf Steiner and anthroposophy: the relationship of the cosmos of the stars to the being whom we call the Christ. Rudolf Steiner has written and spoken in many ways about this great cosmic being, the Christ, who descended and united himself with the Earth in the incarnation of Jesus at the turning point of time. Willi Sucher's work also focuses on this relationship of the Cosmic Christ. It is this relationship that makes possible a new star wisdom and the beginning of that process of speaking to the stars in Steiner's verse. At this point in evolution, it is important that human beings begin to awaken their spiritual consciousness and awaken their new capacities to give birth to the higher self within them. It is this higher, Christ Self who will begin to transform the Earth and ultimately to transform the starry cosmos.

Who is the Christ? Of course, to go into that in great depth is well beyond the scope of this workbook, so here I would like only to look at the nature of this being by considering the Sun. In modern astronomy, we describe the Sun as this ball of nuclear explosions and energy that radiates heat and light into the cosmos—this star at the center of our solar universe. But if we try to penetrate more deeply into the real nature of the Sun, we can come to a realization that the Sun, just as we spoke about regarding the planets, is not a body in the center of

---

* Video: Course 3: Christ and the Stars, Session 1.

our solar system, but the true Sun actually permeates the entire cosmos to the very periphery of the fixed stars of the zodiac. It is that star being(s) who encompasses, and bears and orders the entire solar universe. However, there is an important quality about the Sun not included in modern science. Rudolf Steiner speaks about this nature of the Sun in a very unique way. He states that the Sun is actually non-spatial. In fact, the Sun is negative space, is less than empty space.

What does this picture of the Sun present to us? We can think of this "less than empty space" as being a process that begins at the very periphery of the cosmos, beyond the zodiac. We can imagine a picture of zodiacal and super-zodiacal spiritual substance that continually is streaming, spiraling in from the periphery toward this solar center. Along the way it begins to densify more and more, becoming its most dense on the Earth itself. With the planets Venus and Mercury, already the process of transformation or spiritualization begins, until the substance disappears into this less than empty space, this hole, so to speak, of the Sun, where it is completely spiritualized. What we experience as physical light and physical warmth is really the spatial/sensible by-product of a spiritual process. The Sun actually creates space. Perhaps a parallel can be seen in the way that our own metabolism, through the destruction of material forces we ingest, creates a by-product of warmth in our metabolism and the light of our awake consciousness in the body.

But what becomes of this substance that disappears, so to speak, through the transformative process into the center of the Sun? It reappears at the periphery, beyond the zodiac, and thus the process is continual. So, in the Sun what we have is actually a spiritual activity; an activity of the ultimate transubstantiation of substance into its true spiritual nature where it reappears beyond the zodiac at the periphery again. There is this constant streaming activity from periphery, through the planetary spheres to the Earth and on then to the Sun.

If you have ever looked at the face of a sunflower with the dried seeds, you can see this beautiful large flower head with this kind of aura of little yellow petals around the edge, and yet this spiraling inward and spiraling outward of the seed pattern. This is similar to a flower image of what is actually a process taking place continuously in the cosmos.

In astronomy, if we actually look at the density of the planetary spheres of the planet's bodies, density increases gradually on each planet from Saturn to Earth. But with Venus and Mercury, the density decreases. Thus, our Earth is the densest of all of the planets. Even in this progression of material density, we see a reflection of this transformative process, this build-up of substance to its fullest density, on the Earth and in the beginning of the transformation process. We will return to questions around this Sun later, such as the spiritual beings of the Sun and why the Sun is the center of our universe and the Earth merely a planetary body. There is an esoteric history to the process we will explore with the heliocentric approach out of astrosophy.

Now, if we take this solar process just described, we can in a sense see that activity also expressed in the nature of the "I Am," the ego. As discussed earlier, with our earthly sense of self we have this sense of "I," which we discussed in relation to the planet Mars, the sense of "I," which is the "me that is not that"; the me that is separate and independent. We point to our self bodily when we say "I." So, on Earth we have a kind of spatial concept of our "I" as a kind of "thingness." We associate it with our personality, our character, and the totality of the various identities that define us—career, family role, race, culture, and so on. However, when we really try to elevate our consciousness to the nature of the true "I" of the human being, born out of the Sun, we can come to realize that the nature of the true "I Am" is in fact this less-than-emptiness that is always in process of transformation. This is hard to conceptualize but can be simply held as an imagination of our true nature. I bring this up because in understanding the Sun we can actually have a bit of an understanding of "the Christ," He who in the Gospels refers to himself as "I Am." This being of the Christ is the personification so to speak, the manifestation, the revelation, of this great solar being in our cosmos, who is also the Logos. The Logos—the meaning of the cosmos, the life of the cosmos, the "I Am" of the cosmos in a spiritual sense—descended and became matter, became flesh. This event and its ramifications for our human evolution and for our own true becoming as human beings is deeply profound and is at the center of the work of Rudolf Steiner and the work of astrosophy.

INCARNATION OF THE COSMIC CHRIST*

In traditional astrology everyone says what sign they are, which means where their Sun was at birth. The Sun has this central place in astrology as a kind of "who we are," the basics of our personality. But out of astrosophy we will want to try to elevate this understanding of what the Sun in the chart represents. It represents the true becoming of an "I am," the true nature of who I am as a spiritual being and how I manifest this in my life on the Earth. That is the goal of what the Sun in the chart wants to become.

The personality, or earthly ego that we identify with on Earth, is just a reflection in the world, the space-time biosphere of the true self, which is really in the process of being born in the human being. That capacity for the birth of that human being is now a conscious process, not an unconscious event, but a conscious process in which we participate. That capacity has been implanted into the Earth since the union of the Christ being with the Earth. One could say that the death and resurrection of the Christ being in the earthly body laid the seed force of the Sun into the Earth so that it would not be lost to matter and that humanity would not be lost to the forces of death. Out of that seed force the human being will transform the Earth into a new Sun. This is a mighty cosmic picture to contemplate, but I think it's important at least to touch on it in relationship to the Sun as central to a study of astrosophy and to begin to look at the nature of the Christ incarnation into Earth.

From anthroposophy we realize that though Jesus of Nazareth was a very lofty and highly evolved individuality, the Christ being, the Sun logos only united with this body of Jesus in his 30th year at the event described as the Baptism. During the less than three years of His embodiment, this being totally transformed the sheaths and the very

---

*   Video: Course 3: Christ and the Stars, Session 2.

nature of this earthly vessel, even to going into death and transforming the physical body. Christianity or the Christ impulse then is really not about a teaching, or a doctrine or religion but rather it is about an event; an event that happened for the entire Earth regardless of religion, regardless of race, regardless of nationality. The event of the death and resurrection occurred and is now germinating in the Earth. Any human being can consciously unite with that germination force.

Let us now move on into a more concrete understanding of this being during the three years on Earth and the foundations laid there for humanity's future. We can begin to look at the deeds of this being as archetypes, as seed forces, that the human being can begin to model one's life after and understand one's nature in a deeper way. When we get eventually to the chart interpretation, we will apply what we will now explore—the deeds of the Christ in relationship to the planetary gestures and then to an individual biography. In my own experience and based on the work of Willi Sucher, the relationships to these starry events that are connected to the Christ deeds are some of the most powerful learning tools for someone in understanding their chart, in understanding their challenges and their intentions in incarnation. They can be a real concrete tool for attaining insight and understanding in self-transformation.

So, before we go into these concrete examples, I offer a selection from Rudolf Steiner that addresses what we will be exploring.

> Thus, in Palestine during the time that Jesus of Nazareth walked on the Earth as Christ Jesus—during the three last years of his life, from his 30th to his 33rd year—the entire being of the cosmic Christ was acting uninterruptedly upon Him and was working into Him. The Christ stood always under the influence of the entire cosmos. He made no step without this working of the cosmic forces into and in Him. What took place here in Jesus of Nazareth was a continual realization of the horoscope, for at every moment there occurred what otherwise happens only in a person's birth. This could only be so because the whole body of Jesus descended from Nathan had remained open to the influence of the sum total of forces of the cosmic spiritual hierarchies

that direct our Earth.... He who went about as a being upon the Earth appeared quite like any other man. The forces active within Him, however, were the cosmic forces coming from the Sun and stars; and these directed His body. And it was always in accordance with the collective being of the whole universe with whom the Earth is in harmony, that everything the Christ Jesus did took place. (Rudolf Steiner, *The Spiritual Guidance of Humanity*)

He goes on in this lecture cycle to speak about how the Gospels are really mystery texts, and can be read on multiple levels. In the healings and the various miracles in the Gospels there is a reason it is very often stated that they happened at a certain time, for example "it was the third hour," "it was the sixth day." This is a way of connecting the deeds that were being done in coordination with the starry events that were streaming around, which the Christ was manifesting and using. We will also see going forward how the use of number is a mystery language when we look at the Gospels.

Mercury and the Signs of Christ*

I mentioned earlier when we built up this wave picture of the cosmos, that between the Earth and the Sun, Venus and Mercury already began the transformative process. You could say that Venus and Mercury are of more like nature to the Sun than they are to the Earth. So, they participate in the transformative process and can become for us, as human beings, tools in our own transformative process.

Let us approach Mercury during these three years of Christ's incarnation. When we previously built the form of Mercury, we saw the picture of Mercury in its rhythmical life of weaving around the Earth and the Sun creating this six-pointed star. We saw this imagination of the greater star and the lesser star coming together and uniting into one unified star form. This was a picture of bringing the higher intelligence and its integration into earthly intelligence. This is the activity of Mercury. We have this activity of Mercury beyond the Sun picking up substance from the constellations of the stars and perhaps other

---
*   Video: Course 3: Christ and the Stars, Session 3.

planetary spheres and then coming around between Sun and Earth and handing it off to the Earth. We can imagine that this activity was taken up by the Christ being in a very real and profound way for healing and transforming the Earth.

In Willi Sucher's research, going back to the time between AD 30 and 33, when the Christ was incarnated in Jesus of Nazareth, these loops and conjunctions of Mercury were tracked. By going through the Gospels and looking at the probable dates of these Mercury loops, Willi was able to associate these loops—of which there were seven during the three years, or almost three years, of Christ's incarnation—with what are known in Christian tradition as the seven signs of Christ, which are described in various Gospels.

We will begin to work through each of these seven signs as a healing, not merely a physical healing, but a healing of a whole stream in evolution, a healing of a whole impulse of the past to bring in a new impulse through these astral Mercury forces.

Let's begin with the first sign, which is known as the Marriage in Cana. This sign is associated with a superior conjunction in the constellation of Aquarius followed by an inferior conjunction in the constellation of the Ram, Aries.

Roughly, the story goes that Jesus, his disciples, and his mother had been invited to a wedding in Galilee, in the town of Cana. At the wedding feast they had run out of wine and the mother said to Jesus "They've run out of wine." Jesus says to her "Woman, What weaves between you and I?" Now, that is quite a complex statement to go deeply into about the relation between the mother and Jesus, so for the purposes of this particular study, we will need to leave that. Jesus then tells the servants at the feast to go and get the six stone jars that are used for purification and to fill them with water and bring them to the wine steward of the feast. So, the servants go and they fill the six stone jars of purification with water and they bring them to the steward and he tastes the water and it tastes as if he is drinking wine. He says to the father at the marriage feast, "Most people use the good wine in the beginning and save the poor wine for the end once people have drunk, but you have saved the best wine for last."

There is a lot to this story, but let's just touch a little bit on it. First of all, it's of significance that there are the six stone jars. We have already spoken about Mercury being the six-pointed star. Also, these jars are filled with the water for purification, which is connected to the superior conjunction of Mercury picking up substance from Aquarius, the cosmic waters of life. The image of Aquarius is the man who is holding a stone jar and pouring the waters of life from the cosmos down to the Earth. So already we have a cosmic connection between the six stone jars of the water for purification with Mercury and the water from Aquarius.

Another interesting feature of this healing is that Cana was in Galilee, not Judea. It was a region where there were mixed races. In fact, the word *Galilee* means mongrel or mixed breed. So, it was an area already in Israel that was moving away from the very strict laws of bloodline that the Hebrews throughout their history were entrusted to preserve. The Hebrew people found their sense of "I Am" in the folk, in the continuation of the blood of Abraham. One of their sayings was "I and father Abraham are one." It was essential that this purity of the folk, this sense of "I" belonging to the bloodline, was maintained. It was their special purpose in providing the vessel for the incarnation of the Messiah.

Jesus is at a wedding and alcohol is consumed. In early times alcohol had a certain function that it no longer serves. That function was to loosen the sense of identity from the folk—from the hold of a folk, from the hereditary forces—and to sever the human from its spiritual-folk union. In a certain way it stimulated a different sense of "I am," a different sense of self, which facilitated the separation from the blood forces and the group "I." So, we have in this very simple story, not the conversion of water into wine as some sort of cheap wedding feast miracle, but a profound representation. The new cosmic water from Aquarius was handed off at inferior conjunction in the stars of Aries, . We have spoken before about the Ram being the first constellation, the "I Am" impulse in the cosmos, and that the nature of Christ, which we don't have time to go into now, has a deep relationship to this region of Aries. Aries can also be seen as the Lamb of God.

One way to understand this event at Cana is that the Christ brings the new forces of the "I Am" that will be realized in those people who are freed from the blood forces. And that these new forces of the "I Am" come from the true water that serves as wine for them.*

The second sign is the sign of the healing of the nobleman's son. With this sign there was a superior conjunction in the constellation of Gemini, the Twins, picking up substance from Gemini, and an inferior conjunction in the stars of Leo, the Lion. The story goes that there was a nobleman, in another of the Gospels he is called a centurion or a royal official. In any case we have a person of rank, a person high up the ladder in the hierarchy of the social system. It's important that words matter. The nobleman had a son who was sick and dying. We can think about the nature of the son in relationship to the spiritual son in us. This son is dying and sick. The nobleman, and here is where the language is important, "comes down" to see Jesus and begs him to heal his son so that he doesn't die.

If we think of this as an imaginative initiation picture, we see that the person of royalty or nobility recognized Christ and came to him. When we put this in the context of astrosophy with the superior conjunction in Gemini, we remember that Gemini represents that impulse of hierarchy, of above and below, not only in the relationship of the divine world with the earthly world in the past, but the whole idea of hierarchy. This is the old way of the above/below path, the path of ascending up the ladder. Yet this person high up on the ladder, a royal person, recognizes the true royalty of the Christ being, who as Steiner said was walking about on the Earth as any other man, as a person, not of outer rank, but of spiritual rank. It was this capacity of a nobleman to recognize and "come down" to him, which brought about the healing of the son.

So, you have the superior conjunction in Gemini, picking up this old sense of hierarchy as a path both in social and spiritual development in life, which has been reversed by the Christ. We can think of the washing of the feet as the true image of the changed way of spiritual development, and the reversal of the old path of hierarchy. Now Mercury

---

* Video: Course 3: Christ and the Stars, Session 4.

hands off this Gemini way of the past in the stars of Leo. Leo is the constellation of the true royalty, the kingly sign. We have described the Leo symbol as an image of a center with the line curving out to the periphery and coming back again as a picture of the weaving relationship between center and periphery. In Leo we see the journey of coming to selfhood in the center and with it the danger that one can get stuck in the center, in egotism, as opposed to recognizing the greater periphery as the true nature of the Self and the breathing relationship between the center and periphery, like the heart and breath. The ego-centric self will prefer to succumb to illusions of power and "kingship" out of its own being instead of recognizing and bowing before the True Self in sacrifice.

We come to the third sign. It describes the story of the man who was sick for 38 years. There was a pool called Bethesda with five porticoes, and occasionally the angel of the Lord would come and stir the waters of the pool. Many sick and lame people were gathered around the pool, waiting in the porticoes for that moment when the water would be stirred, and the first one into the water that was troubled would be healed. Jesus came to this pool and there was a man who had been sick for 38 years—he was lame, paralyzed. Jesus asked him, "Do you want to be healed," and the man said, "I've been waiting here for 38 years and there's no one to lift me up and take me to the pool for healing." Jesus tells him to get up, take up his pallet, and walk, and the man does.

This is a somewhat complicated healing to understand, but the key is in the 38 years. Why 38 years? According to the work of Willi Sucher—I can touch on it here, but when we go more deeply into the work it will become more clear—this man was crippled in the will. He had an inability to move, to act, to stand up. He had witnessed something 38 years previously that had deeply troubled him because he had, for some karmic reason, the capacity to sense the significance of this event, but was not able to realize it and to recognize its fulfillment. This event was the star of Bethlehem, which the Magi read as the sign that their great teacher, Zarathustra, was incarnating again. It was a triple great conjunction of Saturn and Jupiter in 6 BC. Sucher, in his book *Cosmic Christianity*, goes into the calculation of this great conjunction in relationship to the birth of Zarathustra, who was the child described in Matthew's Gospel. It is a complicated mathematical process and difficult to understand, but it's related to what is described later in these courses on the Spiritual Nativity. In essence, this great conjunction 38 years previously was the spiritual announcement of the Zarathustra incarnation, which the Magi were able to read.

This Spiritual Nativity is connected to the movement of the Moon Nodes, which take 18.6 years to make a full revolution through the zodiac and are a kind of portal. So, at this moment at the pool of Bethesda, two Moon node returns after the Great Conjunction event, lies this man. The Moon node portal had returned and he now meets the Christ. The meaning of what had made him ill was revealed. This revelation was the healing of that sickness that had eaten into his soul and paralyzed his will even down to his physical limbs. Through this meeting of his "I" with the true "I Am," the Christ, the fulfillment of that star event, he was able through this recognition to regain his ability to walk and stand upright again. What had been a mystery—held back and unknown, which deeply troubled him even to illness—was now revealed. The superior conjunction of Mercury and Sun had occurred in the stars of Virgo, the Virgin, those stars of the great mysteries of cosmic wisdom, the Sophia, who gives birth to the spirit child, and the substance of Virgo was then handed off in the inferior conjunction at the time of this healing in the stars of Sagittarius, the Archer, the stars connected to the limbs and the egoity of the human, exactly at those stars at the tip of the arrow of the Archer.

Here we can see how the cosmic wisdom (the Great Conjunction of 6 BC was opposite the Archer in Pisces), to which this man had been unable to rise, met him at the pool. The point of the arrow of the Archer is you could say the "cosmic aim" of our becoming human, our goal in becoming human, as we rise out of the animal body, the animal nature of the Centaur into our humanity and then aim toward our cosmic goal with the bow and arrow. This man had encountered the Christ, He who is the aim of our becoming human and was through this able to "stand upright and walk" forward in his destiny.

The fourth sign is connected with the event described as the Feeding of the Five Thousand. It is a story that many are familiar with. Jesus removed himself into the hills to be private, and all these people came across the Sea of Galilee in boats and gathered, seeking his teachings. The story goes that he had the people sit down and he taught them. Then he asked his disciples to feed them but they were lost as to how to feed so many. However, there was a young man there with two fishes and five loaves of bread. So, Christ told his disciples to break the fish and the loaves and feed the five thousand people, which they did. After all were fed, there were twelve baskets left over.

Here we have the mystery use of number: two fish, five loaves, twelve baskets and 5,000 people—all cosmic numbers. Rudolf Steiner speaks about the deeper meaning of this "sign" and connects it to the feeding of the people of the Fifth Cultural Age, the Age of Pisces, the two fish, which is our age. In this healing of the 5,000, there was a superior conjunction of Mercury with the Sun in the stars of Aquarius—the cosmic sustenance of Aquarius—which is poured down to humanity. The inferior conjunction was in the stars of Pisces, the two fish, the stars of our Age. So here we have a cosmic gesture of the feeding of the "bread of life," the new food, from Aquarius to the people of the Piscean Age. The remnants left over of 12 baskets filled the entire zodiac.*

We could spend a lot of time going into the details and into the depths of what these signs mean, but this is just to give an indication of these Mercury loops working from the constellations and their relationship to the Christ events.

The Fifth sign is the Walking on the Sea. The superior conjunction took place in the Bull, Taurus and the inferior, again, in the stars of the Lion. We have in the Bull a memory of the Chaldean and Egyptian age, characterized by the Vernal Point in the Bull, as discussed earlier. Here we can see with the great pyramids this real descent into matter and for the first time the use of calculation. The heavy massive architecture nevertheless revealed precise, finely calculated form attuned to the stars. Strongly connected to the Earth yet also with the stars. Even in the imagination of the Bull we have this massive earthly creature with

---

*   Video: Course 3: Christ and the Stars, Session 5.

powerful astral/animal forces but with the two long horns attuned to the cosmos.

Rudolf Steiner speaks in much more depth about this sign of the Walking on the Sea. If we think of the Christ gradually transforming the various sheaths of Jesus into their highest realization, this event represents the transformation of the forces of gravity, on the one hand, and, on the other, astral forces that unite us with the bodily nature. In the story, the disciples were on a boat and the sea was troubled and a storm arose. We can think about the sea in terms of the astral world, our sea of emotions, our surging back-and-forth when we are being tossed by our astral nature. Then they saw Jesus walking across the sea toward them and they had great fear. They cried out to Him, and he said, "do not be afraid; it is I." When he arrived into the boat, the storm ceased and it was calm. Here we have many powerful images related to the "I" and its mastery of the surging sea and storm, the astral body. Steiner speaks about this as that moment when the Christ being had fully transformed the soul and astral nature of Jesus. We can see this overcoming of gravity, overcoming of the forces of being bound up in material life in the soul that tosses us about. In the inferior conjunction in Leo, again we have a picture of the true "I" in the center, the true self that assumes its place as master of the soul.

The sixth sign is described as the Healing of the Man Born Blind. This story, as related in the Gospels, has two components. The superior conjunction of Mercury was in the constellation of Virgo, the constellation of cosmic wisdom, and it came around to inferior conjunction in the constellation of Scorpio. If you recall the two new symbols for these constellations, we saw, in the symbol of Virgo, the Sophia representing the gates to the mysteries of wisdom and life. Scorpio, on the other hand, represents the gates to the mysteries of death and, after Christ, of resurrection. So, we have in Virgo and Scorpio this real polarity with Libra standing between the mysteries of wisdom and life and the mysteries of death. Virgo is also connected in the human form, as we have gone over, to the metabolism, to the transubstantiation of matter into life. Scorpio is connected to the whole death perspective, the fallen eagle, which represents the loss of the human being's understanding of the connection to the divine, marked by death. Yet, also in Scorpio lies, since the Christ event, the potential for resurrection. These are indeed great mysteries.

We have in this sign a story about spiritual blindness, the spiritual blindness of Scorpio, which is healed by the wisdom of Virgo. There are two components to the story. First is the arguments with the Pharisees, who call the man in, ask him who did this to him, blame the parents, ask if he was born this way and why this happened—this whole argument between this person who was blind and was now able to see, with the pharisees, out of their spiritual blindness, attacking the event that had clearly transpired. In this part of the sign, there is this whole exchange that demonstrates a victory over spiritual blindness by the Christ being as he addresses their questions and overcomes their objections.

The second component of the story is the healing when the Christ takes spit and mixes it with clay to make a paste. He places this on the man's eyes and tells him to go wash it in the pool. When he does, the blindness is healed. In the physicality of that gesture we see the beginnings of the metabolic process of Virgo in the spittle. It is the substance that already breaks down the material substance into forces that become part of our life forces. This transformative substance of spittle is mixed with the dead clay of the earth and the union of these two brings about the substance for the healing of the blindness.

The seventh and last of the seven signs is the Raising of Lazarus. Steiner has much to say about this great moment in the Gospels and the being of Lazarus. In the Gospels, Lazarus and his sisters are described as friends of Jesus. His sisters come to Jesus because Lazarus has died, and they ask for his help. But the Gospels say that Jesus waited an extra day, meaning four days, before coming. Why is that? In this sign, Mercury's superior conjunction takes place in the stars of Capricorn, and the inferior conjunction follows in the stars of Pisces. Now Capricorn, in ancient times, was considered the gateway to the gods. It was the constellation through which the initiate went out into the cosmos to receive illumination. Cancer, the opposite constellation, is connected with embodiment, and was seen as the pathway into birth.

Thus, we have the constellation of Capricorn in the superior conjunction, a gateway to initiation, and in fact Steiner speaks of Lazarus' death not as death but as an initiation that had gone wrong. He was being initiated into the Jewish mysteries, and there had been errors in the initiation process. He had not returned into his body after going out into the cosmos for illumination. This process should have happened over three days, but Jesus waited. When Jesus arrives, the famous words are spoken: "Lazarus, come forth," and Lazarus comes out of the tomb. Steiner describes this as a public initiation, the first new initiation by Christ. This event is also connected with one of the Venus signs, which we will go into later.

This event is interesting in that, on the one hand, we have the Capricorn constellation, the gate of initiation, the old form of initiation, which failed. Yet, in this raising of Lazarus, Christ performed the first public initiation, the first new initiation not done in secret. Doing so, he actually started the process of his demise. He had made public what was to supposed to be done in secret, and the punishment for that was death. As the Gospels say, this act infuriated the spiritual rulers, the Pharisees of the Jews, and it was because of this that they sought to have him put to death.

With the inferior conjunction in Pisces, you have this event occurring in the last of the twelve constellations, the culmination of the zodiac. In a certain way, you could say, even in one's chart, when one begins to study charts, Pisces can often be seen as a kind of culmination of a phase of life, depending on the planetary action there. Pisces is a kind of culmination of the twelve before the new year begins with spring in the first sign of Aries. So, in Lazarus, there is a kind of completion of one "life" and the initiation into a new stage of being. Lazarus did go through a transformation. He became John, the beloved disciple, a fundamental change, a new level of existence for him spiritually. So, we see in this seventh sign the healing of the old initiation process out of Capricorn and bringing about in Pisces this culmination and fulfillment for Lazarus in order for him to become a new being, John.

This is a lot to absorb and one needs to live and work with these stories and starry pictures over time. When we get into chart interpretation, one way to take these seven signs is to see if these loops are also in one's chart in the prenatal time. As we shall see, there are about three of these loops in every person's ten lunar month prenatal cycle. Sometimes these loops may correspond directly to these seven signs and sometimes they don't, because they happen often and in different locations. If they relate to these seven signs, this would mean that the superior and inferior conjunctions happen in the same constellations as they did at the time of Christ. It doesn't have to be at the same degree, but in the same constellations. For example, if you have a superior conjunction, as in this last sign, in Capricorn and then an inferior one in Pisces, it would be connected to this event in some special way in your own biography. Meaning in your own destiny you have chosen to come to a kind of personal change and breakthrough that might have its foundations in this Christic archetype. One could think about how, in one's own biography, is there this potential of a kind of Lazarus/John experience, in one's own individual way. Or one might experience the challenge of the resistance against the kind of transformation and culmination of a phase of life. One might even be more prone to the Pharisee response. It can go in different ways, all depending on the karma and the biography of that individual.

If the loops of Mercury in one's prenatal chart are not related to these seven signs, Willi Sucher writes that, at one point in the gospels, Jesus says, "You've seen all of these signs, but I tell you, you will do greater signs than these." This means, that the signs of Mercury outside of these direct archetypal gestures of the Christ being have the potential for us to do our own new signs of healing employing the Mercury forces.

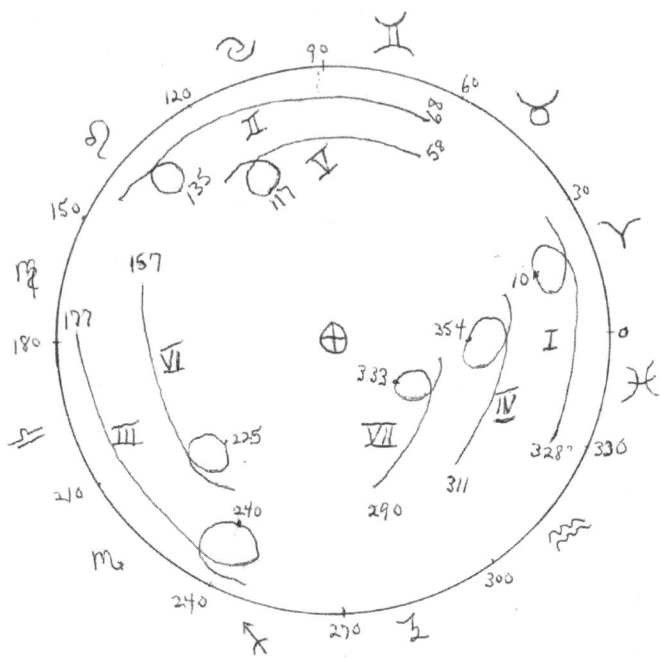

Venus and the Signs of Christ[*]

The Christic aspect of understanding Venus brings us into this turning point in evolution when the human being was in need of a new impulse that the cosmic Sun Spirit brought when He incarnated into a physical body. When studying Rudolf Steiner's work, one reaches a cosmic understanding of the nature of this being and the preparations made in history for His gradual descent to the Earth, as described in the different mythologies and mysteries, until He entered physical embodiment. That embodiment lasted only three years (a little less than three years). That was the maximum that this specially prepared physical body was able to contain this great Sun Spirit. But the purpose of this Sun Spirit was to itself go through physical

---

[*] Video: Course 3: Christ and the Stars, Session 6.

embodiment, go through the experience of separation that humanity had gone through in the experience of death, and to transform death, to transform that physical separation into the foundation for the re-spiritualization and the reunion of the human being with the greater cosmos of being, so that it could come to stand in its full rank in the hierarchy of spiritual beings.

At the core of Willi Sucher's work lies the mystery of these Three Years of the embodiment on the Earth of this being. He follows the deeds of Christ out of a mixture of historical record, astronomical tracking, and the spiritual insights of Rudolf Steiner, to arrive at the cosmic meanings of events that took place in these Three Years of embodiment and even a little bit outside the three years.

We mentioned earlier that Venus is connected with the mysteries, with the old way of the human being finding reunion with the cosmos, with the divine world, through different mysteries. We also built up this five-pointed star, which never changes its form, so it can actually be tracked back to the years AD 30 to 33. In Sucher's book *Cosmic Christianity,* he takes up these events from their cosmological perspective. The whole purpose of astrosophy is to take this Christic impulse that began on the Earth, and out of our work as human beings, bring this Christic impulse back to the cosmos itself, through our transformative deeds.

The Venus pentagram will reveal to us five specific events during the Three Years of embodiment, with two just on either side of the three years. These events represent the founding of the new mysteries, taking the place of the old mysteries and creating the basis for the new mysteries.

If we look at the circle that we created with the five-pointed star, we see that each of these five points are placed as the points created when this star was formed during these Three Years of the embodiment of the Christ on the Earth.

The first of these signs took place in Libra. It occurred at the time of an event before the start of the Three Years, before the Baptism of Jesus, when the being of Jesus had yet to be in-dwelled by the Christ being. The being of Jesus was a very lofty initiate, highly prepared for the sacrifice he was going to make for the Christ Sun spirit to in-dwell that body. This event connects with an experience of Jesus that Rudolf Steiner communicates in a lecture cycle titled *The Fifth Gospel*.

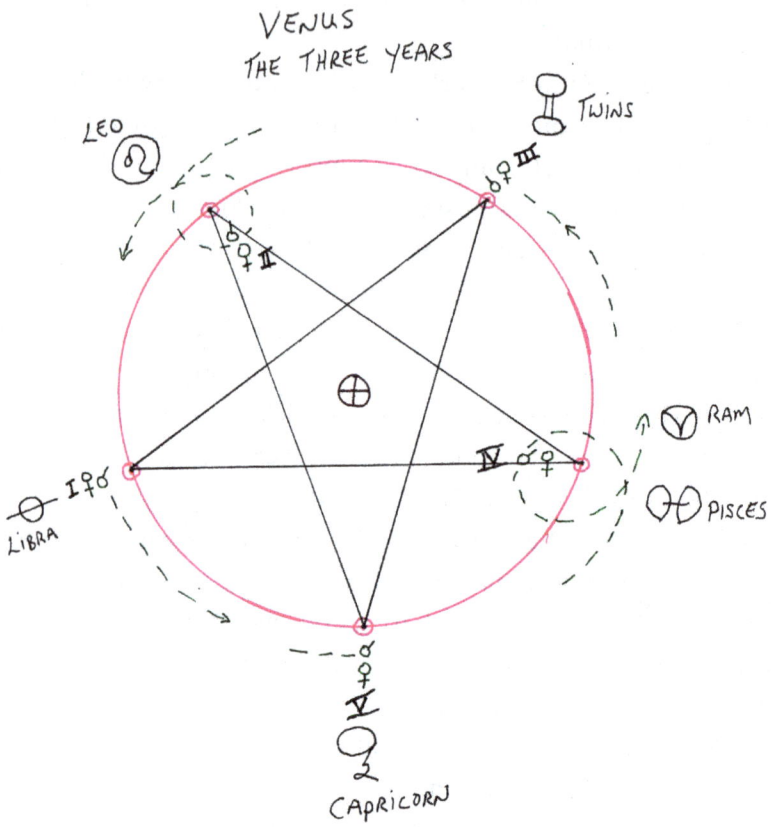

Jesus visited a community near the Dead Sea, which was a group called the Essenes. The Dead Sea Scrolls discovered much about this community. They were an esoteric mystery school within the Jewish tradition. They dwelled in a very reclusive setting and their practices and training involved a kind of strict purification. They separated themselves from the world, enclosed within walls and gates that kept those out who was not members, somewhat like a monastery, where they pursued a path of purification in order to be initiated into higher vision. It is believed that John the Baptist, though not an Essene, had associations with the that group. They continued a lofty esoteric Jewish tradition.

Jesus visits this community, and when he came to the gates to the community, he noticed that Lucifer and Ahriman, those great opposing figures to humanity, were sitting on the gates. They could not get into the community, but Jesus realized that because of this they had been unleashed on the rest of humanity. This experience was somewhat like the Buddha experience of the suffering of humanity. He saw that the old mystery traditions, by separating themselves off for self-purification and ascent to spiritual heights, left the rest of humanity to the suffering inflicted by the adversarial forces of evil in the world. He realized that this was no longer an appropriate as a path. *The Fifth Gospel* says that following this experience he was deeply troubled and saddened and went to his mother (or one could say, The Mother) and had a deep conversation with her. It was after this conversation with the mother and the experience of the Essenes that he was drawn to go to the Jordan River to be baptized. It was at this moment that the individuality who inhabited the sheaths of Jesus sacrificed itself and departed so that the Sun "I Am" could enter this vessel.

Then the Gospels state that immediately after this baptism, emphasis on immediately, Jesus—now indwelled by the Christ—went out into the wilderness. Here He confronted the temptations from those same adversaries who He saw on the gates that the Essene community had let loose on the world. He went out as the Sun spirit, now becoming a human in the flesh, to confront those adversaries and overcome them through the forty days in the wilderness.

All of this is remembered in this corner of the Venus star conjunction in Libra. Libra is the constellation that stands as a portal, a gate, a threshold between the divine wisdom of Virgo and the death forces of Scorpio. In the human form it is the threshold between the upper and lower human. So here we can see this picture of the gates of the Essenes keeping the pure wisdom separated from the dark forces that would destroy it. In this sense is this Venus conjunction a redemption of the old mysteries, a founding of the new mysteries out of the Christ "I Am," who is "the Door," and who steps through the gate into the death forces to transform them, not to keep them away.*

---
*   Video: Course 3: Christ and the Stars, Session 7.

We move now to the second conjunction of Venus, after the conjunction related to the Essene community. Venus goes around the zodiac and catches up with the Sun in the stars of Leo. This conjunction is connected with two events. The Raising of the Youth of Nain and the beheading of John the Baptist. We will only go into the Beheading of John here; however, the raising of the Youth of Nain is deeply connected to the evolution of the new Christian mysteries, even to the Grail mysteries.

Who was John? John was a great prophet, the one who baptized Jesus, calling to the people, "Change your thinking!" You could say that John represents the whole prophetic stream. He was the reincarnation of Elijah. He saw Jesus approaching the Jordan and recognized what his deed was to be, stating that here was One approaching, the thong of whose sandal he was unworthy to untie. So here was this great being of John, with all that came out of the prophet stream, and yet he recognized that the new One to come was greater than he. As he says, "He must increase. I must decrease." John was arrested because he had called out, so to speak, Herodias, the wife of Herod, for her adultery and divorcing her husband, who was Herod's brother, and then marrying Herod. Herodias had a daughter, Salome, who had appeared before Herod at a feast and dance. But this dance was to serve a dark purpose. After the dance of the daughter of the queen, Herod, out of the desire aroused in him, allowed her to ask for whatever she wanted. At her mother's instruction, she requested the head of John the Baptist on a platter. Herod had no choice but to carry out the deed, beheading John and having his head brought in to Salome on a platter, which she then took to her mother, Herodias.

One must always see profound mystery language in the Gospels, with many layers of deep meaning. The head of the human being carries the forces, all the forces, essentialized from the previous incarnation, thus in John from the history of the prophet stream. So, Herodias was participating in dark and decadent mysteries in the use of the forces from the head of John. Herodias, it is noted in the Gospels, was part Phoenician, which is to indicate that she came from the region that was home to the mysteries of Ishtar-Ashtoreth, going by different names. These goddess mysteries were connected to Venus, but they had fallen into decadence and served demonic beings in this time. They were used by dark spiritual powers in order to gain the kind of spiritual knowledge that can be used for egoistic power. Though brutal, we can see in John's death and sacrifice a picture of the end of the old prophetic stream of mysteries. The old way of knowing of the prophets, had to come to an end, was a kind of visionary clairvoyance, whereby higher beings spoke through the prophet. No longer does the spirit stream in from the heights as a kind of prophetic possession of the human, but with Christ the spirit now unites with humanity and the seed is laid for spiritual knowledge out of the "I Am" within. However, Rudolf Steiner goes on to state that, after his death, John the Baptist, in a spiritual form, became a kind of guide and spirit for the twelve disciples during the Three Years. So this prophetic stream was brutally sacrificed, but became of service to the new mysteries going into the future. For students of Steiner, you will know that on a very deep level, there is this special relation between the being of John the Baptist after his death and the being of John the Disciple.

All of these events are connected with this corner of the Venus pentagram in the stars of Leo. As spoken about before, we can see here this gesture from Leo of the human being coming into the center of egoity and the challenge or call of Leo to unite with the higher periphery, the true "I Am" that is the peripheral Self, not the narrow ego of the center. As John said, "He must increase. I must decrease." John's ending became the opportunity to serve the greater impulse of the Christ and the disciples. He sacrificed his individual self for the True I Am. This is the highest gesture of Leo.

Now we move on to the third conjunction of Venus with the Sun in this five-pointed star that occurs in the stars of the Twins, of Gemini. Sucher associates this event with another healing of the old mysteries. It is the story in the Gospels known as the Healing of the Daughter of the Syro-Phoenician Woman.

Again, the details reveal deep hidden meaning. Here it is specifically noted that this was the only time the Christ went outside of the Jewish territory, to the city of Tyre. The Gospels go on to state that He came to a house and there was a woman, she was Greek, of Syro-Phoenician birth. She fell at his feet and begged him to come and heal her daughter who was possessed of a demon. But to test her Jesus said "First let the children eat, for it's not right to take their bread and toss it to the dogs." She replied, "But sir, even the dogs eat the crumbs that fall from the children's table." Jesus says to her, "For what you have said your daughter is healed."

We have a healing, which is of course much greater than just a physical event. All of these events in the Gospels are a kind of merger of historical external event with greater powerful mystery language, spiritual deeds that represents healings on many levels beyond just the physical event itself.

Willi Sucher describes how this healing of the Syro-Phoenician woman's daughter came about because of the great humility that she showed. She fell at his feet. She begged him to heal her daughter. She said "even the dogs eat the crumbs that fall from the children's table." So how can we understand why simple humility would bring the healing of her daughter? As with Herodias, we again have a woman of Phoenician descent, as it is specifically pointed out. The fact that she was Syro-Phoenician points at the connection to certain mystery streams. Her daughter was possessed by a demon. We have the mother/daughter story (like Herodias and Salome). This points us to a relationship to these Syro-Phoenician mysteries, which were associated with the gods known by many names, Baal, Ashtaroth Astarte, Ishtar, and they were particularly decadent at that time. As said earlier, they were characterized by real thirst for power, spiritual power. The moral catharsis and purification required for initiation had been ignored, which opened the door to demonic forces inhabiting the mystery centers and altars of these gods. One could imagine that this "daughter" is both a physical daughter of the woman inhabited by demons as well as the spiritual daughter of the decadent mystery practices, possessed by this absence of moral catharsis and a thirst for spiritual power.

The Venus conjunction associated with this healing is in the stars of Gemini, the stars most associated with hierarchy, the above and below. As mentioned earlier, one can see in the Washing of the Feet, the true reversal of the old spiritual hierarchy. One can think of this woman also falling at the feet of Christ and the total humility shown. On another level one can see in it a picture of the duality between the Tree of Life and the Tree of Knowledge, which you may know of from the story of the garden of Eden. In the decadent form of these mysteries the effort was made to take spiritual knowledge and reach into the tree of life, to gain access to spiritual life forces without having gone through the necessary purification. It was very much associated with black magic. So, in this healing we have a healing of the old mysteries through the humility of the woman, but on a deeper level through the reversal of the arrogance and use of spiritual powers wrongly by asking Christ for even the crumbs from the bread of the children.*

The fourth conjunction of Venus with the Sun occurred in the spring of AD 33, near the vernal point, the crossing over from Pisces into Aries. Already we can think of that as a kind of a transitional point, moving from the conclusion with the final constellation of the zodiac and into the first constellation, the Ram. This conjunction's impact can be seen as taking place during the whole week leading up to the Crucifixion and the Resurrection. It is related to a huge transformation in the relationship of the human being to the spiritual world enacted on the world historical stage in the Crucifixion and the Resurrection. However, in particular, it is related to another one of the mystery traditions that was transformed in the story of Lazarus. (This is also the 7th sign in the Mercury healings.) The story, as related in the Gospels, is that the family of Lazarus (the family of Lazarus were friends of Jesus, including Lazarus himself and his two sisters, Mary and Martha) were seeking Jesus because their brother Lazarus had died. When Jesus heard he had died, he said, "This sickness is not unto death," and he waited two days before going to them. When he arrived, Lazarus had been in the tomb for four days. Mary and Martha said to Jesus that if he had been there, their brother would not have died. A crowd had gathered with the family weeping. Jesus went to the tomb and he called forth these famous words "Lazarus come forth!" And Lazarus came out of the tomb and the crowd was amazed. The Pharisees of the

---

* Video: Course 3: Christ and the Stars, Session 8.

Jewish temple were there and were enraged and the Gospel says that it was at that moment they went to plot how they could take Jesus' life. Why would the raising of someone from the dead provoke Christ's enemies to want to kill Him?

Rudolf Steiner in his lectures on the Gospel of John goes into detail about this event and describes the initiation temple sleep, which was like a death, and lasted for three and a half days. The pupil, the initiate, would be put into a kind of sleep and he would be surrounded and guarded by the hierophants in the temple to protect the spirit and soul and body of this initiate. At that point, the spirit and soul would go out into the spiritual world, just as it does for every human being during sleep, but also the life body would leave, which for anyone else would mean death, but because the hierophants were around the initiate, they sustained the life forces around the body for the three days that the pupil was out, and then when he came back in the body the experiences he had in spiritual vision were imprinted into the etheric body and it became a capacity, which led to his powers as an initiate.

Steiner points out that being in the tomb for three days meant he was in the temple sleep, but the initiation had failed; they feared he had died and would not come out of the temple sleep. Jesus waited until the fourth day to be sure to show the nature of His initiation of Lazarus. When Jesus called him forth, you could say that Jesus performed the initiation in public before all the people. He himself performed the initiation on Lazarus. This is the same Lazarus who would become John. The Pharisees were infuriated, because Jesus had "betrayed" the mysteries. He had performed in public what was forbidden for anyone to see or be aware of, except those in the temple. The sentence for someone who betrayed the mysteries was death. This violation of the mysteries enraged them and caused them to make plans to arrest him and kill him.

In this Venus conjunction and the story of Lazarus we have again the replacing of the old mysteries with the new Christic mysteries. You could say in this picture of the public initiation there were no more closed doors, no more veil over the holiest of holies in the temples where initiation took place. Initiation was now an open secret, in the sense that out of one's own self, out of one's own inner path, one would come to initiation in the future out of the Christic power.

We move now to the final and fifth conjunction in this Venus pentagram. This fifth conjunction occurs just outside of the Three Years in AD 34 in the constellation of Capricorn. Sucher relates it to what happened to Paul, who at that time was called Saul. Saul was in the strict esoteric tradition of Judaism. He was aware that this Jesus had betrayed the mysteries and that this new sect and their talk of a resurrection and the Messiah's arrival was a violation of the truths of Judaism. Saul's work and mission was to persecute the new Christians, the followers of this Risen Messiah. He was traveling on the road to Damascus, where he was to continue these persecutions, when he had this vision of the Christ. He heard a voice saying, "Saul, Saul, why do you persecute me?" He was struck blind and fell from his horse and was in a kind of catatonic state for some days.

Again we have an initiation process; he was blind for three days, in a catatonic state, and afterward he was completely changed. He recognized the truth of the spiritual being of the Christ and was changed from being Saul to being Paul, the greatest of all who those spread Christianity and the first of the new Christian initiates who had not known Jesus during the Three Years. Steiner and Sucher describe this event as the first instance of the future experience of the Christ, toward which every human being may strive. This is Christ appearing not in the physical realm, but in the etheric realm as the Resurrected One. Paul was the first to experience the Christ in this dimension. It is a foundation, foreshadowing the possibility of a new experience of Christ.

This happens in the constellation of Capricorn. Capricorn was always known as the "gateway to the gods." It has historically been that constellation through which the initiates went out into the spiritual world, the portal out into the spiritual world. Capricorn is the constellation of catharsis into initiation.

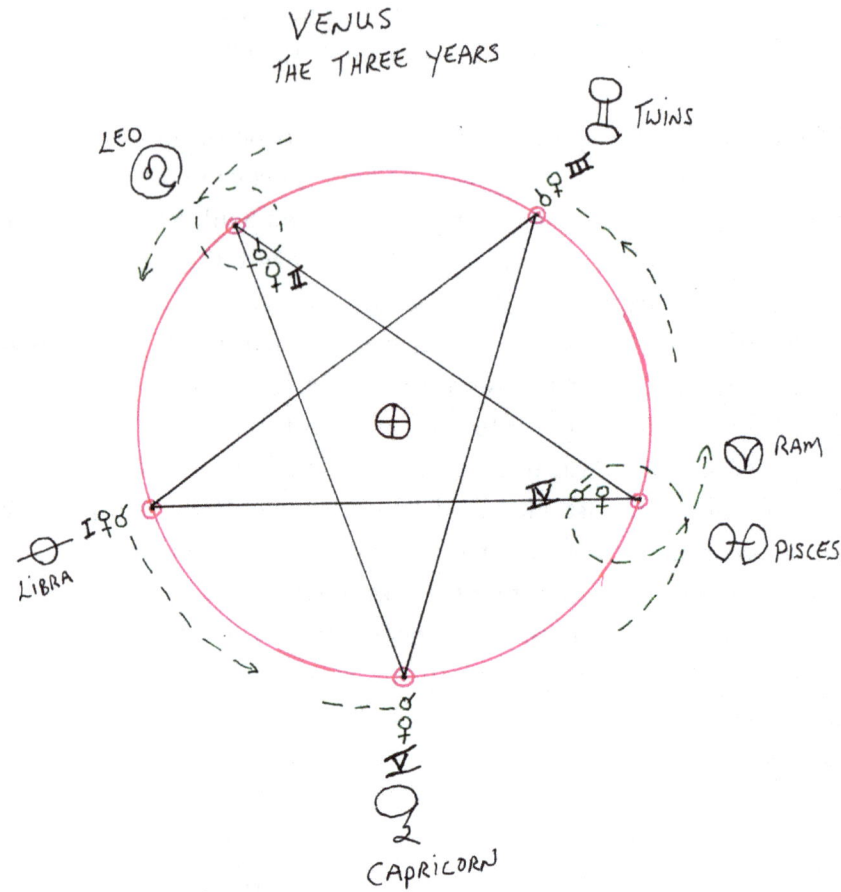

Thus, we have in these five corners of the pentagram of Venus-Sun conjunctions the events of the Three Years. They have been traced back through history by Willi Sucher, following as best as one can with the calendar. Of course there is no exact calendar of the deeds of the Christ during those three years, but from the stories in the Gospels founded on the one date that Steiner did give, which was April 3 AD 33, as the date of Golgotha, Sucher has worked backward through the planetary movements (see diagram).

One of these corners of the Venus pentagram will be found in almost every person's prenatal birth chart. (Since these conjunctions are about 9 months apart, it is possible that the conjunction may occur just before the Epoch or after the Birth—see next course on Chart Construction.) We can actually trace these conjunctions during a person's prenatal time back to the Three Years, conjunction event. Sucher worked with this for many years and taught me. In the many years that I worked with individual charts and biographies, my experience confirmed that, on some profound spiritual level, that Christ event of Venus that one has also in one's chart, in some new way, lives as a deep experience within that human being in their biography. Perhaps it was the event around mysteries of Essenism and withdrawal into a monastic existence for self-purification, and the need to overcome that. Or perhaps it is the opposite, an absolute rejection of anything that is akin to monasticism and wanting to be fully in the thick of the world. Or perhaps the event of the Syro-Phoenician woman, where there was shown this deep humility, spiritual humility. The experience of recognizing that the highest spiritual power comes by becoming the servant of the lowest—this reversal of hierarchy. All past spiritual streams, and many spiritual streams today, still carry this tradition of ascent, of hierarchic rising to heights of spiritual development. But the purpose of the Christ incarnation was to show that this has all been turned around now. The new gesture, the highest, is that one becomes the servant of the least.

So, this concludes the section on the Venus conjunctions and the Three Years. We move next to Jupiter and Saturn.

CHRIST AND THE GOLDEN TRIANGLE*

Let us continue with the Christ events in relationship to the planetary spheres. We have gone through the form of the six-pointed star of Mercury in relationship to the Christ events and the five-pointed star of Venus in relation to the Christ events. In the course on the planets we presented the Golden Triangle created by the conjunctions of Jupiter and Saturn.

Saturn and Jupiter, over a period of 60 years, with one conjunction every 20 years, create a triangle in the heavens. The conjunctions occur in three equidistant corners of the twelve constellations of the zodiac, creating this equilateral triangle. In Willi Sucher's research he connects

---

*   Video: Course 3: Christ and the Stars, Session 9.

these three corners of the triangle with events related to the impact of the Christ in Earth evolution.

This great triangle remains intact and slowly rotates through the zodiac, moving forward about 8° to 10° every 60 years, completing one full rotation in 2,500 years. So, these points of the triangle can, like the Venus pentagram points, be traced back to the time of Christ. Willi Sucher associates them with three fundamental events that are, one could say, themes that each of these corners carry in relationship to the destiny of Earth humanity. These themes that unfold over twenty years are initiated when one of these great conjunctions occur. They are like a call from Jupiter and Saturn, father karma from the past, and father life and wisdom for the future, which emerges from their conference/conjunction as to what is happening with humanity.

The first corner occurred in astronomical 6 BC (it would be 7 BC calendrically, because there is no such year as "0"). This great conjunction of 6 BC is the star of the Magi, the Annunciation of the incarnation of the great being Zarathustra, and his birth on Earth as the vessel in which the Christ incarnates. It is not possible in this course to go into detail about why the 6 BC conjunction is directly related to the incarnation of Zarathustra, but it is related to the Spiritual Nativity, which will be gone into in the Charts Construction course.

Thus, this corner perpetually carries this theme of an Annunciation, a new impulse being born into the destiny of Earth. The great conjunction in 2020 is in this corner and thus of this lineage of great conjunctions. If one goes back every 60 years, one would find this lineage repeating itself. Part of the great work of Sucher is the tracing of these corners back in earthly history, particularly modern history, going back into the fourth/fifth century. I recommend a study of his books for those who wish to find out more about the history of this stream of Annunciation.

The second great conjunction in the next corner of the triangle occurred in the year AD 14. Sucher connects this conjunction with an event described in the Gospels, and that those of you who are students of Rudolf Steiner may recognize in the deeper story of the Matthew Jesus child and the Luke Jesus child, who each carry a different stream in evolution. The Gospel of Luke tells the story of when the adolescent Jesus with his family had gone to Jerusalem for a festival. When his parents and their fellow travelers were a couple of days into their travel for home, they realized that Jesus was nowhere to be found. They went back to Jerusalem searching everywhere for him and were shocked to find him sitting with all the great teachers in the temple who were all listening to him. He was speaking to them and they were all amazed at the wisdom coming out of this young boy's mouth. The parents were also shocked because this was not like the Jesus that they knew, and they said to him, "Didn't you know that we were looking for you; where have you been?" He said to them "Didn't you know I must be about my father's business?"

Steiner describes this event as a union of these two great streams in humanity described in the Gospels of Matthew and Luke. There is a union of these two streams—the kingly stream, described in Matthew, that the Magi came from the East to worship, and the shepherd stream of the child described in Luke, who the shepherds in their simplicity of heart came to worship in the manger. So, this event represents the coming together of the kingly stream and the shepherd stream in the youth Jesus.

In this way, this corner historically carries in a broad sense this theme of the union of two streams, the challenges and karmic necessities involved in this union in the evolution of humanity. The last great conjunction connected with the union of the two streams was in 1980 and the next will be in 2040.

The third corner of the triangle, the third great conjunction, occurred in approximately AD 34, twenty years later. Sucher connects this great conjunction with what was already described in the Venus conjunctions as the conversion of Saul on the way to Damascus. As a representative of the old order of the Jewish temple, he actively persecuted the Christians and aided in their deaths. On the road to Damascus, he had an experience of the Christ, not physically, not in the resurrection body as the disciples had, but in a different sphere. It was then that Saul became Paul, one the greatest leaders and teachers in the Christianity that unfolded.

This event was the first of the new experience of the Christ in the etheric realm, which modern humanity can have. So, this corner of the great conjunction triangle carries this potentiality for a world Damascus, a world awakening in a new way to its future potential and the new experience of the Christ. The great conjunction of 2000 was the repeat of this great conjunction.

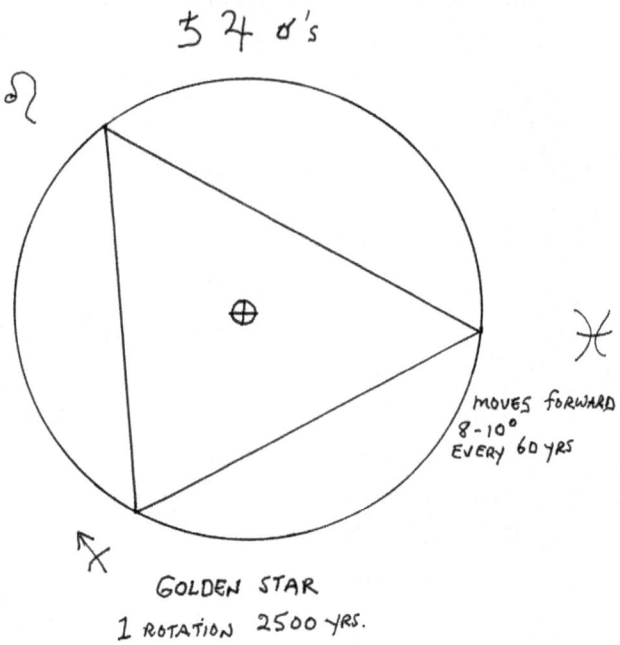

These impulses live in this movement of the triangle of the great conjunctions out of the archetypes of these three significant events in the biography of the Christ impulse in the Earth. They might be hidden to external history, even attacked, but one can begin learning to perceive, or to take up that call consciously in relationship to a great conjunction. They represent 20-year impulses that are to unfold in humanity through the great beings of the Saturn spheres, the Father realm, and Jupiter, the Son realm, or one could say they represent major reevaluations of the past and how the future is unfolding in evolution.

5

Charts Construction

In the sequence of videos, this course on chart construction was recorded first, with the other courses added later. Therefore, in the videos and in this chapter, reference is sometimes made to topics that will be covered that have already been covered in this course, so this may seem confusing.

The Birth Chart: Preparation*

We now begin the process of constructing a birth chart. To construct a chart, you need some tools: a template, which is available on the website and shown below in my hand-drawn template, colored pencils, a compass, and a straight edge. For those who are familiar with astrology and chart construction, you might be able to skip through this lesson, since you already know the process. For those who know nothing about this, I suggest you take your time and go through the process, step by step.

Basically, we need to know three things to begin. We need to know the date, the time, and the location of the birth. There are two options; because of technology and the many resources available online, you can search for a free astrology website, enter that information and get a chart instantly. You may want to do this in any case, either as a backup or as a way to skip through this process.

The other option is to work through this process manually. But whether you create the initial chart online and then transfer it to the template and/or work through the process manually, the online chart

---

* Video: Course 4: Chart Construction, Session 1.

can be a backup reference, so that you know you have the correct ascendant, correct planetary positions, and correct sidereal time. Either way, I recommend that in this new approach to star wisdom you create a mental picture of what you are constructing, so that you know what things mean, such as sidereal time, Greenwich time, ascendant, and so on. This is an important part of the work, because it doesn't bypass the necessary thinking process, which in my opinion and from my experience is necessary to the process of fully entering the whole work of chart construction.

There is something significant about the will activity we use with the thinking process to construct and work through the pictures that provide the end result of the chart. Rudolf Steiner once said that mathematics is actually one of the most valuable sciences as a preparation for spiritual cognition, because it trains the thinking and the will in the thinking for following a process. This engages us inwardly in a necessary way. From my own experience, when there were no technological resources, the manual process of beginning to construct a chart, the mathematical process, would already begin to give a sense of who this person was. It was sometimes even strange, when, for example, there would be certain miscalculations or certain errors, or some calculation processes would be much more difficult than others. Already I felt there's something here that's informing me. Why is this?

It is a fact that when you have the intention of creating a birth chart of a human individual, you are already engaging with the angel of that individuality. We know from spiritual science that it really is the human angel that accompanies the individuality into birth. The angel helps to bring about the incarnation and embodiment process in one lifetime; helps to weave the destiny into the oncoming bodies for the coming life. So, this activity of constructing a chart, of doing the necessary thinking and will activity, is an important process in engaging with the individuality who is the subject of the birth chart that you will be looking into. This will and thinking activity needs to be warmed from the heart. This connects us to what I was reading in an earlier session about devotion and reverence as a fundamental aspect on a path of spiritual cognition.

Charts Construction

When we engage the heart in devotion and reverence toward this individuality and use our thinking and will in our thinking to build the pictures, then we are already in the process of understanding that person. In connection with this, I include an excerpt from Steiner to get us in the right attitude for beginning our process of calculation.

We live in a time when we need calculation. We live with a mind that functions in spatial consciousness—we can no longer clairvoyantly perceive the gods and the divine world. We live separate from that, and now calculation is the tool we can use to begin the process of stepping forward. Calculations are used to build an image, and the image can become a picture that comes to life like a drawing, painting, or tapestry of the incarnation process of the individual. Through further steps of cognition, this picture then can lead us to knowing.

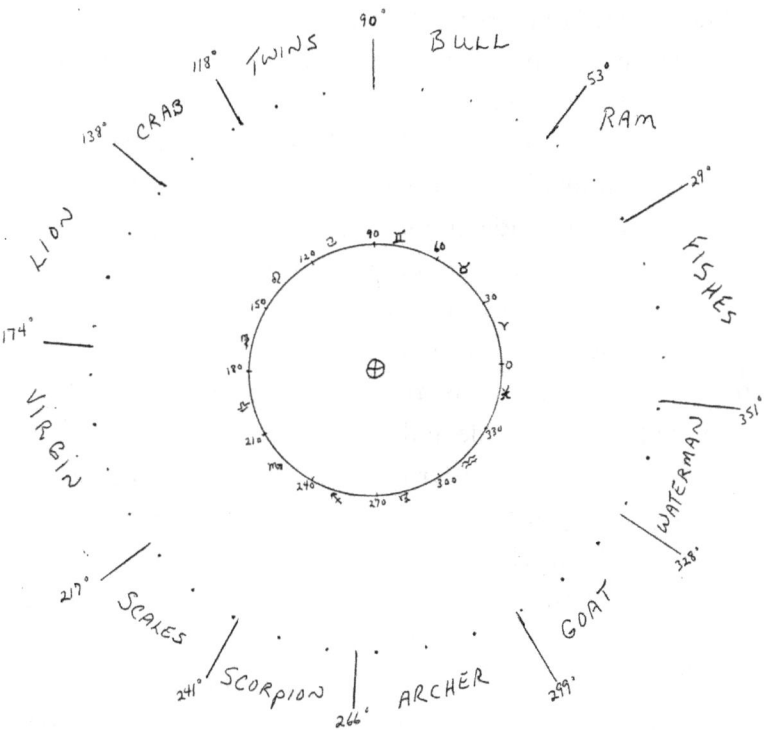

If we make the attempt with the kind of knowledge I have described, we begin to gaze upon the destiny of a single human being with holy awe. For what is it that works in the destiny of each human being? In very truth it is star wisdom—all-embracing star wisdom! Nothing can enable us to behold the working of the Gods in the universe with deeper or truer feelings than to behold it in the destiny of a human being. A world justice flows through Eternity in the existence, the deeds, the thinking of the Gods weaving behind the human being. (Rudolf Steiner, *Karmic Relationships,* vol 6, lect. 6)

The Birth Chart: Time and Place*

For the sample chart that we are creating, we choose the date September 29, 2018, 11:00 a.m. Eastern Daylight Time (EDT), New York City. A human being has been born. A breath has been taken. A new life has entered embodiment, having descended from a long time in the spiritual world.

So, first we need to do three things. We need to identify the location of New York City on the globe. We need to identify the time from two points of view, Earth time and star time. To build the picture, we just step back for a moment and look at the globe of the Earth and find New York City in one location. We want to identify where New York is in terms of the longitude and latitude. You may already be familiar with the fact that the longitudes are the vertical lines along the globe of the Earth, somewhat like the sections of an orange, that measure out 360° in 15° increments around the Earth. This helps us locate positions on a kind of global map. You can do this by either going online and looking up the longitude and latitude for New York City—a very simple process. Or, if you prefer to use a book, there is a book called the *International Atlas,* which lists longitudes and latitudes for locations all around the world.

We come to a latitude of New York City as 40° 71' North and a longitude of 74° 0' west. To being with, write on the template that you printed out, at the top, the person's name (in this case there is no name), the date and time, September 29, 2018, 11:00 a.m. EDT and the location, New York City, and under that the longitude and latitude written out.

---

*   Video: Course 4: Chart Construction, Session 2.

Charts Construction

The second thing we need to do is to convert the local time in New York at Eastern Daylight Time, into what's called Greenwich Mean Time (GMT). In this way we come to this world picture of the movement of time as the Sun appears to pass across the globe. Greenwich, England is the beginning point for the world clock, for 0 hours. So, everything in clock time is based in relationship to Greenwich. New York City is 75° west of Greenwich. That is five 15° time zones across the Atlantic to New York. Each time zone of 15° is one hour change in time. New York being 75° West of Greenwich means it is a change of 5 hours in time. So 11:00 hours (11 a.m.), New York time would be 16 hours GMT. To better simplify working with the chart you should use the Universal time standard of the 24-hour clock rather than a.m. and p.m.

So, we come to a time of 16 hours, 11 hours (or 11:00 a.m.) becoming 16 hours GMT. However, we have a complication. In September we are still in daylight time, so we have advanced the clock an hour for daylight time. Therefore, to be accurate we need to remove that hour from this equation. 16 hours GMT gets 1 hour deducted to give us the Greenwich Mean Time of 15 hours.

Still, we have another slight adjustment, because the standard time, which applies to everywhere within that 15° time zone, is based on the meridian line of that zone. However, every location within that zone is not exactly on the meridian. It can be a bit east or a bit west of that meridian prior to getting to the next time zone meridian. For example, the next western meridian indicates the Central time zone in the U.S. New York City is at 74° west in longitude, the meridian for the time zone is at 75° west. So, New York is actually 1° east, toward Greenwich, of the time zone meridian. That 1° is the equivalent of 4 minutes in time. If 15° equals 60 minutes or one hour in time, then 1° equals 4 minutes of time. So we then need, since it is east of the time zone meridian, to subtract four minutes for that 1° east. We come then to a GMT equivalency of 14 hours 56 minutes. This is the Greenwich Mean Time that you will write on the chart, on your template, as the conversion of New York local time.

Having arrived at GMT, 14 hours and 56 minutes, placing that at the top of your chart template, we now need to move on to what's called sidereal time. In sidereal time we move from Earth/Sun time, or GMT, which is our Earth calculation of time in relationship to how the Sun moves across the globe, to sidereal or star time. With sidereal time we also need to identify the relationship of this location on the Earth, of New York City, at our local Earth time to star time. So we now expand out and we link this place and moment to a star. This is the sidereal time. What does this mean?

Solar time is basically the time it takes for the Earth to rotate around to the same point in relation to the Sun. This is our 24-hour day, which—to be exact—takes 24 hours 3 minutes and 56 seconds. The sidereal day is the time it takes for the point on the Earth to rotate and return to a star point. The star point used as the standard for the calculation of sidereal time is the vernal point, or spring point, where the Sun crosses above the celestial equator on its path through the ecliptic. The sidereal day, then, would actually be slightly shorter than the solar day. The sidereal day is 23 hours 56 minutes and 4 seconds. The reason for this, of course, is that in the solar day the Sun has (apparently) moved a little further along the ecliptic by the next day, so it takes a little longer for that Earth point to come back around to the Sun. Whereas the star point has not moved, so the coming around of the point on the Earth to the star point is a little bit shorter than the solar day.

This equation between solar time and sidereal time is what then gets quite complicated when you're doing the manual calculations to get the exact sidereal time for the moment of birth. However, the sidereal time is quite important because it is the sidereal time that will determine the ascendant and the houses that are based on the ascendant. The ascendant is that point on the Earth plane that extends out along the eastern horizon and intersects a star point. The ascendant, then, is really a wonderful picture of earthly physical embodiment. Imagine the moment of birth; this person is born and at this moment, in this location, if you look to the east along the horizon line, it would meet a particular star point, a wonderful link between Earth and star. We will build more on this as we come to understand this ascendant and how the ascendant plays a crucial role in many more aspects of the birth configuration and the descent to birth.

To go completely into the manual calculation would take more complexities than is necessary now. I recommend going online to get the exact sidereal time, but we will go through the basic process of how to calculate the sidereal time.

If we go to our ephemeris and to the page for September 29, 2018, in the far left column, we see that the sidereal time for each day is listed there. You can see the sidereal time for midnight September 29, 2018, is 0 hours 30 minutes 49 seconds. So, we simply add to this the local New York birth time, but without the daylight time accounted for, which would then be 10 hours local time, not 11. This brings us to 10 hours 30 minutes 49 seconds. This is point when we would get into complex adjustments with the sidereal time based on certain Earth-star calculations. We won't go into that here, but the sidereal time needs slight adjustments to bring it to 10 hours and 33 minutes, the exact sidereal time of the birth. For those who are still interested in what those adjustments involve and why, there are still a few websites (disappearing rapidly) that explain the complete calculations and process for arriving at the exact sidereal time. However, this would require more than is intended for this course.

Now you can place the ascendant and the houses on the template. Again, you can simply do the chart online, which will give you the houses, and you simply draw those on your template. Another option is to use a book, *The Michelsen Book of Tables*.* One goes through the book to find columns in which sidereal times are listed, with a few minutes between. Along those columns are the two sidereal times that either match exactly or fall between. If it falls between those two sidereal time columns, one has estimate where the time would fit. Then, look down the columns and find the latitude of New York, which is 40° North. This will show the ascendant and the houses for that moment.

---

* Neil F. Michelsen, *The Michelsen Book of Tables: Koch and Placidus Tables of Houses: How to Cast a Natal Horoscope*, 2nd ed. (Epping, NH: ACS/Starcrafts, 2009).

On your template, you will complete the information you need to begin constructing the position of the planets. You have the date, time, and location, as well as the longitude and latitude and the Greenwich Mean Time. You have the sidereal time at birth. And under that, you can now write out the degrees of the Ascendant (Descendant would be opposite), the Midheaven and the degrees of the houses. Now, in the Michelsen book and possibly online (I haven't done one online) they will give you only the half of the houses because the other half are formed simply on the opposite degree of the zodiac. So, for example as you draw it, you find the Ascendant degree and use your straight edge to draw it across through the center to the exact opposite location, that would be your descendant. The same with the midheaven and the nadir point and the houses in between. So now you have a chart with the information at the top, and now we can move on to placing the planets on the diagram.

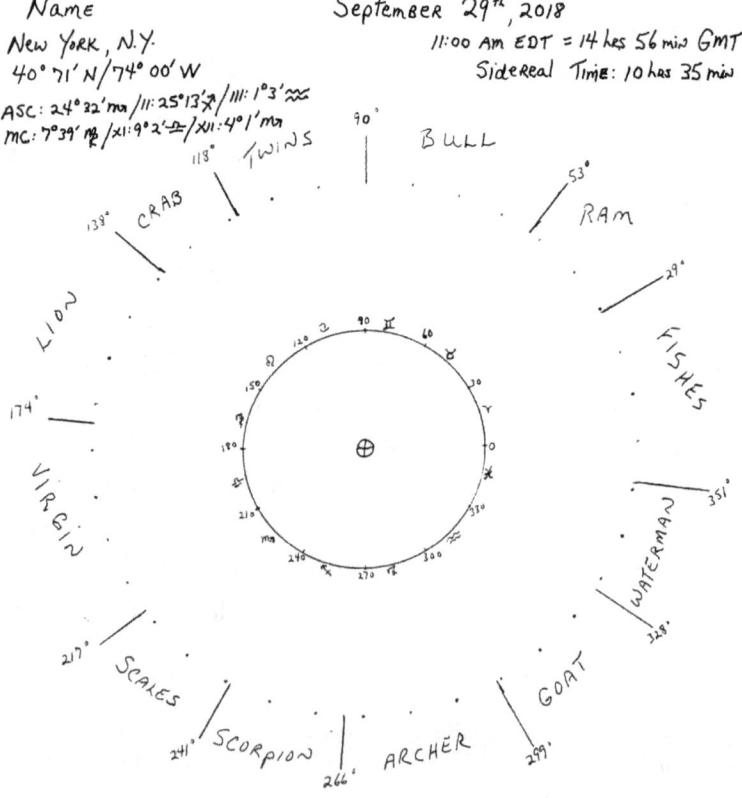

Charts Construction

The Birth Chart: The Planets*

Now we have drawn in the ascendant/descendant line, the primary line to put in on the template, as well as the MC and nadir line. At this point, I suggest waiting to draw in the houses so we have an open chart in which to place the planets first. Now we have a picture in the circle of, we could say, the great cross of the birth event—the eastern and western horizon and the midheaven, the overhead highest point of the ecliptic and the nadir, the point opposite and lowest point below the Earth. This ascendant/descendant line with which we will work is a significant tool.

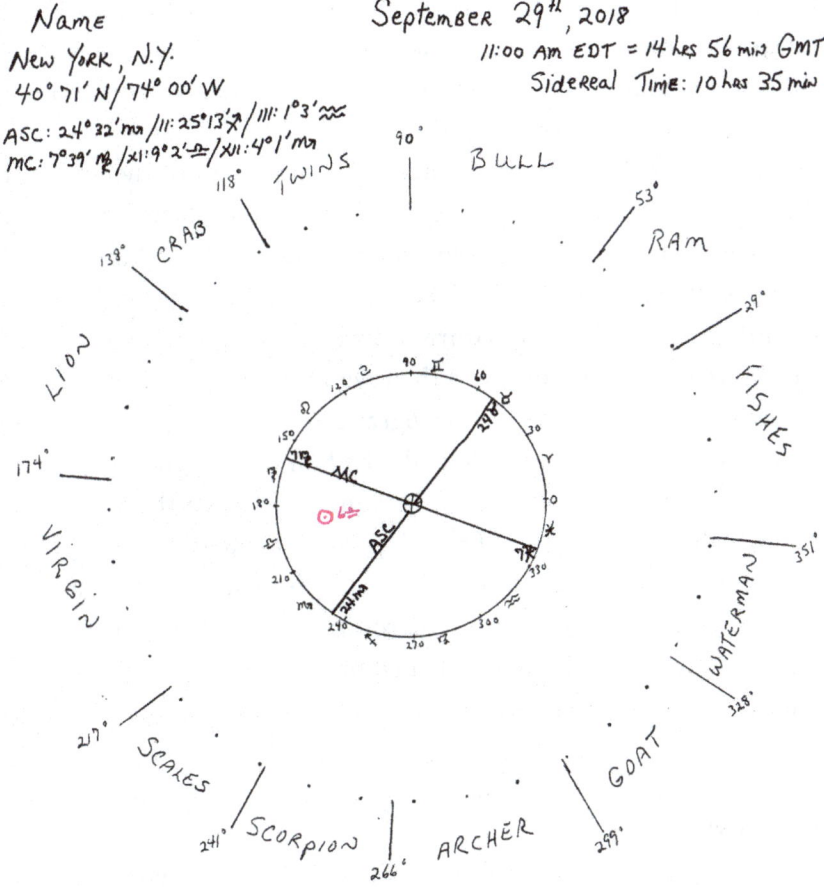

---

*   Video: Course 4: Chart Construction, Session 3.

The next step is to insert the planets onto the inner circle of the chart. I suggest double-checking to make sure you place the Sun first. The Sun in this particular chart is at 6° Libra. The ascendant is at 24° of Scorpio. The opposite then would be 24° Taurus for the descendant. So, we have this line of the horizon, and the Sun would be a bit above this line of the ascendant. If the Ascendant is at 24° Scorpio, we would have the Sun at 6° Libra and the midheaven at 9° Virgo. When we place the Sun, we can see it's a more or less the middle, between the eastern horizon, the point of sunrise, and the noon position. We know that our time of birth is 10:00 (11:00 a.m. daylight time), so we can guesstimate that we are correct with the ascendant, because the Sun in relationship to the horizon looks appears to be where it would be at about 10:00 a.m. This is just to double-check and be sure we didn't miscalculate. The relation of the Sun to the horizon shows us if we are at the right time of day.

Now that we have the Sun placed, we simply go to the ephemeris and follow across the line for September 29th and place the planets. I recommend starting with the outermost planet and working our way in, placing Pluto, Neptune, and Uranus toward the periphery of the diagram's inner circle, then Saturn a little further in, Jupiter in a little more, Mars in a little more, and then we have the Sun. Depending on whether Venus or Mercury are retrograde at the time of this birth, you will have Venus and Mercury outside the Sun toward the periphery, or you may have them very close to the Sun, or between the Sun and the Earth, which is at the center of the diagram. As you are drawing just be aware that you have the space for the planets. You may have a cluster of planets and you need to have the room there to draw them in. So, I would suggest maybe doing it in pencil first in case you need to erase it and move them a bit to give room. Beside each planet, enter the degrees listed in the ephemeris. These are the degrees for the tropical zodiac, which is the circle with the smaller sign symbols, beginning with Aries at 0° to 30°.

An important thing to be aware of is that we are working with a 10:00 a.m. time, whereas the ephemeris is based on midnight, so there will be a little movement of the planets between midnight and 10:00

Charts Construction

a.m., but not enough to require calculations, particularly with the outer planets, which hardly move in a day. With Mercury and Venus, however, there will be a slight movement, so I recommend rounding up the minutes in this chart to the next degree rather than rounding down; this will give us an accurate enough position. We have to use common sense on this, but, in general, for noon or later times I generally round up from the midnight position in the ephemeris, and for morning times I round down if the minutes given are under 30 minutes of the degree. We don't really need to write in the exact degree with the minutes, which is a little more than we need in our work with astrosophy. Next to each planet simply write the degree. For example, if it says 6° of Scorpio, write the 6 with a little Scorpio symbol next to the planet. Now we have the planets in the inner circle at the moment of birth.

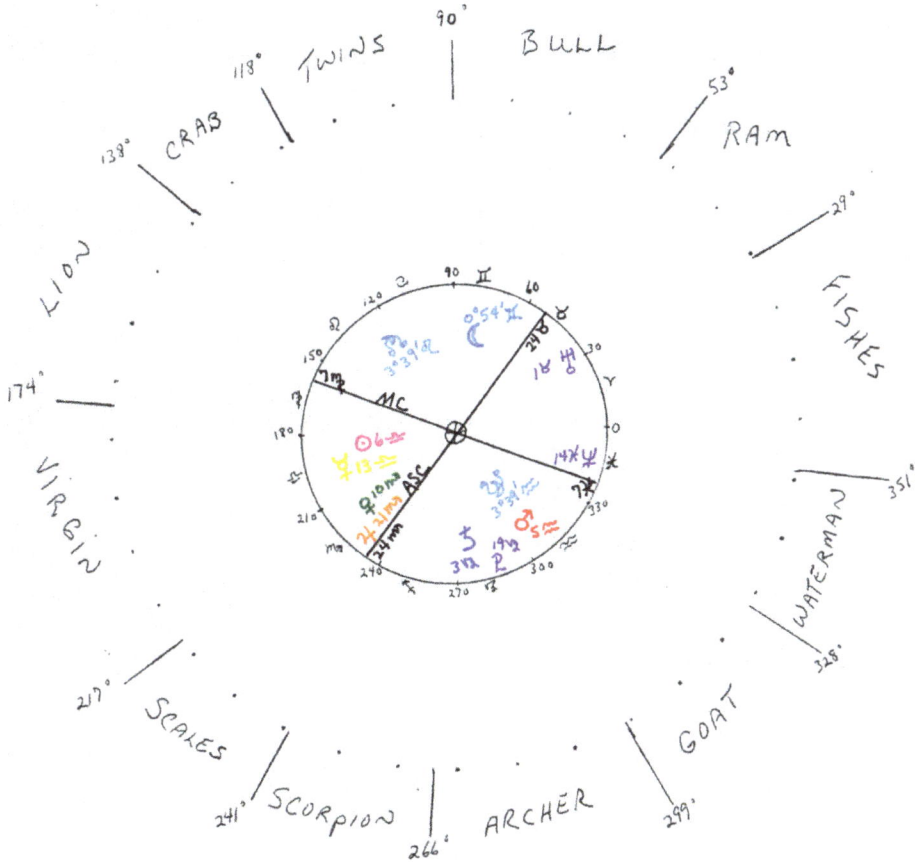

I also recommend that you include the Moon nodes, which are also provided in the ephemeris. In the ephemeris you have what's called the north node, which is the ascending node. The descending node would be the opposite position. You can place them on the chart also, since they will be necessary for later chart work. The symbol for the node is just this little loop and the Moon symbol within the loop as you will see in my example chart on page 117.

Now let's move to the next step, which will be a bridge for us to a whole area in astrosophy that is not taken into account in conventional astrology. We will now need to calculate the position of the Moon. We want to come to an exact position of the Moon because the position of the Moon in relationship to this Ascendant/Descendant line will unveil a secret for us and lead us into the pre-birth journey of the descending individuality into incarnation.

The Moon and the Prenatal Epoch*

Now we need to calculate the exact position of the Moon. This is significant for moving to the next stage of the chart of the incarnation process. One way, again, is to go online and get the position of the Moon from an online chart calculator. You can simply do that, or we'll go through the process to work this out manually.

We know that the birth took place at 14 hours 56 minutes Greenwich Mean Time. We go to the ephemeris to find where the Moon is at 14 hours 56 minutes Greenwich Mean Time. To do that, look at the position of the Moon on midnight September 29th, which was 22° 28' of Taurus, and the position of the Moon at midnight on September 30th, which was 5° 58' of Gemini. This then tells us how far the Moon moved in one day. In general, the Moon moves about 13° in one day. Depending on whether it's at its apogee or perigee, it may go a little slower or a little faster. The Moon on this day from midnight to midnight moved 13° 30'. That's from 22° of Taurus to the end of Taurus, which was 7° 32', and then 5° 58' into Gemini for a total of 13° 30' movement. Now we want to know where the Moon was at

---

* Video: Course 4: Chart Construction, Session 4.

14 hours 56 minutes Greenwich Mean Time. We can round off to 15 hours, as the 4 minutes difference there is not enough to affect our calculations.

Fifteen hours is 0.625 of a full 24-hour day (15/24). So now we want to convert the distance the Moon moved, which was 13° 30', into minutes to facilitate our calculation. So 13° times 60 minutes will give us 780 minutes, plus the 30', meaning the Moon moved a total of 810 minutes during the 24-hour period. We multiply that amount times the portion of the day of our birth time, which is 0.625, and we come to the Moon moving 506.25 minutes between midnight on the 29th and our birth time of 14 hrs. 56 min. Greenwich time. Now if we convert this back to degrees, dividing the 506.25 minutes by 60, we come to 8° 26'.

This is how far the Moon moved from midnight on the 29th to our birth time. So, we take this midnight position of Taurus on the 29th and we add the 8° 26' and it brings us to 0° 53' of Gemini. 30° 53' would be the total, so the 30° takes us to the end of Taurus and brings us 53' into Gemini. So, the Moon at birth is at 0° 53' of Gemini. Now you can place the Moon on the chart.

With the planets, I use the colors that are traditionally associated with the planetary realms. I use certain shades of Violet and purple for Uranus, Neptune and Pluto as the new planets, the traditional colors are: Saturn, dark blue; Jupiter, orange; Mars, red; Sun, pink; Venus dark green; Mercury bright gold-yellow; light blue for the Moon and Moon nodes.

Now you have the completed birth chart in this particular template format. Everything is now within the inner circle of the signs. All the positions are given for tropical zodiac signs. Now we need to take the next step, and that requires working with the Moon and the Ascendant/Descendant line, the horizon line at birth.

Why are we working with the Moon? In a study of the life between birth and death and between death and rebirth, the Moon sphere is the realm that the human being enters last before the incarnation process. The Moon, of course, reflects the Sun's light, but more than sunlight, which we can see, the Moon goes around the Earth as a kind of spiritual recorder, a mirror, reflecting the gestures of the planets on the backdrop of the constellations.

We know that the Moon doesn't rotate, therefore the same side of the Moon always faces the cosmos and the other side always faces the Earth. The far side of the Moon is like a recorder, or receptor, of the activities of the movements of the stars. It thus records the descent over time of the individuality. The Moon sphere is the sphere of the work of the angels as they engage in preparing the biography of an individual in the sojourn to birth, to be woven into the destiny of the forthcoming incarnation.

Then comes a moment when the human being has contracted, so to speak.* We can imagine this kind of contraction over time for this human individuality who has been expanded out to the periphery before beginning the return journey to Earth to become embodied in a physical, human form.

The whole journey culminates in the individual's arrival in the Moon sphere, where an event takes place that we can calculate. (In the next session we will go into this.) It is an event called the epoch, a moment when the transition occurs between the descent of the human being—the contraction of the human individual in preparation to enter the Moon sphere and the process of uniting with embryonic development on Earth. The human individuality begins to weave into the life body and the embryo and hereditary forces. This gives us an essential picture of the journey of the human being toward weaving into the forthcoming body for incarnation. It's an awe-inspiring, living picture. We need the Moon, because the Moon is the recorder. The Moon sphere is the realm that carries this process into embodiment on the Earth, which, as we've said, is connected to the Ascendant/Descendant plane of the horizon, so that the human being eventually steps down onto the earthly plane.

We will next learn how to calculate that moment. Then we will move from the inner circle on the template of the actual birth positions

---

* Here again we are using spatial concepts for non-spatial activities. These are needed so we can form concepts and images, but we need to bear in mind that we are really speaking of consciousness and states of being.

to the outer circle and the drawing in of the gestures of the planets as a kind of microcosmic memory of the long journey of the human being through the cosmos to birth.

The Prenatal Chart*

We ended the last session with the completed birth chart. The inner circle of the template is now peopled with the positions of the planets at the moment of birth, with the Ascendant/Descendant line and the calculated position of the Moon. We spoke about the importance of the ascendant and the Moon in the chart that would lead us into another mystery about the incarnation of the individual. Here we quote Rudolf Steiner to get us started:

> At birth a being who has contracted to the minutest dimensions, but has drawn into itself the forces of the wide expanse of the whole cosmos unites itself with the physical human germ. We bear the whole cosmos within us when we incarnate again on Earth. It may be said that we bear this cosmos within us in the way in which it can unite with the attitude that we, in accordance with our earlier Earth existence, had brought with us in our souls on the outward journey when we were expanding into the spheres. (*Life between Death and Rebirth,* lect. 5)

We move now from this spatial picture, a fixed moment in time, the birth, into a time picture; into an imagination that is not a frozen moment in time, but is a weaving of the planets together over the whole time from conception to birth. This is called the prenatal period, and the beginning of that period is called the epoch. So, what is this transition moment that determines the epoch? There is an experience that occurs as the human being contracts, so to speak, descending ever more toward this oncoming incarnation, when at a certain moment it arrives into the Moon sphere.

One important consideration when we speak about the planets and the Moon and the Sun is that on the one hand, we look at them as if they are bodies in space. We talk about Jupiter as a body in space

---
* Video: Course 4: Chart Construction, Session 5.

and the Moon is this body we see in the sky, but from the perspective of spiritual science the planets are really spheres of being. Within the entire sphere bounded by the orbit of that planet, if you want to make it into a spatial concept, is contained all the activity of the beings associated with that planet. The planet is really a whole sphere of beings, of activity of beings.

The soul now descends and it enters the Moon's sphere to await birth. Something then happens. Below are additional references from Steiner, which we will elaborate. The term *physical germ* was already mentioned in the previous quote:

> ...The spiritual seed of the physical body, which we were preparing, falls ever farther from us and disappears.... So, it is in all reality. The physical body's germ shrinks and contracts and falls into the stream of generations—into a physical father and mother upon Earth—while we ourselves as soul and spiritual being are left behind, feeling that we belong to what has fallen from us, yet cannot unite with it directly. (*Spirit as Sculptor of the Human Organism*, lect. 7)

The spiritual germ of the physical body has already descended to Earth, whereas we still dwell in the spiritual world. And now a vehement feeling of bereavement sets in. We have lost the spiritual germ of the physical body. This has already arrived below and united itself with the last of those successive generations, which we have watched. We ourselves, however, are still above. The feeling of bereavement becomes violent. And now this feeling of bereavement draws out of the universe the needful ingredients of the world ether. Having sent the spiritual germ of the physical body down to Earth and remained behind, we draw etheric substance out of the world ether and form our own etheric body. (*Man's Being, His Destiny, and World Evolution*)

Rudolf Steiner here describes the experience that every human being goes through, and he talks about the spiritual germ of the physical body. What is this germ? He refers to it in the same way that we look, in a sense, at an acorn or the seed of a tree, and we realize that though the seed is physically tiny, the whole adult tree is contained in that germ, in a spiritual, invisible way.

The spiritual germ of the physical body is not small, per se (again we're getting into this spatial vs. non-spatial difficulty). The germ of the physical body is really the twelvefold zodiac. If we study the zodiac in relationship to the human form, we find that the origins of the human form we all share is the twelvefold zodiac. From the very periphery comes the germ of the physical body, and this germ contracts, so to speak, in a certain way and at a certain point in its approach to incarnation. This spiritual germ of our true human form falls to Earth and unites with the hereditary substance.

This experience of the loss of the germ, as he describes it, is a kind of bereavement or a feeling that something inherently part of us and forming us has left and we remain above in soul and spirit. That experience of loss instigates a transition; we turn our attention from the cosmic activity and toward Earth and the coming incarnation, uniting with the physical germ. This transition facilitates the beginning of our weaving into the etheric body, the karma, the experiences we have gone through in our descent through the planetary spheres toward birth. This moment is called the *epoch*. This occurs approximately ten lunar months prior to our physical birth. This is somewhat coincident with physical conception, but we should not mistake this moment with physical conception. Physical conception occurs on the Earth and instigates the process by which the germ leaves the Moon sphere to unite with this process on the Earth. However, it is not exactly the same moment.

The epoch has been discovered through research that has come down to us from early Egyptian ancient writings, from the sacred text called the Hermetic Corpus. It was given by the high initiate called Hermes Trismegistus, a name that means "thrice-born Hermes." Thrice-born is a title of initiation, and we think of initiation as a kind of birth into the spiritual world.

This rule for determining how to find the epoch moment, this moment of transition, was laid out in the Hermetic Rule. The rule is based on the relationship of the Moon and the ascendant at birth, which is why we talked about the significance of finding the exact position of the Moon and the exact position of the ascendant. The ascendant is that bridge from the Earth to the Moon sphere that connects our Earth existence to cosmic existence and the Moon where we are weaving now the etheric body into the physical embryo.

This Hermetic Rule presents four conditions by which we determine the epoch date, based on the relationship of the Moon and the ascendant. The Moon can be waxing and above the horizon or waxing and below the horizon. The Moon can be waning, meaning going toward new Moon from full Moon, above the horizon or waning and below the horizon. When the Moon is waxing, it would be at the position of the ascendant at the epoch, and when the Moon is waning it would be at the position of the descendant at the epoch. Whether it's above or below the horizon will determine whether it's a bit longer or a bit shorter than 273 days (10 lunar months).

This image explains these four options.

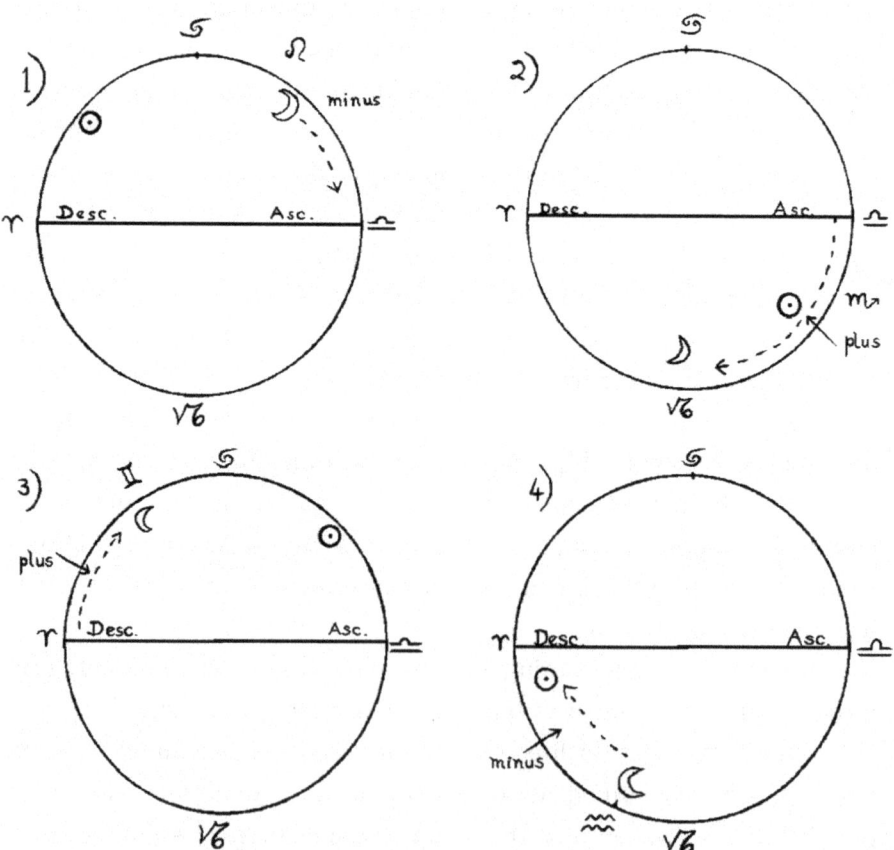

Charts Construction

HERMETIC RULE

1. The Moon is waxing and above the horizon (designated by the horizontal line from ascendant to descendant). Then, at the so-called epoch of conception, the Moon would have stood in the sign that appears as the place of the ascendant—in this case, in the sign of Libra. The epoch will be shorter than 273 days because to return to where the Moon is at birth is less time than returning completely to the ASC (Libra).
2. The Moon is waxing but below the horizon. At the epoch the Moon would have also stood at the ascendant at birth (Libra). The epoch would be longer than 273, because it would take longer than 273 days to move past the ASC in Libra and on to Capricorn.
3. The Moon is waning and above the horizon. Then, at the so-called epoch of conception, the Moon would have been at the place in the zodiac that appears as the descendant at birth (Aries in above diagram). The Epoch would be a little longer than the 273 days, the time it takes to go past the Desc on to Gemini.
4. The Moon is also waning but below the horizon. The epoch would have also been at the descendant of birth. The epoch would take less than the 273 days it would have taken to return to the Desc (from Aquarius to Aries).

We can now look at this particular chart. Where is the Moon in relationship to this horizon? Is it waxing or waning? Above or below the horizon? In this particular chart we have the Moon at 53', just at 0° of the Twins, and it is a waning Moon above the horizon. This means we would go back to when the Moon was in the descendant position. We start at that point and work our way back 10 cycles, 10 lunar months of 27.3 days each, noting each time the Moon returned to this descendant position.

In this particular chart with the Moon waning and above the horizon, this occurred within the same day, as it was not so far from the descendant line. So, we would start on the birth date on September

29th and go back 27.3 days through the ephemeris and find when the Moon was again at the position of the descendant. The descendant was at 24° of Taurus. If we go back, one by one, through ten lunar months, and we track and write down the dates when the Moon returns to this descendant position, we come to December 30th, 2017, as the date of the epoch after 10 lunar cycles.

Next, we go to the ephemeris for December 30, 2017, and place the Sun to start with in the outer circle. With a compass we can trace the path of the Sun for the 273 days. Begin with the Sun at 8° of Capricorn, at the epoch, and trace it around to the birth Sun position. We have now the beautiful curved arc of the Sun. When we move on to interpretation, this Sun path is a kind of spiritual spinal cord, a spiritual formative shape from which the body is formed, containing a memory of the head from the previous incarnation.

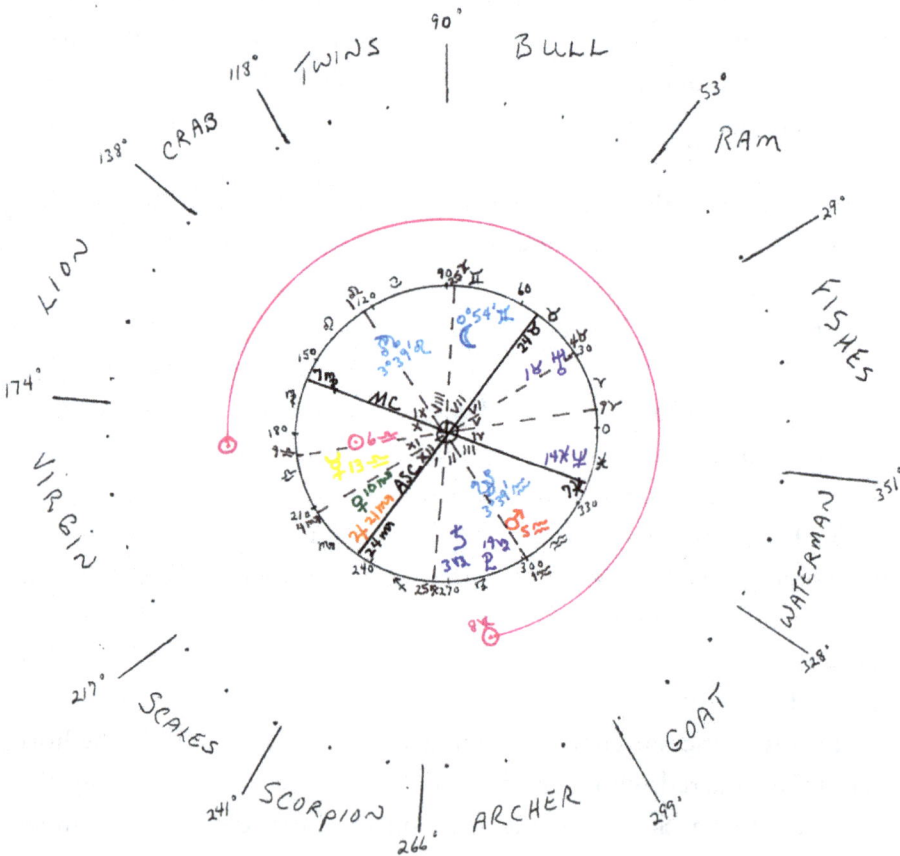

Once we have the epoch date, December 30th 2017, then you simply go to the birth chart in this outer circle, between the tropical zodiac and the constellations of the fixed stars, and trace in the movement of every planet for the ten lunar months. This tracing of these planets is, you could say, a kind of extract or compressed imagination of the activity of the human being in those planetary spheres through the whole descent through incarnation. It is like a little memory tableau capturing the essence of the gifts, the potentials, the challenges of each planetary sphere as it works into the biography, into the soul life and the etheric body of the individuality who is incarnating. To read this prenatal weaving of the planets takes us from this spatial image at birth to a real living, weaving imaginative world. As one can imagine, we can look at it and we can follow one planet at a time, but then try to imagine holding all of them in our consciousness as they move simultaneously in relation to one another, coming into conjunction, into opposition, before the Sun and looping around it, while at the same time opposing another planet. This is a pictorial language of the soul's activity.

THE FULL PRENATAL CHART*

Let us look at the following chart (page 128) and follow some of the prenatal movements during. We began at the birth, September 29th, and went back to when the Moon was in the descendant 27.3 days earlier, September 1st, then earlier to August 5th, earlier to July 9th, earlier to Jan 11th, earlier to May 15th, and still further back to April 8th, March 21st, February 22nd, January 26th, and finally arriving at December 30th, a day before New Year's Eve.

Clearly, when we place the outer planets on the periphery of this outer circle, they move very little. But we need to keep track of when a planet goes direct or retrograde as we go back through the ephemeris. It is helpful as we go back through the ephemeris to make a list for each planet, indicating significant moments such as conjunctions and oppositions to other planets, as well as retrograde and direct dates. We

---

* Videos: Course 4: Chart Construction, Session 6.

will need this when we create our next chart. For example, its important to know when Pluto moves a couple of degrees during the prenatal ten months or to note when it goes retrograde or direct. What are those dates? The same goes for Neptune and Uranus. When we get to Saturn and following the movement, it begins at 1° of Capricorn at the epoch, moves forward, stops and turns backward, and returns to the birth position of 3° Capricorn. So, it makes a little hairpin curve there. Jupiter also does a kind of hairpin loop. It begins at 16° of the sign of Scorpio, moves forward to 23°, stops, turns backward, goes back to 13°, stops, moves forward again to 21°.

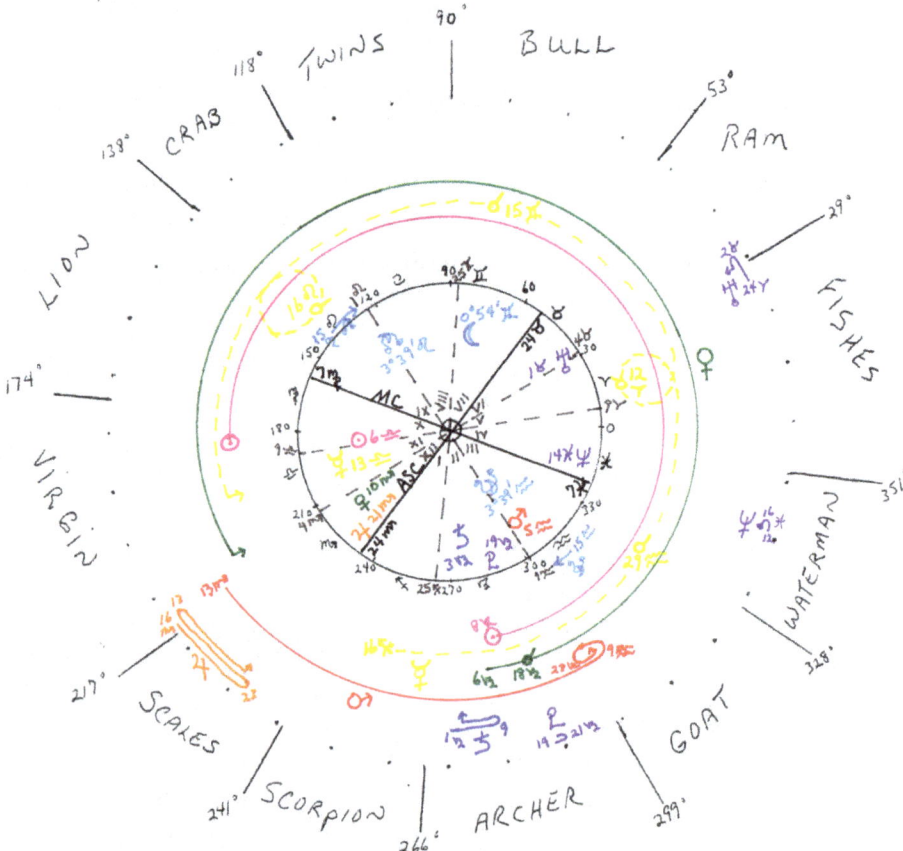

Each of the planets is making its movements. Mars in a prenatal chart will sometimes go completely in a straight circle around and sometimes it will go into a looping gesture. These all have different meanings. In this particular chart, Mars begins very near where Jupiter began at the epoch and then comes forward into Aquarius, and then does a loop around, coming back at birth into 5° Aquarius.

The Sun goes from 8° of Capricorn all the way around to the birth position of 6° Libra. Venus begins at 6° Capricorn, very close to the Sun at the epoch. Then it makes a full movement around and comes back at birth at 10° of Scorpio. With Venus, in almost every chart there is a conjunction with the Sun. Sometimes this conjunction is what we call a superior conjunction with the Sun, which means that Venus is on the far side of the Sun from the Earth. Sometimes it is what we call an inferior conjunction with the Sun, which means it loops between the Sun and the Earth during a retrograde period. In this chart, you can see shortly after the epoch there is a superior conjunction of Venus with the Sun at 18° of Capricorn, where Pluto is located.

Mercury begins at 16° of Sagittarius. Mercury moves quite quickly, so in the Mercury cycle during these ten months, you will have a few conjunctions with the Sun—superior, inferior, superior, inferior—two to three loops of Mercury. You can see those also on the chart. It conjuncts, beyond the Sun, comes around in a loop for an inferior conjunction and then goes back out again beyond the Sun.

So, here we have this amazing weaving tapestry, from the moment of the epoch to the moment of birth. What is the difference between these two moments? We can think a little bit of the epoch as the "cosmic idea" for the coming incarnation. It remembers the moment when the human being made the decision, so to speak, with the help of the higher hierarchies to return to incarnation. It remembers this urge to return to Earth life, to achieve certain goals, to develop in certain ways, to transform certain karmic challenges. The epoch carries the "idea" or plan of what is to be carried forward to take up the karma from the past. Then the process of the descent begins through the spheres, encountering in the Saturn sphere, the Jupiter sphere, the Mars sphere, the Sun sphere on down, the aspects of the spheres that work their way into the soul and etheric body. Then at the moment of birth we have this kind of stepping down onto the Earth. We are here with the task, "How am I going to realize in my life this idea or plan that I had at the epoch?"

A quote from Willi Sucher sums up this section on the prenatal epoch:

> We thus have, during our life on Earth, a silent "star companion" next to us, made of the details of the celestial configurations between epoch and birth, who participates in everything that we do or we fail to do, who looks upon us as a being of whom is expected answers and spiritual, moral deeds, in facing the issues concerning existence in a physical-material world in relationship to a spiritual cosmos. (*Practical Approach I,* Jan. 1967)

So, one can look at this star companion in the sense that we mentioned earlier, that when we began to do the chart work on the individual, we are in a sense elevating our consciousness to the angel of that person. Because this silent companion is really carried by the angel-being who stands above and behind us with this picture of our plan, of our intentions, our goals, but does not intervene, but simply karma presents the opportunities and we are then free in how we meet or don't meet these opportunities and challenges.

THE MOON GRAPH*

Having now drawn this prenatal epoch-to-birth chart in that outer circle of the template and seeing the movements and gestures of the planets, we can take this prenatal chart and transform it into another form, the Moon graph. This chart basically takes all the curving, weaving paths of the planets and lays them out in graph form. What does this present? Each of these 10 lunar cycles of 27.3 days can be correlated to the ten seven-year developmental life cycles of the human being during their biography. Those of you who have studied child development in Waldorf education or from an Anthroposophical perspective can recognize these seven-year cycles in life that are related to the development of the different stages of the human body, etheric body, soul life, etc.

If we begin with the first lunar cycle of the prenatal epoch, starting at the epoch and through the first 27.3 days we have the time from

---

*   Videos: Course 4: Chart Construction, Session 7.

birth to the seventh year. This is the time associated with the Moon and embodiment, the development of the physical body. From age 7 to 14 we have the unfolding and developing of the life body of a child; at about 14 puberty begins and until 21 we have the unfolding and development of the astral body. Age 21 to 28 and the following two seven-year cycles to age 42 are connected with the unfolding of the ego within the soul life. As the first three cycles are connected with Moon, Mercury and Venus, these middle cycles are all connected with the Sun, the "I Am" forces in the soul, as the sentient soul (21–28), the mind soul (28–35), and the consciousness soul (35–42). Then we move into the Mars years (42–49), which are sometimes called the "confronting karma" years, the "life challenges" years, as well as the time when the personality really makes its mark in the world. Not that there are not challenges throughout life, but maybe particularly in these years is a kind of confrontation with destiny in certain ways. Also during these last three cycles is the potential of the "I" developing higher levels of consciousness through the work of the higher ego. Though this development is not restricted to these years, one can see a kind of evolution or metamorphosis connected to these planetary spheres. In the Mars years is the potential for the transformation of the astral body into what's called the Spirit Self, or in Eastern tradition, Manas; in the Jupiter years (49–56), the years of wisdom dawning hopefully, the potential to develop Life Spirit or Buddhi; and the Saturn years (56–63) the potential to develop Spirit Human, or Atman. It's during this time that Saturn makes its second return to the place of birth. Saturn takes 29.458 years to make a full orbit, so most of us can have two Saturn returns, one at about age 30 and one again at about age 60. It is also the time for looking back, for reaping what has been sown in life.

We can take the movements during the prenatal time and draw them out. One may need to find graph paper that suits the purpose but a template is available on the website (astrosophy.com).

Along the vertical column, as you can see on page 132, you would enter the zodiac on the left and divide it into the 30° for the tropical signs. Outside that you need to draw lines across the graph to indicated the unequal constellations as you can see above. Along the top

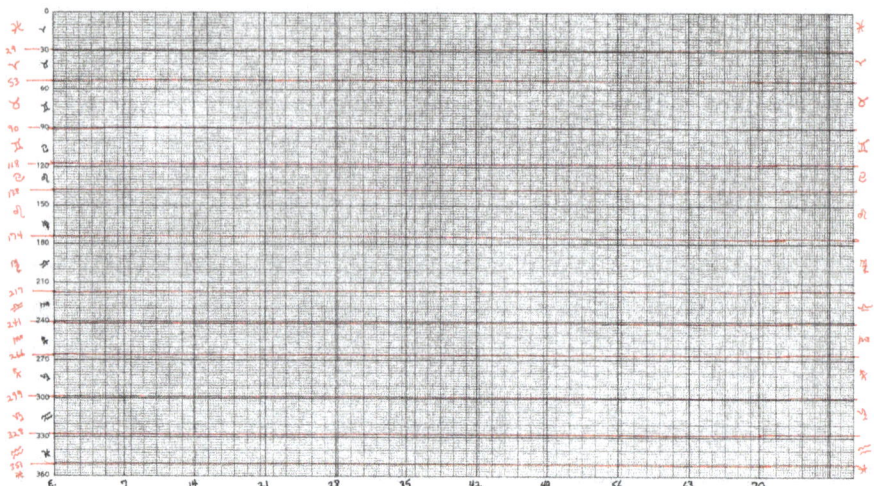

you start with the epoch date, then count 27.3 small cubes and make your first line down for the first seven-year cycle, the next prenatal date after the epoch, then 27.3 little cubes and second line down to the next cycle, and so on across the page. You then have the dates of the seven cycles from epoch to birth across the top. Along the bottom, you can write the ages corresponding.

Then you go to the ephemeris, just as you did in the circular weaving of the prenatal chart, and you start with the position of the Sun at epoch and you literally chart it on the graph like any graph is charted. Go to the next date line and mark the position of the Sun, the next line, etc. Then you can take the straight edge and connect the points and the Sun curve. The joy of the Sun curve is that it creates a straight-line angling across the graph as a kind of central spine (see the sample opposite). Then you do the same with each planet. It's very detailed and complicated work. Some people may choose to simply do it for a particular segment of the biography rather than for the whole biography so as to work with different segments at different times. As you draw this out you should follow conjunctions, oppositions, retrograde movements, and so on as they show up within the biographical timeline of the human life. These all reflect a picture of when these planetary events will be encountered in the karmic unfolding of the biography.

Charts Construction

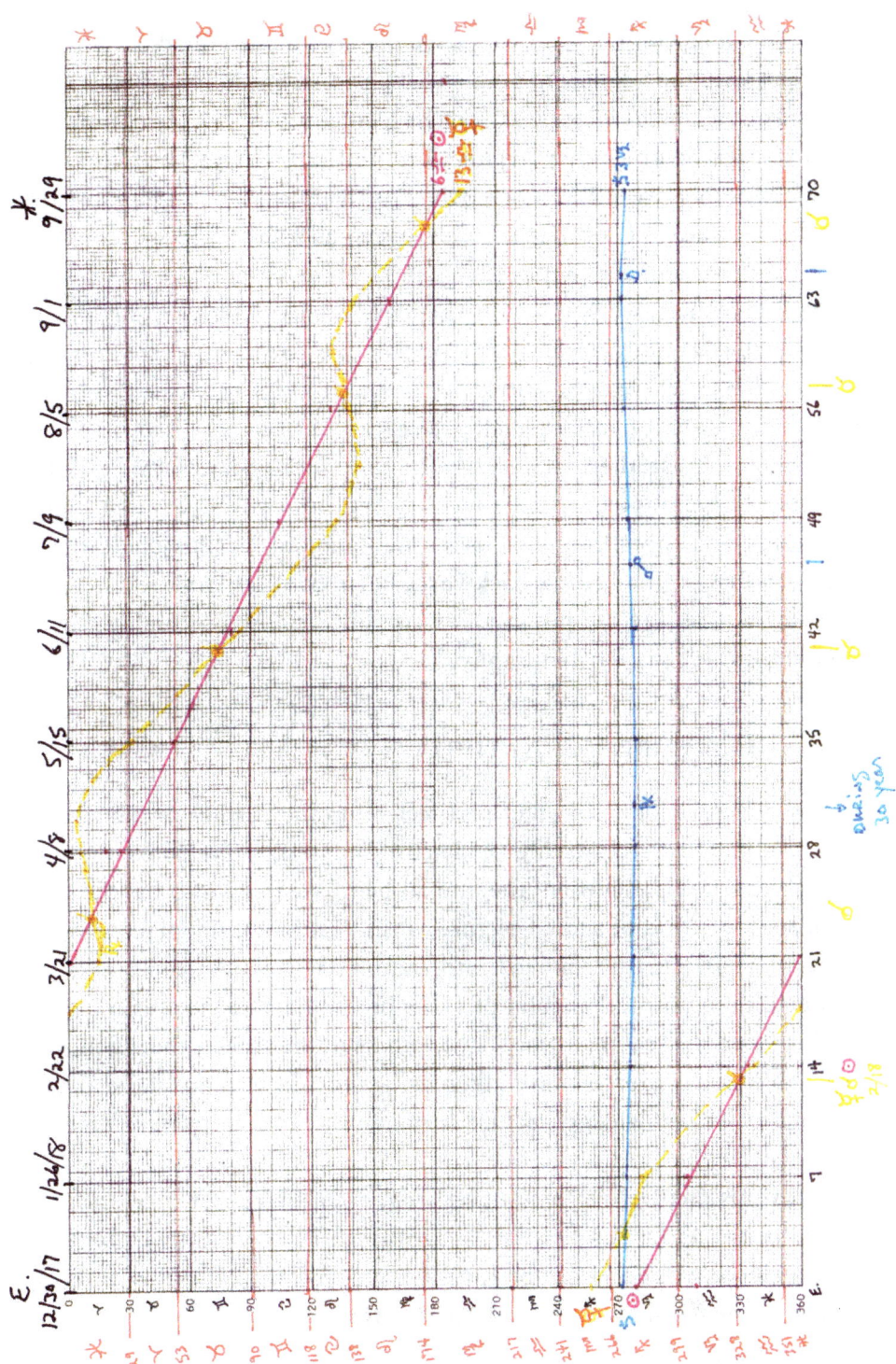

The image on the following page includes a partially drawn Moon graph, with the Sun line in pink and the Saturn line in blue. Clearly, the Saturn line angles very little, though it might move forward and then go retrograde and begin to curve up a little bit, as we can see in the blue. But then we see Mercury, which is the most difficult, because the path becomes like a hill and valley sweep as Mercury moves forward, goes retrograde, goes forward again, goes retrograde. As we draw in the full planets, we will see, as they are moving along, exactly where these conjunctions occur as the paths cross each other, or we might need to find where oppositions occur, and so on.

This is a more intensive chart creation. I think it's used very well in biography studies as a picture of how this cosmic weaving intersects our biography, what happens in the early years versus the later years. On a more complex level one can look at this chart going forward as well as going backward, but that is for a more intensive study course. Let me just say, it's complicated. Why shouldn't it be complicated? It's our biography!

The Spiritual Nativity and the Sun Realm[*]

Now we move on to another perspective on the journey of the human soul and spirit into its life on Earth. Thus far, we've looked at the birth chart, this picture of the human being stepping into the physical plane. It's a kind of spatial picture of the relation of the planets to the Earth itself. Then we moved into the prenatal epoch, you could say, transitioning from the realm of space on the Earth to the realm of the Moon and the realm of time. The rhythms of the planets during the ten prenatal lunar months have taken us, you could say, into the realm of imaginative knowledge, picture forming, to more deeply understand our cosmic biography.

In this chart we take another step, even outside of time and outside of space. In this sense it's a bit difficult to speak about because though we will be using the tools of calculation to find this moment, this moment eludes calculation to a certain extent. Also, though it is

---

[*] Videos: Course 4: Chart Construction, Session 8.

an event that occurs in time, it also stands outside of time as we experience time as a continuum of sequenced events. This may sound a bit difficult, obtuse perhaps, but this event was discovered by Willi Sucher based on his study of Rudolf Steiner. It is an event that is a continuation of the Hermetic Rule.

With this event, we move from the Earth at birth, from the lunar realm during the prenatal time, and now enter into the solar realm, the realm of the Sun. In human biography there is a kind of fourfold development in star charts: the earthly birth chart into the physical, the prenatal lunar chart weaving of the etheric/soul formation, and the solar chart that we will explore, taking us outside of time and space into the pure spiritual thought realm, and the fourth would then be the Saturn chart that would point us to previous incarnations and their relationship to the current life.

Just as the lunar prenatal chart takes us into the cognitive realm of imagination, living pictures, the solar chart takes us into the higher cognitive realm of inspiration. The Saturn chart would then take us into the highest realm of intuition. We will not go into the Saturn chart in this course. It is something not found by calculation, but rather goes beyond the tools of calculation and must be entered by intuition, which can then be followed by calculation as verification.

The chart we will explore now is the solar chart that is the Spiritual Nativity. Sucher received his inspiration for understanding this chart primarily from lectures Steiner gave in January 1914 in Berlin, published as *Human and Cosmic Thought*.

In this lecture cycle Steiner speaks about the relationship of the human soul to the world of cosmic thought, expressed in the great world of the philosophical perspectives. He presents the relationship of different philosophies to the twelve constellations of the zodiac as well as to the seven planets. The interrelationships of these philosophies become a kind of awakening in the human being of the cosmic thought realm that he experienced in the world of the Sun. This then works into the biography as a fundamental configuration of philosophical outlook on the world.

Willi Sucher began to research this question of the world philosophic thought penetrating into the human being. How and when and is there a vehicle for calculating this? To begin, we shall refer to Rudolf Steiner on the topic:

> If we can find the relation of thought to the Cosmos, to the Universe, we shall find the relation to the Cosmos of what is most completely ours. This can assure us that we have here a fruitful standpoint from which to observe the relation of man to the universe. We will therefore embark on this course; it will lead us to significant heights of anthroposophical observation....
>
> I remark expressly, so that no misunderstanding may arise, that these constellations are of much greater importance in the life of the person than the constellations of the external horoscope, and do not necessarily coincide with the "nativity"—the external horoscope. For the enhanced influence that is exerted on the soul by this standing of Mysticism, in the sign of Idealism waits for the propitious moment when it can lay hold of the soul most fruitfully. Such influences need not assert themselves just at the time of birth; they can do so before birth or after it. In short, they await the point of time when these predispositions can best be built into the human organism according to its inner configuration. (*Human and Cosmic Thought*, lect. 1 & 4)

This was the starting point for Sucher. What does he mean by "waits for the propitious moment when it can lay hold of the soul most fruitfully"? Did he mean to await an auspicious time before or after birth for the cosmic thought world to be incorporated into the human biography? He looked to the Hermetic Rule. According to the Hermetic Rule, the Ascendant is significant. The Ascendant, this horizon line, is the bridge from the Earth to the cosmos, starting with the Moon sphere. We used the Ascendant to find the prenatal epoch through its relationship to the Moon. But the Hermetic Rule continues: the Moon is also our key to finding the Ascendant and the Descendant of the epoch.

In our working chart, this prenatal epoch moment we have calculated as December 30, 2017. The epoch also has its own Ascendant/Descendant. It is another bridge. It's the bridge, or one could say the portal, from the Moon sphere to the Sun sphere. The Moon at birth will tell us the direction of this portal, which is the direction or path, so to speak, of our departure from the Sun sphere into the Moon sphere. The Hermetic Rule indicates that the Moon position at birth equals the Ascendant or the Descendant of the epoch. So, we have the indicator of the birth Moon as the Ascendant/Descendant of the epoch, but we need to now know when does this gateway from the Sun sphere to the Moon sphere activate or open? Rudolf Steiner states that this can occur before or after birth. So, there must be a time when it happens. The birth Moon gives us the indication of direction, which can be from the same direction as the Moon or the opposite direction, but it does not tell us when this occurs.

The Portal to the Sun[*]

To explore this, let's look first at the relationship between the Sun sphere and the Moon sphere from an astronomical perspective. We know that the Moon orbits around the Earth, and the Moon orbit is tilted, like all the planetary orbits, to the ecliptic, or Sun's path through the zodiac. The Moon orbit then intersects the ecliptic plane at two points. These two intersection points are called in astronomy the lunar nodes. There is an ascending node and a descending node, sometimes called the North node and the South node. These nodes are the portals, the gateways between the Moon sphere and the Sun sphere. We will go into further detail about the nature of the nodes in the heliocentric course following. Now we can move to finding when these node portals open by looking to when they have a relationship to either the waning or waxing Moon at birth. We already know that the Moon at birth points us to the Ascendant/Descendant of the epoch, which is the bridge from the Sun realm to the Moon realm. Now we know the Moon nodes are the general portal between these spheres. So now we need to find when this portal comes into relation to the Ascendant/Descendant of the epoch, which is indicated by the Moon at birth.

These Moon nodes move over time. Those who know a bit about astrology have heard of the Moon node return. These Moon nodes

---
[*] Videos: Course 4: Chart Construction, Session 9.

take 18.6 years to make a full revolution along the twelvefold zodiacal path of the Sun. These 18.6-year Moon node cycles are again another rhythm in which the human biography unfolds that one can explore. We have one full revolution in 18.6 years, and therefore we have 9.3 years for a half revolution, meaning for the north node for example to come around to the position where the south node had been. Age 9 is also a significant time in childhood development, related to the movement of the lunar nodes. In one sense we can see these lunar nodes cycles as related to a process of developing ego, or self-consciousness, a function really of the Sun nature in us.

Let us look more deeply at the Sun to further understand this Spiritual Nativity. In our time we look at the Sun as a "thing," a place in space, the central point of the universe. This is, you could say, a spatial-centric Sun that has certain manifest qualities. It offers manifest warmth/heat and manifest light. However, there is also a spiritual Sun. We might call it the peripheral Sun, and the peripheral Sun bears unmanifest heat and unmanifest light. The unmanifest, or perhaps you could say non-physical heat, is what we could call warmth of the heart, or the creative fire of being. The unmanifest light is what we mean with enlightenment, and enlightenment has this connection to thought, to awareness in consciousness. So, one could look at the unmanifest Sun as that realm of the thoughts of the gods, as Steiner points out in these philosophies. This unmanifest, or peripheral Sun permeates the entire universe to the periphery, to the zodiac. One could even say that the peripheral Sun is what streams through the diversity of the twelvefold zodiac from a unity beyond the zodiac, into the solar cosmos, permeating all the planetary spheres. The manifest Sun rays out from a central point generating heat and light for physical existence.

Now if we return to our chart, we have a waning Moon at birth, 0° 54' of Gemini. According to the Hermetic Rule, this means that since the Moon is waning, the "direction" of the soul from the Sun sphere would then be opposite this Moon at birth that is at 0° 54' of Sagittarius (the tropical sign of Sagittarius), just at the entrance to the stars of Scorpio.

To now discover the Spiritual Nativity, we would look for when the Moon nodes, following their movement in the ephemeris, crossed the point of the 0° 54' of Sagittarius, the opposite point of the Moon of birth. Then the portal would be open to the Sun sphere. But we have two Moon nodes, so we must also look to when the opposite node comes around to the same point 0° 54' of Sagittarius. Then another opening would occur. Thus, there are possibly two times that can be the Spiritual Nativity, and as Steiner indicated, it can occur before or after physical birth.

In this particular chart when do the two portals open? One opens about six years before birth and the other a few years after birth. This then is the tool that Sucher determined as the means for discovering the time of the Spiritual Nativity. But which of the two times is it?

Looking at the diagram on page 140, we see the Moon node falling back along the zodiac and crossing over this 0° 54' of Sagittarius, right about at the crossing point of the fixed stars of the Scales transitioning into the fixed stars of the Scorpion.

So, we can calculate the two dates when these two portals opened. One would be on August 19, 2012, six years before birth. The second would be January 5, 2022, three plus years after birth. Now one must construct two charts for those dates. This is when the process of inspiration can inform us correctly. One must then identify the philosophical framework of these two charts. For example, what constellation is Jupiter in? What constellation is Saturn in? Then configure the philosophies. Then one observes both charts in relation to the birth chart, or better, one begins to meditate on these two charts in relation to the birth chart and then...listen! This is the process of inspiration as one awaits something to speak, revealing which of the two. As Steiner said in the quote earlier, this takes us to the heights of anthroposophical research.

Having finished our Spiritual Nativity chart, we come to a conclusion of our chart calculation "how to" and the application of astrosophy to birth charts. Perhaps this gives a sense of the profound depths to which astrosophy journeys in its efforts to reach a true understanding of this most magnificent relationship that we have as human beings to this great world of the stars.

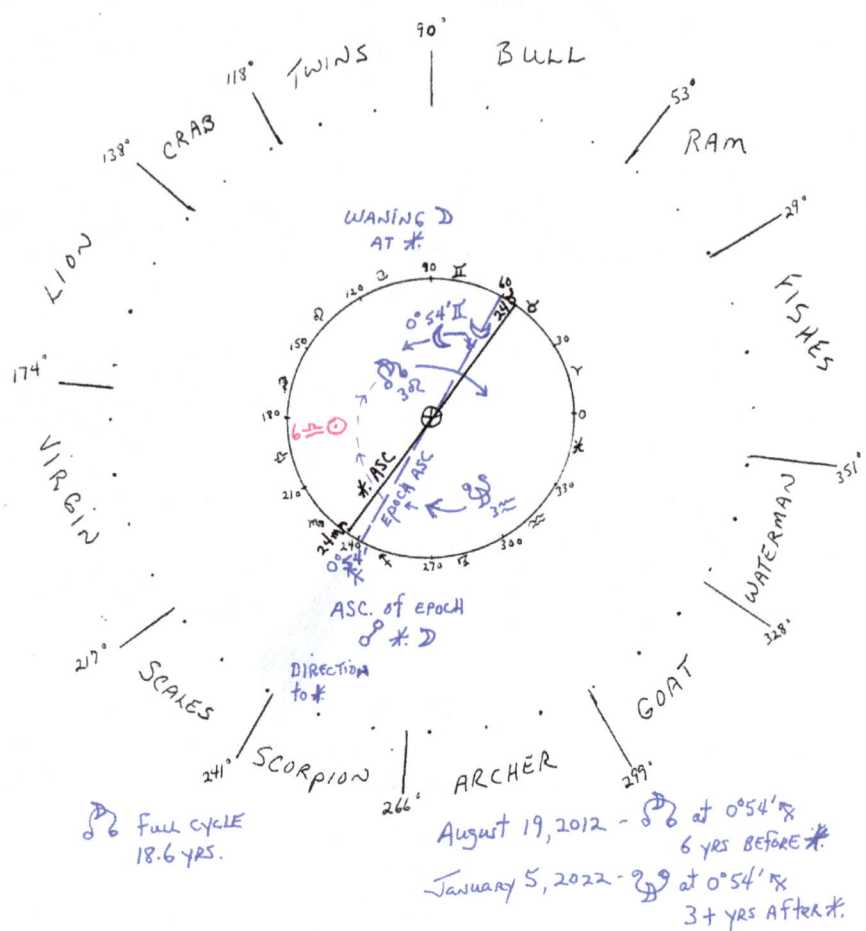

We end this chapter with an important key verse by Steiner on our new relationship to the stars, as well as a few final thoughts on this area of work.

> Stars once spoke to human beings
> It is world destiny they are silent now
> To become aware of the silence can be pain for Earth humanity
> But in the deepening silence there grows and ripens
> What human beings speak to the stars
> To become aware of this speaking
> Can become strength for spirit human

This stands as a clear reminder that the significance of astrosophy is not in determining what the stars are "doing to us." We have reached a point in evolution where there has been a kind of inversion. What once guided from without, determined from without, shaped from without has been handed over, and now it is up to us, as we develop our sense of our spiritual ego through a path of inner development, to take up these star configurations within us and transform them so that we may be of service to the greater world of the hierarchies. We are in fact the tenth hierarchy, and the hierarchies above us and below us are awaiting our activity. We have a special place in the cosmos because we are that hierarchy, the only hierarchy, who is able to say no, to develop freedom and out of freedom, a new form of love.

The focus of a new astrosophy is on how do we now return something to the cosmos, because our returning something to the cosmos actually changes the cosmos. As we explored in the Christ and Stars chapter, central to this transition and central to astrosophy is the event that occurred in the Earth as the major turning point in time. That is the event described as the union of the Christic Force, the Christ being, with the Earth. That event is not the teachings of Jesus, but the death and resurrection of the Christ being. That transition is central to the entire body of astrosophy as developed by Willi Sucher. This event was no less than the Sun "I" uniting Itself with the Earth. And now the Sun shines from within the Earth as a seed force and within us as a seed force, out of which we transform the Earth into a Sun over long ages of time.

I conclude this chapter with a short quotation from Rudolf Steiner that summarizes speaking to the stars:

> It is no longer the same being once present as the cosmos that will receive its illumination from humanity. As the divine-spiritual passes through humanness it will experience a quality of being not previously manifested. (*The Michael Mystery*)

6

Heliocentric Astrosophy

In this course, we introduce heliocentric astrosophy, meaning a Sun-centered astrosophy.* This astrosophy from the heliocentric perspective, as developed by Willi Sucher, is a totally new approach to how we bring about a spiritual perspective in star wisdom based on a model that is essentially materialistic—the heliocentric model. What is the basis of heliocentric astrosophy? What is its purpose? How does it relate to the Copernican model, about which Steiner had few good things to say?

Copernicus (1473–1543) first circulated his model, or theory, of the heliocentric universe around 1514, but it wasn't until shortly before his death, the last year of his life, that he published it. But his theory was not accepted by most astronomers until about 1700. It took nearly two hundred years for the Copernican system to be accepted as the worldview concerning the nature of our cosmos. Even Tycho Brahe argued against the Copernican model.

Nevertheless, there was a heliocentric model even in ancient times that was based on a certain mystery wisdom. In the third century BC, Aristarchus of Samos (310–230 BC) wrote on the idea that the Earth revolves around the Sun. The Pythagoreans also understood this heliocentric model of the universe, though, of course, those earlier individuals still retained a relationship to the reality of the spiritual world and to the spiritual nature of cosmic spheres. It was really with Copernicus that we fully entered an abstract worldview—mathematical abstractions no longer related to experience and perception.

---

* Videos: Course 4: Heliocentric Astrosophy, Session 1.

I will begin with a couple of quotations from Steiner about the Copernican system, as well as one from Sucher on how one would be unable to accept the abstract materialistic Copernican system and still find a path spiritually into a heliocentric concept in relation to birth configurations or as a means to understand human evolution.

> The intrinsic character of spiritual life as it is in the present age arose for the first time when modern natural science came upon the scene with men like Copernicus.... The very ground slipped from under men's feet when Copernicus came forward with the doctrine that the Earth is moving with tremendous speed through the universe! We should not underestimate the effects of such a revolution in thinking, accompanied as it was by a corresponding change in the life of feeling. All the thoughts and ideas of men were suddenly different from what they had been before the days of Copernicus! And now let us ask: What has occultism to say about this revolution in thinking? One who asks, from the standpoint of occultism, what kind of worldview can be derived from the Copernican tenets, will have to admit that, although these ideas can lead to great achievements in the realm of natural science and in external life, they are incapable of promoting any understanding of the spiritual foundations of the world and the things of the world—for in fact there has never been a worse instrument for understanding the spiritual foundations of the world than the ideas of Copernicus—never in the evolution of the human mind! (*Esoteric Christianity*, lect. 7)

> The Copernican worldview pictures the universe in a way that, if followed to its logical conclusion, would tend to drive all spirituality out of the cosmos in humanity's concept of it. The Copernican world picture leads us at length to a mechanical, machine-like conception of the universe in space. It was, after all, in view of this Copernican picture of the world that the famous astronomer said to Napoleon: "He had searched through all the universe and he could find no God. It is, indeed, an entire elimination of spirituality." (*Karmic Relationships*, vol. 4, lect. 6)

For Sucher's perspective on this, one can find more in his many books, particularly in *Practical Approach I*.

Here we might as well indulge for a moment in a discussion about the difference between the geocentric and the heliocentric perspectives, their merits and their limitations.... The Earth is also a part of the solar cosmos, and therefore we expect it to participate in the concerns of the solar cosmos as a whole. We know there are even people who would be inclined to regard the heliocentric perspective as being wrong.

It is certain: the Copernican world conception has put a final end to the ancient worldview of a living universe of spheres, apart from the visible planets, in whom divine beings lived and moved. Copernicanism has indeed denuded the universe from all notions of the presence of spiritual beings behind it and in it. It has become, in our modern view, a gigantic mechanism.

However, we make a sharp distinction between Copernicanism and a heliocentric world conception. There is no need to mix them up, and even the elements of the spheres, with all possible aspects of spiritual reality working in them and through them, can be maintained in the heliocentric perspective, and in our eyes, even more effective than in the geocentric. We are, of course, fully aware of the claims of Christianity, wanting to see the Earth, and with justification, in the center of the universe and view of the Deed of Christ.

However, we still contend that our planet is not yet the center, that we can only hope that it will in future step into that place once the Deed of Christ is raised to realization in the hearts and deeds of the human race. On the other hand, we can imagine that our planet occupied, at some past stage of evolution, a different position in the universe and that it sank from it for the very reason that Christ's Deed of Redemption became a cosmic necessity....

Thus, our conviction has grown that, together with the "breathing" rhythms that we see in the geocentric approach as they are indicated, for instance, by the loops and conjunctions with the Sun, we can again break through to a realistic and yet spiritual conception of the spheres of the planets. In other words, we can apply the geocentric aspect in all those concerns that intend to find the realization of cosmic events in matters of Earth life, both with regard to Earth space and time. The heliocentric approach will lead us to perceive how these events are related to the life of the solar universe, dynamically and spiritually. (*Practical Approach I*)

Here, Sucher points to this shift—from the geocentric to the heliocentric—as a move from the egocentric, Earth-centric perspective in astrosophy, you could say, to a cosmic solar universe perspective, whereby the Earth is a participant with the other planetary spheres in relation to what we described earlier as cosmic intelligences.

So why this shift from the geocentric to the heliocentric? Again, I include a couple of quotations, one in which Steiner presents an understanding of why the heliocentric model came into prominence out of a spiritual, esoteric decision or recognition by the Rosicrucians in the 15th and 16th century. This will lead us into an understanding, from a quotation from Sucher, on how we then work with the heliocentric astrosophy, both in relationship to the individual chart as well as to an understanding of world events in this new context of the redemption of the Earth and its place in the solar universe.

> In the 15th, in the 16th centuries, and even later, there was a Rosicrucian school isolated, scarcely known to the world, where over and over again a few pupils were educated, and where above all, care was taken that one thing should not be forgotten but be preserved as a holy tradition. And this was the following—I will give it to you in narrative form.
>
> Let us say a new pupil arrived at this lonely spot to receive preparation. The so-called Ptolemaic system was first set before him, in its true form, as it had been handed down from olden times, not in the trivial way it is explained nowadays as something that has been long ago supplanted, but in an altogether different way. The pupil was shown how the Earth really and truly bears within herself the forces that are needed to determine her path through the Universe.
>
> So that to have a correct picture of the World, it must be drawn in the old Ptolemaic sense: the Earth must be for Man in the center of the Universe, and the other stars in their corresponding revolutions be controlled and directed by the Earth. And the pupil was told: If one really studies what are the best forces in the Earth, then one can arrive at no other conception of the World than this. In actual fact, however, it is not so. It is not so on account of man's sin.

> Through man's sin, the Earth—so to speak, in an unauthorized wrongful way—has gone over into the kingdom of the Sun; the Sun has become the regent and ruler of earthly activities. Thus, in contradistinction to a World-system given by the Gods to men with the Earth in the center, could now be set another World-System that has the Sun in the center and the Earth revolving around the Sun—it is the system of Copernicus. (*Rosicrucianism and Modern Initiation*, lect. 4)

Sucher writes:

> Thus, I arrived at the following conclusions: Heliocentric astrology ought to be developed as a means to help us to get onto the road leading to the healing and redemption inaugurated by the Deed on Golgotha. It can eventually become something like a means for the diagnosis of human nature in a wider sense, because of the involvement of individuals in the "great sin." A deeper understanding of the Events in Palestine and on Golgotha at the turning point of history, particularly with regard to its spiritual-cosmic aspects, ought to enable us to eventually unite with the Christ impulse, the impulse toward redemption of the "great sin."
>
> Thus, it may even be possible in the dim future to bring the Earth back into its "righteous" position as the center of the universe. But to simply deny heliocentric cosmology seems to me like blinding oneself against the consequences of the Fall and the need for its redemption. (*Practical Approach III*, Nov. 1970)*

Now we have an idea of what heliocentric astrosophy represents. Through the Fall, as described in the Book of Genesis, humanity was no longer able, so to speak, because of the "great sin," as Rudolf Steiner calls it—sin meaning separation—to carry the Earth in its proper place in the universe. So, leadership had to be taken over by the Sun until a time that the redemption of humanity could take place, and human beings could gradually mature into responsible caretakers of the Earth as the center of the solar universe. Thus, the heliocentric approach is a picture, a proper picture, of the true role of the Earth now in the cosmic order, with the Sun as the center and

---

* Video: Heliocentric Astrosophy, Session 2.

the Earth as a body among the planets in relationship to the Sun. When we go, in the next course, to the lemniscate perspective, we will see an astronomical model that already, even in its astronomical form, begins the process of this coming together of the Earth and Sun on the road to reunion.

One might take some time to review the quotes thus far given about the heliocentric view and think about the profound impact of the Copernican model on human consciousness, and our sense of who we are in the cosmos. It addresses what Rudolf Steiner often spoke of as an ahrimanic picture of a mechanized, materialistic, meaningless machine. Yet, through a heliocentric astrosophy and an understanding of the role of the Sun "I" or the Christic "I" in the cosmos, we can begin a process of transforming that Copernican mechanistic model into a spiritual perspective of our relationship to the hierarchies and to the Sun.

If you read Willi Sucher, you will see that, throughout his work, the bulk of it is done from a heliocentric perspective, in terms of human incarnation asterograms and historical events, all relating to what are called the elements of the spheres. What are these elements of the spheres that are astronomical phenomena but cannot be viewed from a spiritual perspective?

In the geocentric perspective, we looked at the apparent path of the Sun, which we call the ecliptic plane. It's the plane through which the Sun and planets move on the backdrop of the Zodiac. In the geocentric perspective, we on Earth are in the center looking up at this phenomenon of movement of the Sun and the planets along the ecliptic plane. When we shift now to the heliocentric model, the Sun is stationary and the Earth is revolving and the ecliptic plane is the plane of the orbit of the Earth. Heliocentrically the Earth and planets move along this ecliptic plane through the zodiac.

We know from geocentric astronomy that the angle of the Earth's orbit tilts at an angle to the ecliptic plane. Heliocentrically, the Earth orbit is the ecliptic plane, with all of the orbits of the different planets tilting at slight varying angles from the ecliptic plane, the plane of the Earth orbit. This tilting of the orbits of the planets shows heliocentrically what we spoke about in the geocentric model as the relationship between the orbit of the Moon and the Earth. The intersection of the ecliptic plane with the lunar orbit is the tilt of the lunar plane to the solar ecliptic plane. In the heliocentric model, we have the same picture. As in the geocentric model, we spoke about the nodes of the Moon, which move in time and make a full revolution about every 18.6 years; so in the heliocentric model, the planetary planes tilt to the Earth plane, which is the ecliptic. Each planet then has its nodes in relationship to the Earth plane. Below is an image of the solar universe with the Sun in the center and the different orbital planes of the universe going out to Pluto. Even though it doesn't really show in the image, you can imagine that each of these orbits is tilted at an angle to the Earth orbit.

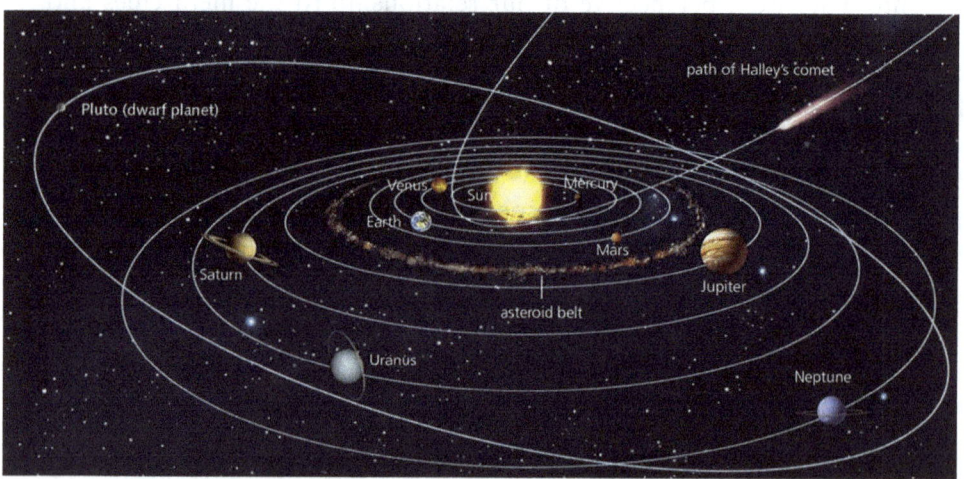

The second image is a slightly more focused picture of these two planes intersecting, and you can see these two points on either side of the circle; at one point, the planet comes around and descends below the plane of the Earth orbit, and then ascends above the plane. These two intersection points are called the ascending and the descending nodes. This is an astronomical phenomenon. We talked about the lunar nodes in the geocentric model, so in the heliocentric, these nodes are portals or connecting points between the planetary spheres and the Earth sphere.

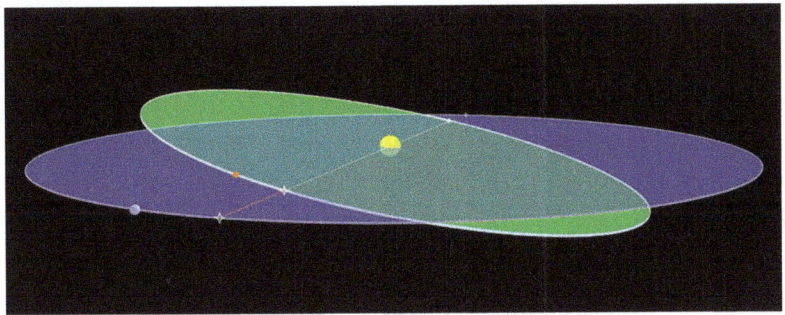

When a planet is in a particular node it is, one could say, communicating in a certain way with the Earth sphere, and various planets in various nodes have over time revealed their characteristics through history. Each planetary node also carries the general impulse or intent of the beings of that planetary sphere. For example, if the Earth enters the node of Jupiter, which is at a certain degree on the ecliptic plane, the Earth will stand in a particular relationship to the sphere of Jupiter intelligences, or Jupiter beings. In addition, through Willi Sucher's research, these nodes also retain and carry certain memories of events in the world, which we will look into later. So, here we have a picture of the nodes as spiritual entities, spiritual gateways between the Earth's sphere, the human sphere, and the hierarchies or the cosmic intelligences, or planetary beings, of the other spheres.

We also have a picture used in heliocentric astrosophy to help us understand these spheres. From the Copernican system, we know that planets do not revolve in circles around the Sun but elliptically. Thus, there is one point of a planet's orbit that is closer to the Sun and another point at which it is the farthest from the Sun. We have the same situation with the Earth, which is part of the reason for our seasons. Picture the shape of the ellipse as if looking down from above at the elliptical orbit and place the Sun in the center. The portion of the ellipse that comes closest to the Sun is called in astronomy the *perihelion* (*peri* = near; *helio* = sun). The portion of the ellipse that is farthest from the Sun is the *aphelion* (away from helios). Sucher has placed a kind of human form within this ellipse, the form of a cosmic-size being, with the Sun in the heart and the activity in the region of the perihelion as akin to human head activity, thinking. The aphelion is related more to the will, as if the planetary beings in the aphelion area want to break away from the orbit and go their own way. In the perihelion they hold close to the Sun. With imaginative thinking, we can in this way differentiate the qualities of the activity of the beings in the planetary spheres: the aphelion related to the will, or is comparable to what we experience as will, and the perihelion related more to what we might consider thinking, or head activity.

In the solar cosmos, this heliocentric perspective, we know astronomically that all of these elements do not remain fixed and stationary like a machine, but like all life and being, they are in constant movement and change, however gradual that might be. So, the nodes of the planets move slowly along the backdrop of the zodiac over time. Also, the perihelion and aphelion shift very slowly over time. These movements of the perihelion and aphelion and of the nodes in relationship to each other and through the zodiac over vast periods of history have been the bulk of the research of Sucher. For example, the node of Venus comes into the same position in the ecliptic as the node of Mercury, further out in space, of course, but at the same degree. This means the node of Venus conjuncts the node of Mercury at some point in history. This will have significant meaning for humanity. Or the perihelion of Jupiter might move from one constellation and cross into a new constellation over vast periods of time, thousands of years. These macrocosmic rhythms, over centuries and thousands of years, reflect changes in human consciousness that have taken place at these transitions, or at these meetings of the nodes, or a node with the perihelion, or the movement of the nodes and apsides into different constellations. This is a major component of Sucher's research into the evolutionary journey of the Earth as humans over time work to regain their "center" in the spiritual cosmos.

As we can see, heliocentric astrosophy is a vast work for exploration. There are two ways to work with this heliocentric model. One is a study of the history of world events, cosmic-size world events, in relation to the movements of the elements. The other is working with individual heliocentric birth charts. We will go into how to construct an individual heliocentric birth chart next.*

---

* Video: Heliocentric Astrosophy, Session 3.

One of Sucher's magnificent research projects that he has developed over time has to do with the heliocentric planetary positions of famous personalities at their birth and at their death in relationship to these elements of the spheres. Much of his later chart work involved sitting with a person and reviewing both the geocentric chart and the heliocentric chart. He would give what he called "historic similars." For example, someone's Mars at birth might be in the node of Venus, and perhaps Darwin had his Mars in the node of Venus at death or maybe Copernicus had his Mars in the node of Venus at birth. He knew the historical personalities who had similar planetary positions in relationship to these elements. He did this because it characterized the evolution of human consciousness and the task of human beings to take up what the greater cosmos of these planetary spheres and the hierarchies carry. Steiner spoke about how we go through various processes when we excarnate at death, but eventually expand, so to speak, in consciousness into the various planetary spheres, each of which carry certain qualities and histories. During this process, we hand over the fruits of our earthly life—our earthly goals and intentions—to the planetary spheres with which they are associated.

Then, on the path to birth, we pick up these impulses, metamorphosed as they may be, to bring into the new incarnation. We continue with the development of what has been done in our previous lives but perhaps in a very different way. Additionally, other people who also traverse these spheres and carry similar impulses, similar karmic goals, can also pick up what one has left off and carry it forward in their incarnation. There is this communion with souls and spirits working and striving toward similar goals and aspirations karmically in their incarnations. In the following quote, Steiner gives an example of this, which led Sucher to this work with "historic similars."

> We look at the period following that of Leonardo da Vinci. We find that Leonardo continued to work through a number of those who lived after him. Even externally there can be found in Leonardo's writings things that later on were demonstrated by scientists and also by artists.... We then see that the inscribed imperfections [meaning here, inscribed into the planetary spheres in the

spiritual world after death], worked as inspirations into the souls of Leonardo's successors, into the souls of people who lived after him.... What has not been perfected is the seed of the following divine evolutionary process.... Imperfection, however, imperfection originating in great men and women whose influences have remained for posterity, helps to promote creative activity in the following period. (*Life between Death and Rebirth*)

Let us now go into these two approaches just to give you an idea of how one might work with them. Let's first start with the historical approach.

To start, refer to the two images of the heliocentric astrosophy model. The first one is a color image with the elliptical shapes drawn in, as if we are looking down on the solar system and the planetary orbits. It was done by a friend of mine because I don't have the technological skills to do it. It gives you a colored, truer elliptical picture with the zodiac. The second image is my old original drawing with which I used to do heliocentric charts. Here there are no ellipse shapes, only simplified concentric circles of the planetary spheres with the elements added in and the constellations around the periphery. In both of these models, you can see that Saturn is the outermost orbit. This is simply done because of space on the page and because the movements in a chart of Pluto, Uranus and Neptune are insignificant. So, I place their elements and their positions outside of the Saturn circle, on the outer boundary, in the area of the constellations. This is just a technical explanation of these diagrams.

In this picture of the heliocentric model in color you can see, on the outer boundary, the new symbols for the constellations with their names and the unequal sidereal boundaries of these constellations by degree. Then you have the blue sphere of Saturn and in it the perihelion of Saturn at 92°, and opposite it, the aphelion at 272°. In all of these elements, of course, the perihelion and aphelion are 180° opposite and the nodes are 180° opposite. The current position of the ascending node of Saturn is at 113° in the Twins and the descending node of Saturn at 293° in the Archer.

Heliocentric Astrosophy

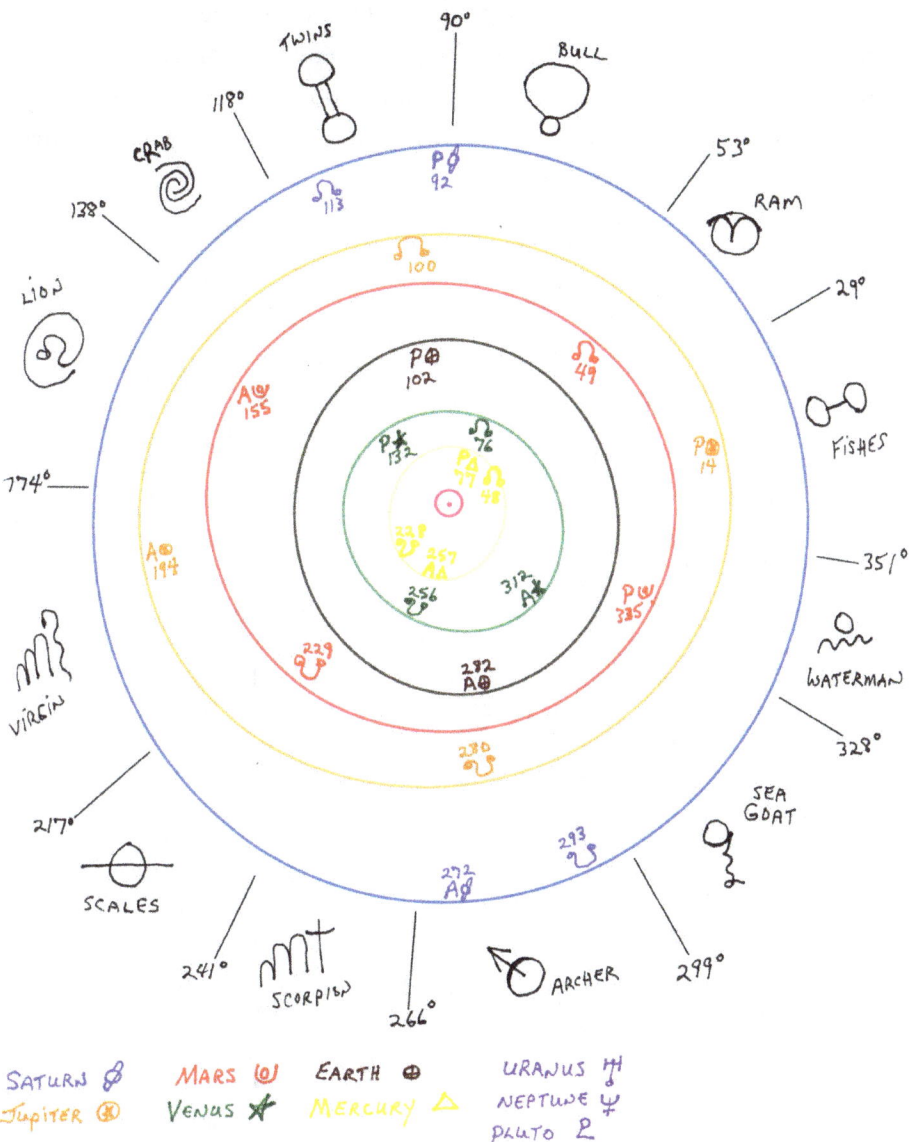

I have not put in the elements of the outer planets, but at the end of this Heliocentric chapter I will insert a list of all the positions so that one can draw them in for oneself. I won't go through each planetary sphere, but you can see for yourself the locations of the elements in each sphere. (Many of these templates are available on the website astrosophy.com for download in the notes under each video.)

The second image is then the template I use for the heliocentric chart construction in black and white. You can see again on the periphery the new symbols for the constellations, the boundaries for the constellations, and the elements in the various spheres beginning with Saturn.

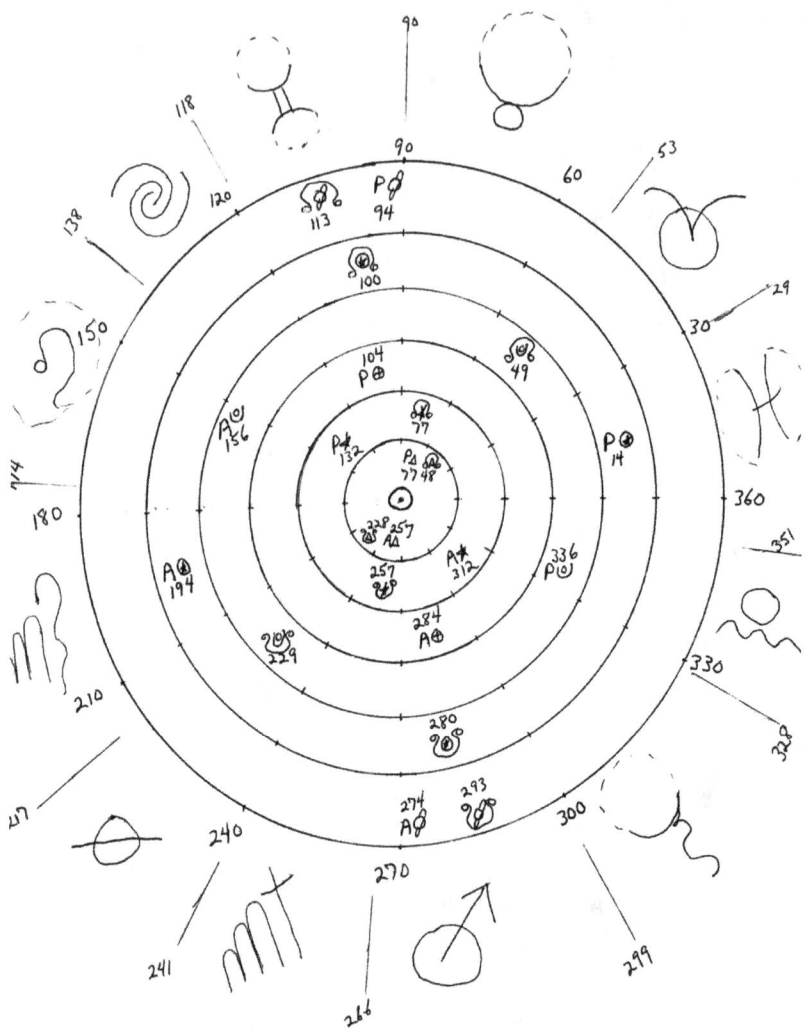

I will just point out that the planet symbols in these templates are different than the traditional symbols. Sucher began to develop new symbols for the planets that were more of a picture of what they represent. So, you can see that Saturn is really an image of this body with the ring around it; Jupiter is this sphere with the five-pointed star in the center, which indicates the future Jupiter stage of evolution, when the true Christian mysteries will be realized, which Jupiter carries on a cosmic scale; the image for Mars is like a U with a circle in it, which is a kind of hieroglyph of Ancient Moon evolution (crescent moon with a sphere), which is connected with Mars; Venus is a five pointed star, which is the form that Venus creates in the heavens; and Mercury is the small triangle. Mercury creates a double triangle in the heavens geocentrically. So, these are some new planetary symbols with which Sucher began to work.

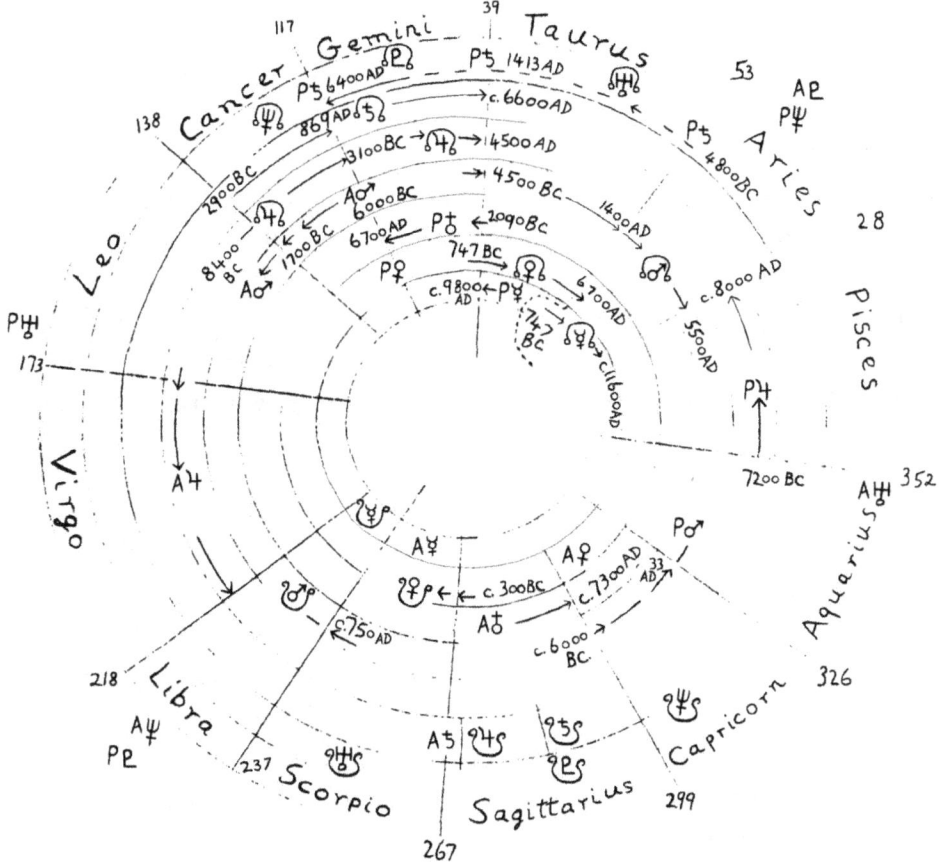

Above is chart from *Practical Approach III* by Willi Sucher. He goes into great detail about the elements of the spheres. I would refer anyone to that book and that section where he describes each of the planetary spheres—their elements and their history, as well as a sample of the historic similars with the births and deaths of different historic personalities in relation to those elements. The quality of the image may not be strong as it is a copy from a copy of a book, not an original image.

Out of many, many examples, I present several here that indicate how to work with the historical movements of these elements. In the diagram from *Practical Approach III* we see the various elements and arrows with dates that indicate their movement. They encompass vast periods of time. For example, near the top we see the movement of the node of Saturn. It entered Cancer in 2900 BC and will go through only two constellations of the Zodiac, entering Taurus in AD 6600. We see the vast scale of time involved with the slow cosmic movement of those elements. It gives us a sense of the great macrocosm and the long period of our evolution.

Note, too, that the perihelion and aphelion slowly move counter-clockwise, whereas the nodes move clockwise. The slowness of their movement is enhanced by the shift in the degrees of the constellation boundaries owing to the precession of the equinox. And we see the apparent change in degrees slowed even more because of the compensation for the shift in the precession of equinoxes, which changes the degrees of the constellations.

Let's consider several examples:

1. The perihelion of Jupiter moved from the constellation of Aquarius into the constellation of Pisces in 7200 BC. It will move out of the constellation of Pisces into the constellation of Aries in AD 7900. This perihelion of Jupiter stays in Pisces for basically the entire fifth post-Atlantean Epoch, from the beginning of Ancient India until the end of the seventh Age. Sucher speaks about this perihelion of Jupiter in particular (and the aphelion opposite, but particularly the perihelion) as carrying the primary impulse of the fifth post-Atlantean age, which is spiritual freedom.

2. The node of Jupiter in the constellation of Gemini: At the Baptism of Jesus, when the Christ being indwelled him, Saturn

stood in the ascending node of Jupiter. At Golgotha Jupiter itself moved into the ascending node of Jupiter. Sucher characterizes this as the ascending node of Jupiter carrying, in a spiritual etheric essence, the memory of the entire mystery of the Three Years. So, in interpretation, if a planet enters this node of Jupiter, there is an activation of this memory and a potentiality connected with that for an individual or a historical time, in relation to the particular planet that enters this node.

3. The perihelion of Mercury came into alignment at the same degree as the ascending node of Venus in 1879, the beginning of the Age of Michael. Here we have this quality of the sphere of Mercury, active cosmic intelligence coming into alignment with Venus, the healing brought about through the new Christian mysteries. This alignment reflects the impulses at the beginning of the Age of Michael and its task to redeem intelligence through the Christ impulse.

4. The ascending node of Mars—we know that Mars is connected with the larynx and speech, as well as to the emergence of the natural scientific age with its development of the mastery of the material world of objects. The ascending node of Mars entered the constellation of Aries in 1413, the beginning of the Consciousness Soul Age. It is the time of the emergence of the thinking that brings about our spiritual freedom. Aries has a deep relation to thinking, both a spiritual thinking for the future as well as the descent of thinking into the brain and the senses. So, a certain kind of intellect out of the Mars sphere that is connected to the mastery of the object world takes this thinking impulse of Aries in a particular direction, which evolved into the natural sciences.

5. We spoke about the ascending node of Jupiter and its relationship to the Christ mystery. It will move into Taurus in AD 4400. This has a relationship to the Maitreya Buddha, whom Steiner states will advance from Bodhisattva to Buddha around AD 4500. With this event, the potential for the power of the magical creative word will arise. The word will

become a force of creating good in the world. So, we have this Jupiter connection with the evolution of the Christ impulse and its force in the world moving into Taurus, the sphere of the throat and larynx.

These might sound farfetched. It is esoteric history and these elements move very slowly. But if one were to really study the comprehensive work of Willi Sucher in this area, one would begin to see this amazing weaving of the planetary spheres in relation to each other and to the zodiac in the shaping and movement of evolutionary streams in the great panorama of world history.*

We will close this course on the heliocentric perspective by looking at how to create a heliocentric birth asterogram as a complement, an elaboration, of the geocentric birth asterogram. Here you can see the heliocentric chart template. The process of creating the heliocentric chart, once you've done the geocentric chart, is quite simple. You already have calculated the two significant dates, the epoch and the birth. So, in the heliocentric chart, using a heliocentric ephemeris, you simply take the planet position on the epoch date, place it into the corresponding circle that you see below, and then you use your compass to draw that planetary movement from epoch to where it comes to at birth. In the heliocentric, there are no loops, there are no retrogrades, it's not complicated, it's a single curving line.

It's important when you're drawing this to convert the tropical positions given in the heliocentric ephemeris, since they do not correspond to this heliocentric model. You will need to convert the tropical positions into the 360-degree circle that you can see on the chart. For example, if the heliocentric ephemeris says a planet is at 10° Pisces tropical, you know that tropical Pisces begins at 330, so you would add 10° to 330 and place the planet at 340° on this particular chart. Alternatively, if the planet is at 4° Cancer, for example, it converts to 94°. It is a fairly simple process if we have a geocentric tropical template to help us recall the tropical sign's degrees that we convert onto the sidereal 360° template.

---

* Video: Heliocentric Astrosophy, Session 4.

Heliocentric Astrosophy

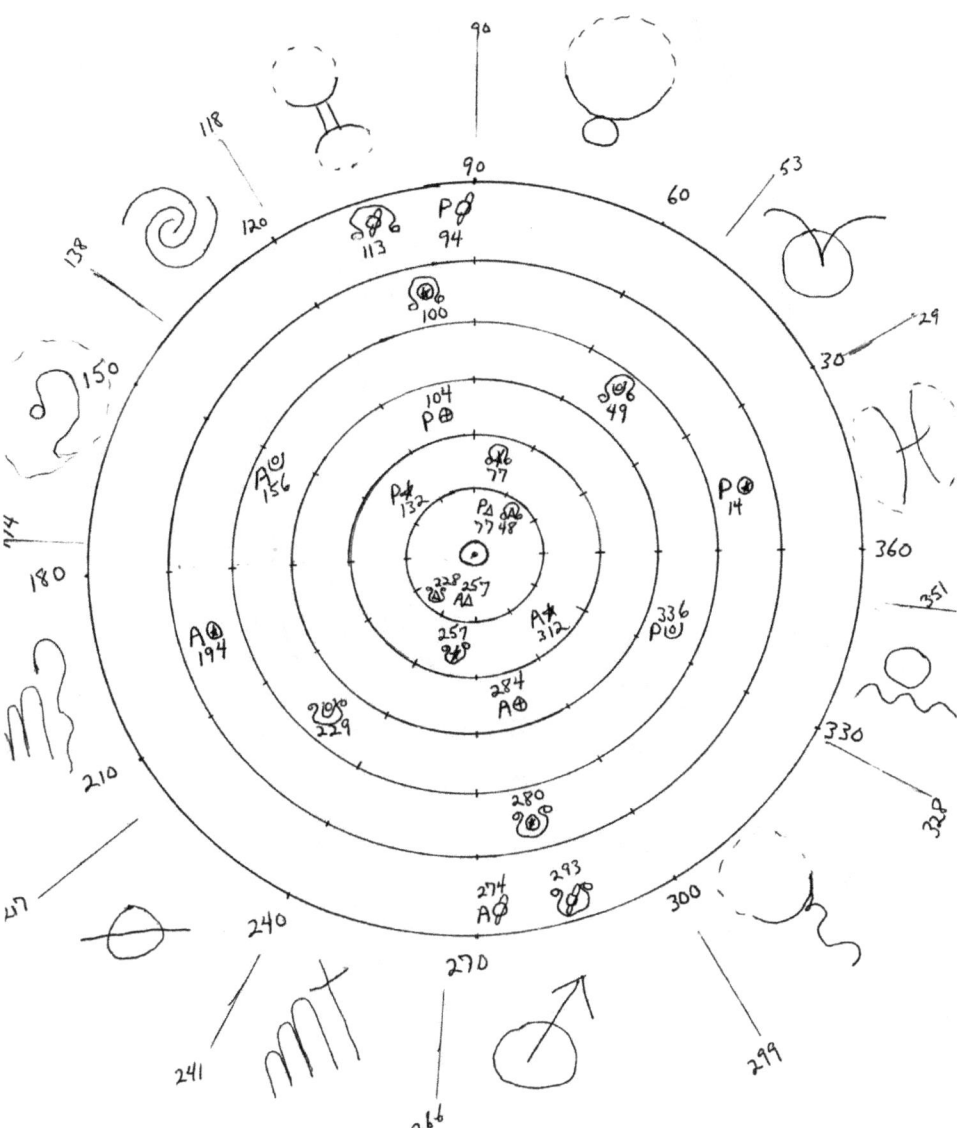

Then, we have the heliocentric chart. On the next page is a heliocentric chart with the colors and movements of the planets. Next, of course, it's a matter of understanding the chart, which includes primarily the meanings of the elements. Let's look at the sample birth chart, which is an epoch and birth chart from 1947. It is not possible to go into this in depth, but a few examples will give an idea of how we can work with the heliocentric birth chart.

Let's focus on two spheres of activity—the Mars sphere and the Venus sphere.

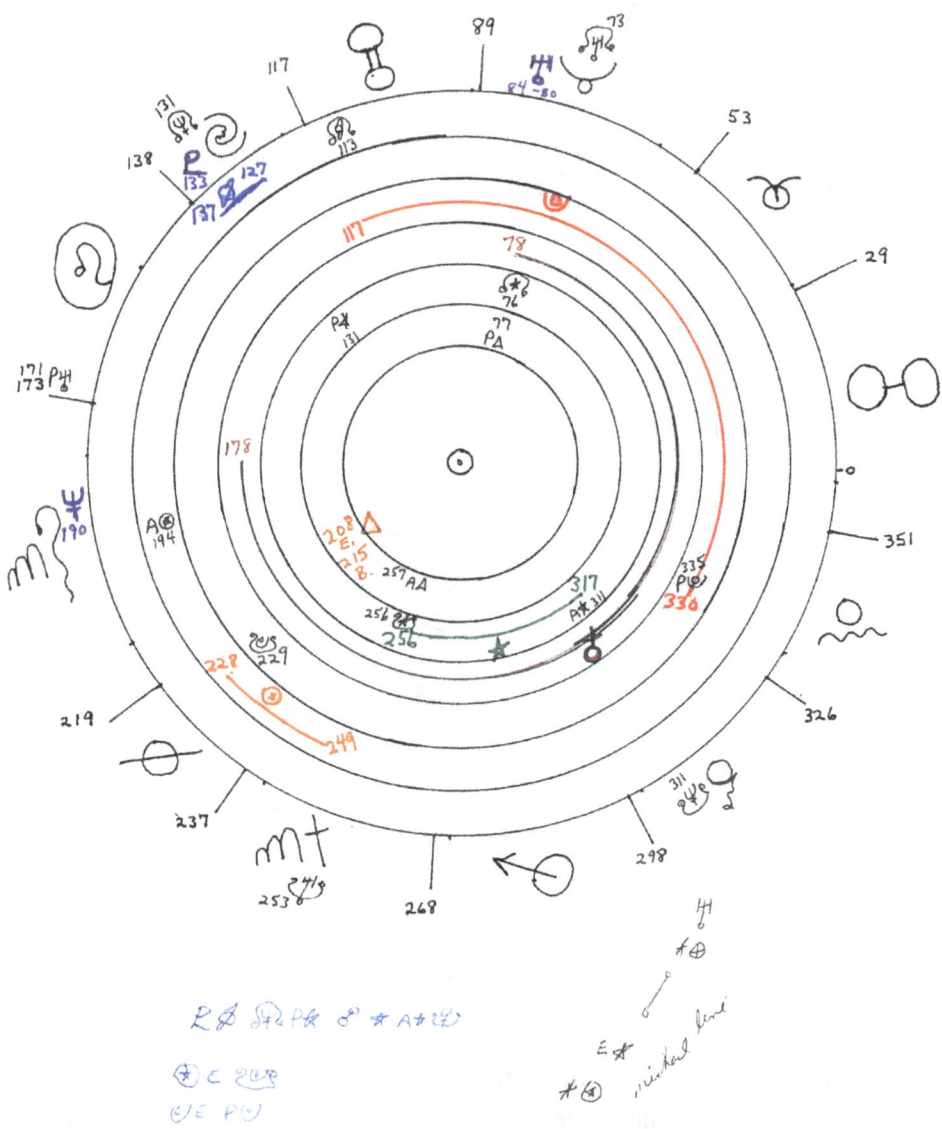

Looking at this chart, we see the planet Jupiter near the bottom in orange. We see that, at the epoch, Jupiter begins in the descending node of Mars and then at birth comes into Scorpio. In the Planets Course the nature of the Mars sphere and its relationship to our object consciousness was presented. We have in Mars the kind of thinking that is oriented toward the development of the object consciousness and human freedom, the path of separation from the divine. This Mars sphere is then also deeply connected with the development of the natural scientific worldview. Very often scientists have this kind of relationship to the Mars sphere in the heliocentric chart. So, one could understand this Jupiter in the descending node of Mars at the epoch as a kind of intent, from a past incarnation for the coming incarnation, to take up this new kind of thinking—Sucher describes it as "clairthinking"—which the Jupiter sphere carries, and bring it into this Mars sphere.

The node of Mars is in the stars of Libra, which is this constellation connected with the activity of Michael. So, again, this reflects the call to take fallen earthly intelligence that is bound to matter, the intelligence from the Mars sphere, and lift it to cosmic intelligence through Jupiter, as that sphere of living thinking, creative wisdom. Jupiter, of course, moves very slowly; thus, many individuals will have this one particular configuration/impulse. This is why one aspect, particularly if it's an outer planet, isn't definitive of the chart. We consider the whole context of the heliocentric and geocentric chart.

Now look more closely at the Mars sphere in this chart (the upper, red arch). Mars at the epoch also activates the Mars sphere by being in the perihelion of Mars, that point closest to the Sun in the elliptical orbit. Mars is at 330°, just 5° out from the perihelion of Mars. Here again, we have this picture of Mars at the Epoch (in this particular person's chart), connecting itself with the Mars sphere, the impulses of encountering the material, and separating from the divine, to come to freedom and egoity. Then it comes at birth close to the ascending node of Saturn, which you can see in the Saturn circle at 113°. Mars comes to 117° in the Gemini constellation.

This is when the historical perspective on these elements can be informative when reading the chart. The node of Saturn crossed into the stars of the Twins from the Crab in AD 869. Some readers might be familiar with Rudolf Steiner's description of what happened in AD 869. The Fourth Council of Constantinople took place in the Catholic

Church, which moved from a trinitarian view of the human being to a dualistic view. It removed the spirit and proclaimed that human beings are composed of body and soul, though the soul has some spiritual qualities. This proclamation set a course that led to the emergence of a materialistic worldview and a dualistic separation of faith and knowledge. The threefoldness of the human being was made to become twofold. This polarity, reflected in Gemini in the sphere of Saturn, is connected to world karma. So, in this person's chart at the epoch, Mars begins in its own perihelion and then arrives at birth in this node of Saturn to address this question, in the realm of Mars, which has taken up this whole dualistic object consciousness.

Another perspective on heliocentric chart interpretation, as I mentioned, involves historical similars—looking at the epoch and birth and death planetary positions of various historical personalities in relation to these elements. This was Sucher's practice of when reading charts. This offered some similars with whom that person could feel a connection to help them understand how these elements worked in others. Of course, this is something only the person could know for themselves. For example, let us look at this position of Jupiter in the descending node of Mars in Libra at the epoch. Copernicus had this configuration at birth; Henry Ford had this Jupiter in the node of Mars at birth; Napoleon had this Jupiter in the node of Mars at birth, as did Vladimir Solovyov. You can see that it is never completely one-sided. Many in this selection were individuals who developed this materialistic science as part of the industrial revolution. However, others were great authors who struggled with questions of the nature of our humanity, like Solovyov and Leo Tolstoy. They tried to lift these Mars questions of self into this higher Jupiter perspective. Similars to the position of Mars in its own perihelion at the epoch in this chart are: Henry Ford with this Mars at his death and Novalis at his birth.

Historic similars for Mars in the ascending node of Saturn at birth shows one quite significant individual who was central to the development of the Mars perspective in human thinking. Francis Bacon had this Mars at his death. Francis Bacon is really, one could say, the father of binary thinking and the father then of a materialistic scientific approach. Ben Franklin had Mars at this position at the epoch. Yet, Mahatma Gandhi, too, had this Mars at the ascending node of Saturn at birth. In these individuals, we can see in their life paths certain major contributions to world karma.

As another example of how one might understand and interpret a chart of the heliocentric perspective, let's consider the Venus sphere, whose impulse is different from that of the Mars sphere. Mars brings us the whole journey into separation and freedom and the development of materialistic natural science through object-consciousness. Venus is the sphere that now wants to reintegrate the human being with the divine spiritual. It carries the impulse of the new Christian mysteries, which for me is another way of speaking about the impulse of anthroposophy, the infusion of the Christ-consciousness into earthly life.

In this particular chart, we have Venus, which you can see at 256° and the epoch (in green). This is in the descending node of Venus and the aphelion of Mercury that have aligned. The meeting of the aphelion of Mercury and the descending node of Venus occurred in 1879, so the alignment of these two elements of the Mercury and the Venus sphere carries the impulses of the Michael age. Mercury is connected with cosmic intelligence; this winged intelligence as one sees in depictions of Mercury. Venus is connected to the new Christian mysteries. So, this coming together of these elements reflects this uniting of Michael's task with intelligence with the founding of the new mysteries out of the Christ impulse that was inaugurated in 1879 at the start of the new Michael Age. This person has Venus in this line at their epoch. Here we have potentially a real Michaelic impulse in this individual.

Here, of course, the green line is very short, but we can imagine that Venus has gone completely around once, and that this is a continuation of it, since Venus takes less than a year to go completely around the Sun. We see that Venus at the birth comes into the aphelion of Venus. We have here this very special picture of Venus at the epoch in its own elements in the Michael line and at the birth again in its own element, the aphelion line. Also significant, at birth, it stands opposite Saturn, or the path of Saturn during the prenatal, and opposite Pluto.

This configuration at birth—Venus opposite Saturn and Pluto—would take us too deeply into this chart for now, but it's a powerful configuration to pursue fully when sitting with a birth chart. In fact, I see this as a central theme for this individual to focus on in the chart.

Now, to add one more element, if we look at the Earth, the brown line, we can see that it comes into the position at birth opposite where Venus was at the epoch, as well as in the Michael line. Thus, depending on who this person was and incorporating all the other factors of the biography, it is possible, if the person is karmically connected with the stream, to work in a real Michaelic way, specifically in this incarnation as a karmic choice to redeem the fallen intelligence and lift it into a more spiritualized way of thinking and truly transform the Mars sphere. For historic similars in relation to Venus in the Michael line at this epoch, Dostoyevsky, Ralph Waldo Emerson, and Rembrandt all had this in their epoch.

So, in this brief introduction to the heliocentric chart, I intended indicate how we can dig into a chart as a kind of perspective that does not contrast to the geocentric chart, but allows both of these pictures to come to life. An understanding of the spheres of the planets, as well as the history of the planetary elements, gives a complex and illuminating picture, to which individuals can relate or find meaning through their own biographies and experiences.

We have now moved through the geocentric and the heliocentric perspectives, and this concludes our heliocentric course. Next, we will step into the future.

HELIOCENTRIC ELEMENTS LOCATIONS

Heliocentric Mercury
Perihelion 76.8°   Aphelion 256.8°
Ascending Node 47.9°   Descending Node 227.9°

Heliocentric Venus
Perihelion 131.0°   Aphelion 311.0°
Ascending Node 76.3°   Descending Node 256.3°

Heliocentric Earth
Perihelion 102.3°   Aphelion 282.3°

Heliocentric Mars
Perihelion 335   Aphelion 155.3°
Ascending Node 49.2°   Descending Node 229.2

Heliocentric Jupiter
Perihelion 13.7°   Aphelion 193.7°
Ascending Node 100.0°   Descending Node 280.0°

Heliocentric Saturn
Perihelion 92.3°   Aphelion 272.3°
Ascending Node 113.3°   Descending Node 293.3°

Heliocentric Uranus
Perihelion 170°   Aphelion 351°
Ascending Node 73.8°   Descending Node 253.8°

Heliocentric Neptune
Perihelion 44.3°   Aphelion 224.3°
Ascending Node 131.3°   Descending Node 311.3°

Heliocentric Pluto
Perihelion 224.2°   Aphelion 44.2°
Ascending Node 109.9°   Descending Node 289.9°

7

The Future Lemniscate Perspective

We come to the final course in this introduction to astrosophy.*
Now we move into a model of the universe that Rudolf Steiner spoke of, one that will take us into the future of astronomy and astrosophy—a new dimension of understanding our cosmos.

Thus far, we have gone through the geocentric perspective, into the nature of the zodiac and the planets. Then we took up a basic introduction to the heliocentric perspective and traveled the journey of human consciousness in evolution. From the time of the great myths and archetypes, the gods and sagas, which the zodiac and the planets all represent, we moved into the modern consciousness in which human beings were no longer the center of the world and surrounded by the world of the gods. Instead, the human being was completely separated from the cosmos and became "speck of dust" in this great mechanistic, heliocentric cosmos, no longer having a relationship to the divine spiritual.

Steiner describes these three stages of the evolution of consciousness in his *Anthroposophical Leading Thoughts,*** also published as *The Michael Mystery*. He describes the phases of cosmic history. One he calls "heavenly history," which Owen Barfield describes as the time of "original participation." In that time, there was no need for gods or

---

* Video: Course 6: The Lemniscate Perspective, Session 1.
** *Anthroposophical Leading Thoughts: Anthroposophy as a Path of Knowledge: The Michael Mystery* (Rudolf Steiner Press, 1973); see also, Carl Unger, *The Language of the Consciousness Soul: A Guide to Rudolf Steiner's "Leading Thoughts"* (SteinerBooks, 2012).

myths and no star wisdom, because human beings lived in an instinctive union with the higher divine world and did not need any representations. Steiner describes the next phase as "mythological history," the time going back to the later ancient Indian era and the Vedas, and on into the myths and stories of the gods from the various cultural ages, from which the geocentric perspective of the universe arose. He called the third phase modern history, or "earthly history," which is our current object consciousness and our sense of separate selfhood, detached from the world of the divine and viewing the cosmos as only matter.

What comes after "earthly history? Next, we move into the model of the lemniscate cosmos, which Steiner discusses in his *Interdisciplinary Astronomy: Third Scientific Course.** Because this model is quite a complex and difficult to fully grasp with our current consciousness, we will use a lot of images. As you will see in some quotations from Steiner, we are entering a consciousness that is no longer brain bound and object oriented. It is a new consciousness to be developed that can "see" into the life realm of time. It is a synthesis, really, of the material perspective, or the object consciousness, and the life consciousness, which is germinating now in human beings, and will be required to develop our human consciousness.

Let's begin with a couple of quotations from Steiner, before building up this system using some images of this lemniscate model.

> The two streams—the spiritual and the materialistic—drifted further and further apart. In the Mysteries, the words that later came to denote the external heavenly bodies had always referred to supersensible worlds, to a sequence of spiritual realms. The outer world always understands the words to mean the material aspect, and this is true even of the contemporary mythology—I use the word deliberately—we call "astronomy." Spiritual science recognizes the full value of all mythologies. Thus, it also appreciates the worth of the mythology called modern astronomy that sees only space filled with physical cosmic bodies.... A time will come when people will say of modern mythology, "In the past, there were human beings who thought it correct to place the material Sun in

---

* See also Steiner's *Astronomy and Astrology: Finding a Relationship to the Cosmos,* ed. M. Jonas (Rudolf Steiner Press, 2010)

the center of an ellipse and to rotate the planets in ellipses around it. They constructed a cosmic universal system even as earlier people had done before them. But today, we know that it is all mere saga and legend." Indeed, a time will come when, no matter how much the old mythologies are now despised by the modern world, it will be considered absurd to speak of a Copernican mythology. (*The Spiritual Hierarchies and the Physical World*, p. 13)

In short, men are entirely convinced that Copernicus, for example, finally established the fact that the Sun stands still, or perhaps has a movement of its own. In any case, it does not move around the Earth every twenty-four hours, but the Earth itself revolves, and also moves around the Sun in the course of the year, etc. These things are well known. They are understood today as if man had finally cast off the ancient superstition of the Ptolemaic world conception and had set truth in place of the former error.... Earlier humanity believed all sorts of stupid things because it trusted its senses.... At last, one knows that in the course of the year the Earth revolves around the Sun, and so on. In fact, one has made wonderfully fine progress! We are no longer far distant from the time in which we will understand what all this means. The true reality was of no consequence at all to the spiritual powers upon whom Copernicus, Kepler and Galileo were dependent; it was rather to bring definite faculties into the human head. What matters is the education of mankind through the education of the Earth....

Thus, mankind was to be obliged for a time to think in this way about the cosmos in order to be educated in a certain way through thoughts. It is with this that the wise guidance of the world is concerned.... One will say, "Good, now we have a physical cosmic system; when we study it, we must, as we know, calculate it and treat it geometrically as is taught today in practically every elementary school."

But spiritually, things are otherwise. You see, to an observer able to behold the spiritual, the following is presented, for example. He comes upon a certain movement of the Sun; it takes this course. (*Inner Impulses of Evolution,* last lecture)

Following is an image of this lemniscate form. It is the drawing by Steiner that follows this quote. We will continue with this quotation and the further development of this drawing. Here you see the very beginning of this form of the lemniscate, which he puts on the blackboard. But it's not quite so simple as just thinking about it in a physical way. One must now begin to create images, but realize that these images are only images of a non-spatial reality projected into space.

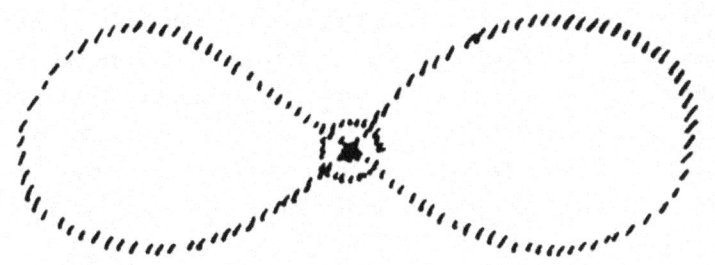

Physical science speaks of a movement of the Sun; and it can do so, for within the spatial picture of the Cosmos that surrounds us, we perceive by certain phenomena that the Sun is in movement. But that is only an image of the true Sun-movement—an image cast into space. If we are speaking of the real Sun, it is nonsense to say that the Sun moves in space; for space itself is being radiated out by the Sun. The Sun not only radiates light; the Sun creates the space itself. And the movement of the Sun is only a spatial movement within this created space. Outside of space it is a movement in time. What seems apparent to us—namely, that the Sun is speeding on toward the constellation of Hercules—is only a spatial image of the time-evolution of the Sun-being. (*The Festivals and Their Meaning*, June 4, 1924)

How can we understand what Steiner is talking about here? There's a gentleman named Roland Schrapp, who has written a booklet called *The Lemniscatory Path System*.* He a comprehensive scientific study of the Lemniscate model Steiner presents, and I highly recommend it for those who want to delve into the astronomical science of it. I am including a selection from this booklet that will begin to take us into

---

*   It is permissible to download it here http://www.rolandschrapp.de/The_Lemniscatory_Path_System.pdf.

how we can understand this new idea of a different kind of space connected with time.

> ...the further development of the Copernican system toward a lemniscatory path system or system of formative forces,...based on Rudolf Steiner's specifications, will also take place. But as great as the resistances will be, ultimately humanity will have to take the step toward understanding the cosmic formative forces of the planetary paths in order to ascend from the realm of the dead form to the realm of the moving life, the ethereal, out of which the form observable with physical senses is first born. In this sense, Rudolf Steiner points out the necessity for today's humanity to rise from pure formal thinking to a thinking in movements. (*The Lemniscatory Path System*)

Here we begin an exploration of what we can call centric space, Earth space, Euclidean and peripheral space, counter space, negative space. Below is a quote from the Goetheanum website on projective geometry, which I think will help us. Then we will move into how Willi Sucher develops his picture of the lemniscate.

> Counter space is the space in which subtle forces work, such as those of life, which are not amenable to ordinary measurement. It is the polar opposite of Euclidean space. It was discovered by the observations of Rudolf Steiner and described geometrically by George Adams and, independently, by Louis Locher-Ernst. Instead of having its ideal elements in a plane at infinity it has them in a "POINT at infinity." We call this point the counter space infinity.... It appears thus only for a different kind of consciousness, namely a peripheral one that experiences such a point as an infinite inwardness in contrast to our normal consciousness that experiences an infinite outwardness.

This is really interesting to contemplate: this point of infinite inwardness and the infinite outwardness of our object consciousness in which we are the centric point.*

In a previous section, I presented Willi Sucher's "wave theory" of the cosmos, which presents the heliocentric picture of the periphery

---

* Video: Course 6: The Lemniscate Perspective, Session 2.

of the Zodiac and the streaming in from the Zodiac of zodiacal substance. Let us try now not to think materialistically, but see this cosmic substance that begins to densify as it approaches the Earth. On Earth it achieves greatest density. Ideally, on the Earth this densified substance begins a process of transformation and spiritualization, and then on Venus and Mercury the process is facilitated further until it disappears into the Sun. Steiner calls the Sun less than empty, or negative space.

Willi Sucher, in this wave theory, describes how the substance then disappears through the "hole" of the Sun. What we experience as physical light and warmth is merely a byproduct of a spiritual activity. The true sidereal substance becomes completely spiritualized in this central counter space, this negative space of the Sun. What happens to it? It reappears at the periphery, and the wave process begins again. Here we have this kind of perpetual flow, a coming together, from peripheral life into substance, centric substance, then through the "hole" of the Sun, through the negative space, and reappearing as periphery.

Patiently try to picture these things without analyzing or intellectualizing; just hold this as a picture. Then you can build this forward. Sucher, in an article in *The Living Universe*, builds a picture of how this lemniscate is formed. He begins by describing how the lemniscate is really an archetypal form of life. When we study plant morphology, the growth of a plant in nature, we find a kind of lemniscate weaving form.

So, let's look at how Sucher builds the rationale behind this lemniscate form. The following quotations are all from a lecture of January 12, 1956 (in *The Living Universe*).

> Now, first of all, I should like to work a little on the idea of the lemniscate. Why just this form? Why of all forms in the cosmos this particular one? You see, it is bound up with the very principle of life. If we think of two spheres of different quality in the cosmos, for instance, of that sphere of emptiness we have been speaking of, the Sun, that "hole" in the cosmos. What kind of Sun would that be? It is very interesting to go right through this idea. We have that "hole" in space, the Sun in the heavens that we see in Fig. 3a.

Here he presents figures 3a and 3b, side by side. Figure 3a shows the Sun. We see in this picture what we just read about in projective geometry as the point at the periphery. The center is the periphery, and the "hole" is the surface. Juxtapose this with the Earth-centric, Euclidean space shown in 3b, where there is a center and a surrounding periphery.

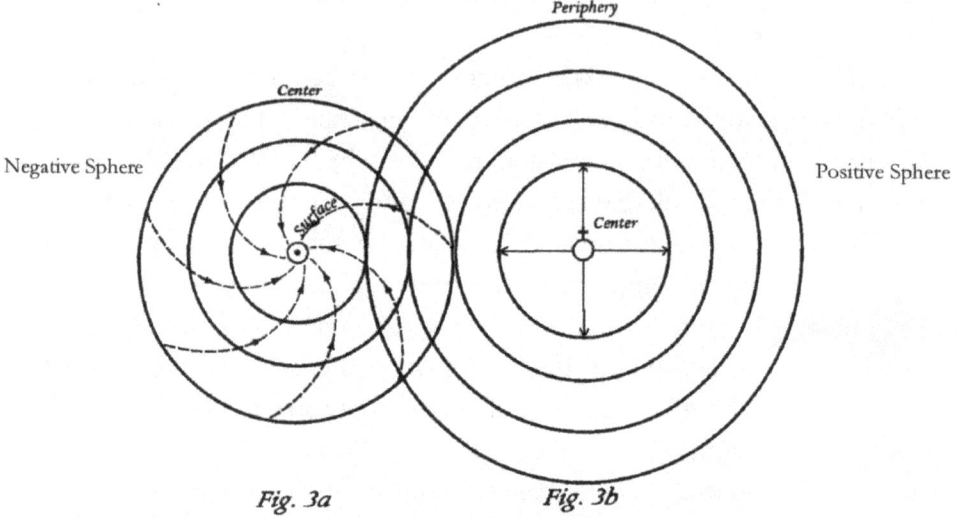

Fig. 3a   *Fig. 3b*

It would draw in the sidereal zodiacal "substance" that is out here beyond this circle. This is obviously a sphere with a negative character, which does not do what you expect from this second sphere, indicated in Fig. 3b, a sphere that starts from a center point and goes out toward the periphery—this is the general aspect we develop if we speak of a sphere. But this Sun in 3a is just the reverse, it comes in from what we would [ordinarily] call a periphery, though it's not exactly so, and finally comes to what we can call a surface. I mean, this [outer circle] is not really a periphery in 3a. If we take a circle and turn it inside out, obviously the center moves out of the middle, doesn't it? Where would it move to? — into what we see in 3b as the periphery. But in 3a it is the center of that sphere and this [center point], well, if you think of it as a globe, would be its surface. Can you follow?

Now I shall call 3a a negative sphere and the sphere that would start from its center and move out, expanding toward the periphery, a positive sphere (3b).

Then he continues on with this image:

> Now if we have two such spheres intersecting, and if these two entities were made to move, we would get a lemniscate. In the points, where the concentric circles clash, you would find the foundation for the drawing of a lemniscate. The "points of clash" between these concentric circles would be the points that you would have to use in order to draw a Cassini Curve or lemniscate—a figure eight.

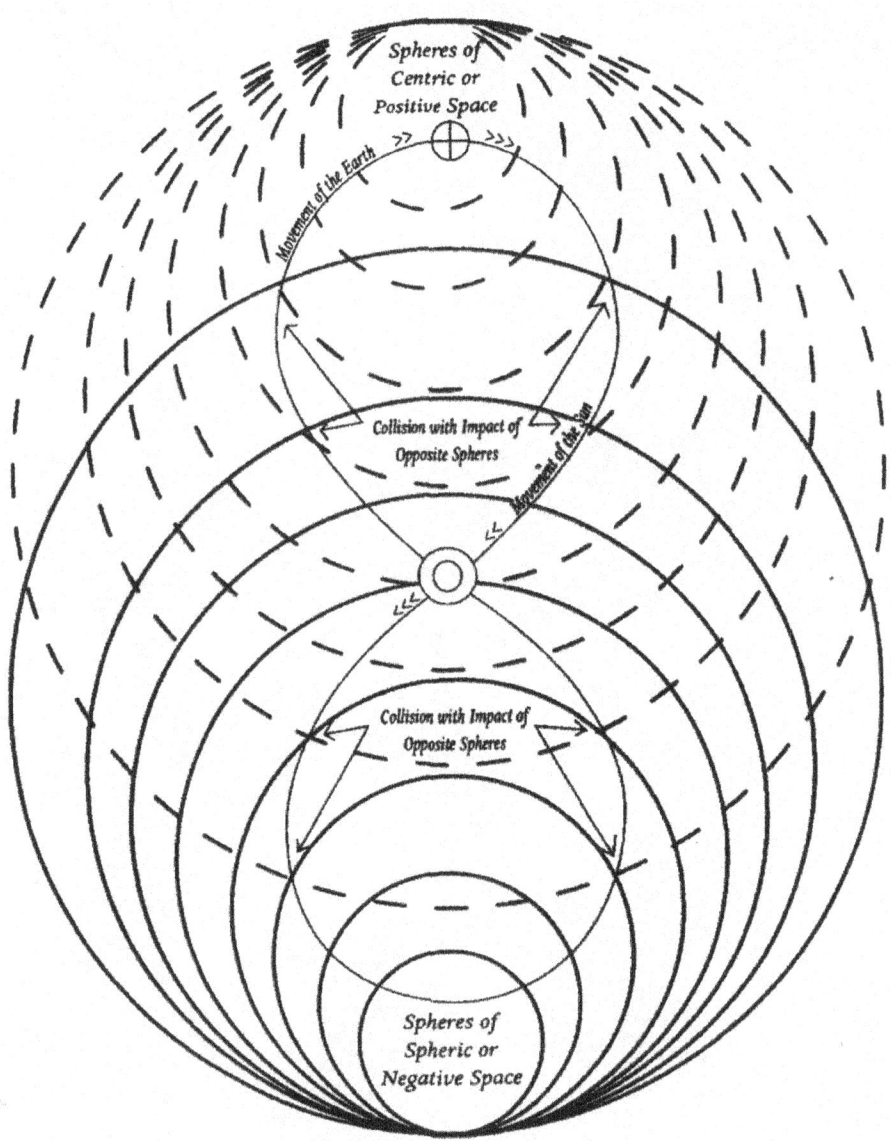

In this lecture then, Sucher describes how the lemniscate form arises from the convergence of these two spheres of centric and peripheral cosmic space.

Now look at the drawing by Rudolf Steiner (below), in which he takes the basic lemniscate shown on page 169 and adds a complication. He shows not just one lemniscate but also a second lemniscate, forming a double lemniscate, one created by the path of the Earth and one by the path of the Sun. These two lemniscates converge only at the shared center point. We begin to see in this picture that we have a moving cosmos of Sun and Earth in a mutual relationship, and at one point during each year the Sun stands in this central crossing point of the Cassini curve, the figure eight, and at another point of the year, the Earth stand in the same place.

Let's continue with what Steiner has to say and look at this rendering of the image he drew on a blackboard:

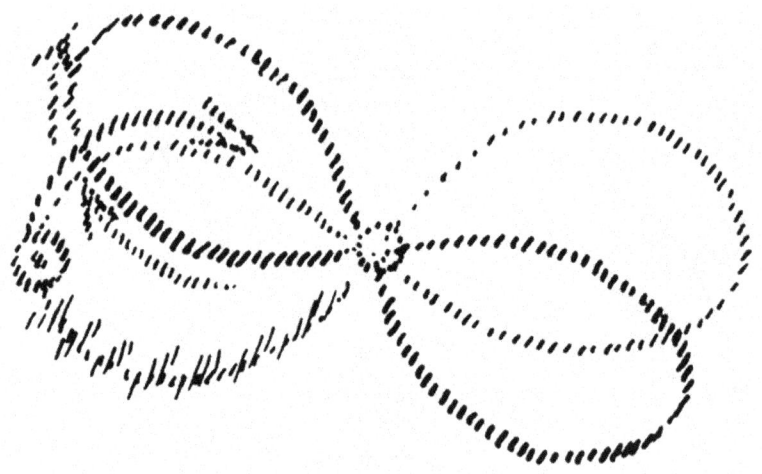

Seen from a certain point of view, it is the Sun's course. But when I draw this line here and bring the Sun back again, the point does not fall exactly on the earlier point. It lies somewhat above it. This is a real movement of the Sun that can be perceived spiritually, but the Earth, too, makes certain movements in the course of a year. Observed spiritually it describes this orbit. You must picture it in three dimensions.

You can see in the lower curve a circle with the dots and the arrow moving toward the center, the path of the Sun. Then the heavier slashed line is the path of the Earth with the arrows moving from the center and forming a second lemniscate.

As Steiner says, picture this in three dimensions. I have an hour glass at home, which helps me to think of this two-dimensional picture as spherical and three dimensional. We have the continuous paths of the Sun and Earth in a three-dimensional double lemniscate, crossing at the center. Yet the central point doesn't remain the same, because, when the Sun returns to the center, it will have moved a little further on. This is what Steiner refers to by saying this whole lemniscate moves forward, so to speak; it moves toward the constellation of Hercules. But we must remember, as he said, that this is a spiritual reality that we project into space. We have an incredible dynamic of the Sun and Earth weaving a figure eight in the course of a year, while at the same time, moving forward so that it never returns to exactly the same central point. A few more quotations might help to make this clearer.

> We have to draw the path of the Earth with the Earth tending in a sense toward the place where the Sun has been, and then the Sun tending toward the place where the Earth has been. We thus get the one half of the lemniscate—Earth, Sun, Earth, Sun. When this has gone around, then it goes on. They move past each other, as you see.
>
> Thus, we obtain the true path of Earth and Sun if we alternately imagine the Earth to be at the place where in our usual drawings we are accustomed to put the Sun, and the Sun at the place where we are accustomed to put the Earth.
>
> The fact is, we don't get the true relation between the motions of the Earth and of the Sun if we assume either the one or the other to be at rest. We have to imagine both to be in movement, whereby the one follows the other, yet at the same time they go past each other. So then we have to imagine it such that, seen in perspective, the Sun is alternately in the center of our planetary system and then again the Earth is where we normally conceive the Sun to be. They change places, taking turns as it were. But it's complicated, because, needless to say, in the meantime the planets have also changed their

situation, which gives rise to considerable complication. (*Interdisciplinary Astronomy,* pp. 256–57)

"No little complication." It's difficult to carry this picture. He speaks about how the Sun, in a sense, pulls the Earth behind it, so the Earth is always one quarter of the lemniscate back. So, when the Sun is at the center point, the Earth is at the outermost point of its curve. When the Earth comes into the center, the Sun is in its outermost point of one half of the curve. Then the Sun comes back into the center and the Earth is out. I can't even do it with my hands on this camera. But you can see how the weaving takes place.*

Let us continue with another quote from Rudolf Steiner:

But, as you see from this, there is a point in the cosmos, where the Sun and the Earth are both together, but at not the same time. When the Sun is there on its path, or rather has left this point by a quarter of its path, the Earth begins its movement at the point that the Sun has left. After a certain time, we are, in fact, on the spot in cosmic space where the Sun was; we follow the Sun's path, cross it and are, at a certain time of the year, at the very place where the Sun has been. Then the Sun and Earth go forward and after a time the Earth is again practically at the spot where the Sun was. Together with the Earth, we actually pass in space through the spot where the Sun has been. We sail through it. We not only sail through it, however, because the Sun leaves behind results of its activity in the space it has traversed, so that the Earth enters into the imprints left behind by the Sun and crosses them—really crosses them. Space has living content, spiritual content, and the Earth enters and crosses, sails through, what the Sun has called forth.

You see, this is how the matter looks spiritually. Spiritually one must draw lines like these when one thinks of the orbits of Earth and Sun.... We have now the external picture, the purely geometrical picture. The other picture will be added, and only from a combination of the two will a later humanity attain the concept it must have. (*Inner Impulses of Evolution,* continuation)

---

* Video: Course 6: The Lemniscate Perspective, Session 3. This text comes from the video course in which the hands are used to create the movement.

This quotation has been a focus of study for me for quite some time. Willi Sucher speaks about it and tries to develop it in the lecture I mentioned. Also, Roland Schrapp takes this up and develops it. Both the Sun and the Earth are on different paths on this lemniscate, at angles to each other along a kind of hourglass form except at the center. Steiner speaks here of this central point, where the Sun leaves an imprint of what it has brought for the Earth to step into a quarter of a year later. Here we have the amazing spiritual activity of the relationship between the Sun and the Earth. It is central to what I have tried to take up in my work with the cycle of the year and the Christic festivals.

Steiner at one point did speak about how there were festivals in the earlier times that celebrated this event, but he didn't identify those festivals. However, it seems clear that they are in relationship to Solstice and Equinox points. When one planet is on the periphery point and the other is in the center, is this the solstice point when the Sun is furthest away or is it when it is closest the Earth? Or is it the Equinox point when the Sun is in the center and vice versa. My own work in living with the cycle of the year is to think about this as the core of what astrosophy is all about, which is the relationship to the fact that the deed of Christ took place on the Earth. The Sun being united His essence with the Earth being. This is a spiritual picture of the union of solar reality with earthly reality and the beginning of the transformation that this lemniscate picture is an imagination of—this interrelationship of Sun and Earth working together. This brings a new understanding that transcends the heliocentric with the Sun in the center, and the geocentric with the Earth in the center, and the Sun enveloping it. So, we have this question: What is the moment in the year when the Earth stands in the spiritual imprint that the Sun has left? I will not go further into this question here but simply present the picture of this astronomical lemniscate system as Steiner developed it.

The mathematical astronomical aspects of this new system are frankly beyond my expertise, as I do not have a scientific or astronomical background. However, I have familiarized myself with it enough to begin to carry it as a picture.

One can imagine how the lemniscate relates very much to the Christic year and the relationship of this lemniscate movement to the festival year. Before I present a little treasure to share on camera here (in the video, a model of the lemniscate form built for Willi Sucher is shown),

I want to return to this thought of heavenly history, mythological history, and earthly history. We can picture it in the form of a U-curve with heavenly history at the top of one side of the U-curve, then moving down through mythological history to the bottom of the U-curve, earthly history. This is the point of separation, of egohood, feeling within one's "I." This is the beginning of the turn up of the U-curve. Not back to a mythological history, but into the realm of Imagination and new picture consciousness, like that from which the mythologies arose, but now in a new, conscious way. Then we eventually move on to a kind of consciousness that no longer needs an astronomical model, because it then moves into the new form of participation, heavenly history, but in a fully conscious way.

I will share one quotation from Steiner about this, and then we can look at the model.

> It would not have been possible to make any calculations relative to the constellations and star orbits in the ancient epoch; they were then an expression of the free intelligence and the free will activity of divine-spiritual beings. In future they will again become incalculable. Calculations are significant for the intermediate period only. (*Anthroposophical Leading Thoughts*, Jan. 4, 1925)

Now I'd like to share this treasure with you. This is a wooden model made for Willi Sucher, which I feel extremely blessed to have in my possession. We will try to look at it a little more closely, if the camera can zoom in a bit. It is a double lemniscate, with red numbers on the Sun lemniscate and the blue on the Earth lemniscate with the crossing point in the center. The whole lemniscate also moves in this kind of direction, sort of walking forward, through the cosmos, toward, as Steiner says, the constellation of Hercules.

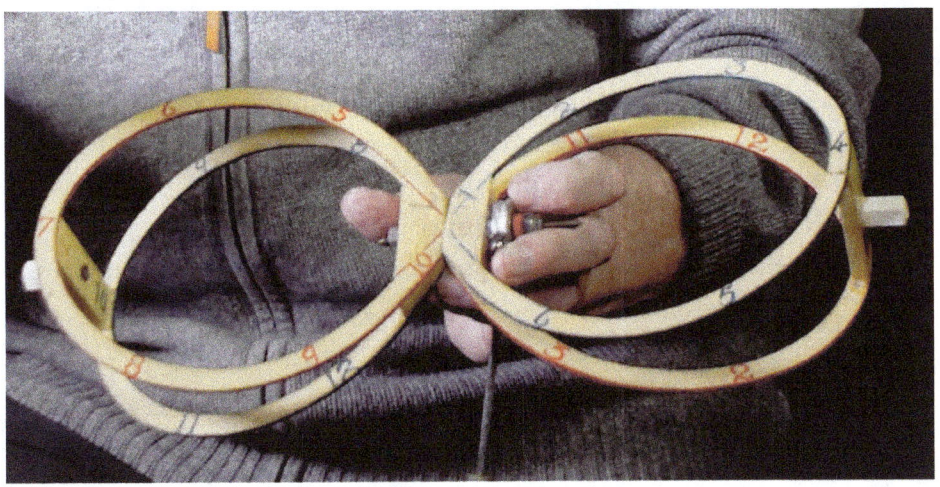

We can see on the model here how the numbers progress: 1, 2, 3, 4, 5, 6, 7 would be here crossing over, going under 8, 9, 10, 11, 12 for the 12 months of the year. Then the Sun has its own lemniscate. So, we have this movement, and around it on the periphery we have the zodiac, which is this realm of duration, the fixed stars that don't weave. However, the solar cosmos of the planets makes these lemniscate forms in the backdrop of the twelvefold zodiac.

We must think about it in the sense that when we look—say, in spring—we have the Sun with the stars of Pisces behind it, which means the Earth is in the opposite constellation. And then, as the Sun and Earth move forward, they are in the opposite constellations. So, somehow we have to work this lemniscate form so that the Sun and the Earth continue to be in those opposite constellations of the zodiac. You can imagine that it's quite complex.

We must also consider the planets in their motions. I will include a final image as we wrap up this course. Steiner mentions in one of the quotations that including the planets adds another level of complication, since Saturn, Jupiter, and Mars also participating in these lemniscate forms, outside and around this Earth/Sun lemniscate form. In addition, Venus and Mercury make smaller lemniscate forms following the lemniscate paths of the Sun and Earth. We can try to picture this living beautiful weaving of all the planets, creating these life forms in the cosmos, between space and counterspace.

To conclude this very basic introduction, below is one of several drawings, which Willi Sucher made, that will blow your mind. There are many of these drawings in which Willi attempted to create this Sun/Earth lemniscate path as a kind of cross form. This one has the path of Saturn around it. You can kind of see on it the constellations in the positions where the constellations of the zodiac would be.

With this image for the future, we complete this course as an introduction to astrosophy. I hope it has led you on a journey that can become fruitful for you.

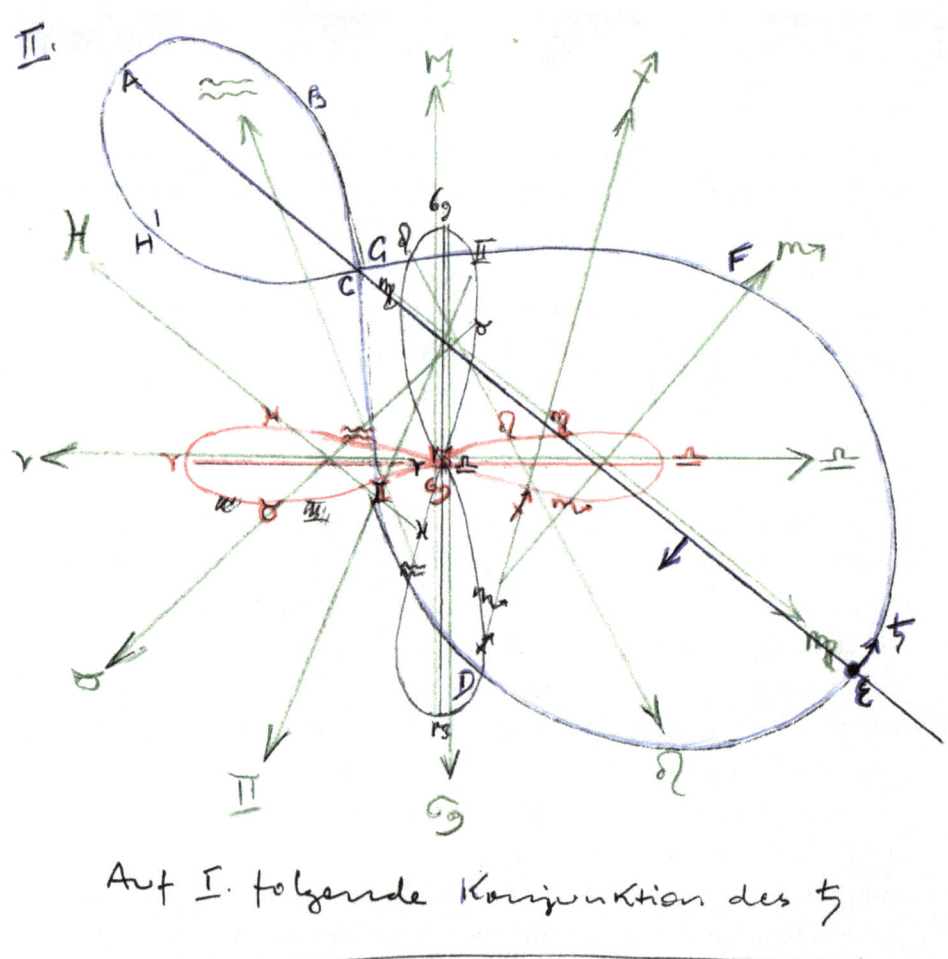

Appendix I: Selected Quotations by Rudolf Steiner on the Stars

The following quotations are only a selection of the expansive knowledge provided by Rudolf Steiner on the cosmos of the stars from many perspectives. There might seem to be contradictions or a variety of points of view. This only goes to show the complexity of the cosmos and the interweaving life of the beings who dwell there. It requires us to perceive with the eyes of Imagination and hear with Inspiration, rather than applying our brain-bound object consciousness in attempts to create an orderly "table" of what the stars "mean." However, on entering these spheres we can begin to perceive how what might appear to be contradiction arises from one reality seen from different perspectives.

General Stars and Zodiac

What is a Star?

> To speak of a "physical" star is not really correct. For what is a star? Physicists imagine that combustion of gas or some process of the kind is taking place in the sky. But as I said, if they could actually get there they would be amazed to find no burning gas in the Sun but actually a lacuna, a gap in space, in a condition infinitely more rarefied than any particles of earthly matter could ever be. Everything is Spirit, pure Spirit. Nor are the other stars so many bodies of incandescent, burning gas, but something entirely different. Bordering on this Earth with its physical substances and physical forces, is the universal Cosmic Ether. We are able to perceive the Cosmic Ether because, as we gaze into it, our field of vision

is circumscribed and the surrounding ether appears blue. But to believe as materialistic thinkers do, that physical substances are roaming around up there in the Cosmos is just childish fancy. No physical substances are moving around, for at the place where a star is seen, there is something altogether different. The farthest reaches of the etheric would lead out of and beyond space, into the spheres where the Gods have their abode. And now picture to yourselves a certain inner relationship that may exist between one person and another and comes to physical expression. Picture it quite graphically. You are caressed by someone who loves you. You feel the caress but it would be childish to associate it in any way with physical matter. The caress is not matter at all, it is a process, and you experience it inwardly, in your soul. So it is when we look outward into the spheres of the Ether. The Gods in their love caress the world. But the caress lasts long, because the life of the Gods spans immense reaches of time. In very truth the stars are the expression of love in the Cosmic Ether; there is nothing physical about them. And from the cosmic aspect, to see a star means to feel a caress that has been prompted by love. To gaze at the stars is to become aware of the love proceeding from the divine-spiritual beings. What we must learn to realize is that the stars are only the signs and tokens of the presence of the Gods in the Universe. Physical science has much to learn on its path from illusion to truth! But men will not achieve self-knowledge nor will they understand their own true being until this physical science has been transformed into a spiritual science of the worlds beyond the Earth.

Karmic Relationships, vol. 7 lect. 2 (CW 239)

Stars as Beings

The third aspect presents the boundary of visible space: this is the aspect of the stars. But the stars do not appear as they do to physical sight. For physical sight the stars are points of radiance at the boundaries of the space in the direction toward which we are looking. If we have acquired the faculty of Intuitive Knowledge, the stars are the revealers of cosmic beings, spiritual beings. And with Intuition we behold in the spiritual Universe, instead of the physical stars, colonies of spiritual beings at the places where we conceive the physical stars to be situated.

Karmic Relationships, vol. 5, lect. 5 (CW 239)

Zodiac and Cultural Ages

Each individual cultural epoch, as it relates to the evolution of consciousness for each nation, is connected with the progression of the Sun through the zodiac.

You know that the time of transition from the third to the fourth cultural epoch was represented by the sign of the Ram or Lamb. The Babylonian-Assyrian epoch gathered together in the sign of the Bull all that was important for its time. The previous Persian age was designated in the constellation by the sign of the Twins. And if we go still further into the past we would come to the sign of the Crab for the Sanskrit culture. This epoch, in which the Sun was in Cancer at the time of the spring equinox, was a turning point for humanity. Atlantis had been submerged and the first Sub-Race [cultural epoch] of the fifth Great Epoch had begun. This turning point was denoted by the Crab. The next cultural epoch similarly begins with the transition of the Sun into the sign of the Twins. A further stage of history leads us over into the culture of Asia Minor and Egypt, as the Sun passes into the sign of the Bull. And as the Sun continues its course through the zodiac, the fourth cultural epoch begins, which is connected in Greek legend with the Ram or Lamb (the saga of Jason and the search for the Golden Fleece). And Christ Himself was, later on in early Christian times, represented by the Lamb. He called Himself the Lamb.

We have traced the time from the first to the fourth-cultural epoch. The Sun proceeds through the heavens, and now we enter the sign of the Fishes, where we are ourselves at a critical point. Then [in the future], in the time of the sixth epoch, the time will arrive when man will have become so inwardly purified that he himself becomes a temple for the divine. At that time the Sun will enter the sign of the Water Carrier. Thus the Sun, which is really only the external expression of our spiritual life, progresses in heavenly space. When the Sun enters the sign of the Water Carrier at the spring equinox, it will then be understood completely clearly for the first time.

Thus proceeded the High Mass, from which all the uninitiated were excluded. It was made clear to those who remained that Christianity, which began as a seed, would in the future bear something quite different as fruit, and that by the name Water Carrier was meant John [the Baptist] who scatters Christianity as a seed, as if with a grain of mustard seed. Aquarius or the Water Carrier means the same person as John who baptized with water in order to prepare mankind to receive the Christian baptism of fire.

The Temple Legend, pp. 141–42 (CW 93)

Sun and Zodiac: Center Reappearing at Periphery Related to Cosmic Wave

Imagine a piece of matter pressed more and more into the central point, where it disappears. It is not being pushed through to the other side. At the center, it actually disappears into nothingness! In other words, eventually the Earth, as its material aspect presses in upon the middle point, will disappear into the center. But that is not all. As much as disappears at the center, so much reappears at the extremity. Matter disappears at one point in space—the center—and reappears at another, the circumference. Everything that disappears into the center emerges again at the periphery. Everything has been worked into this matter. The beings who were at work on the planets impressed everything into the matter. Naturally, the matter is not in its present form, but in a form that it received by means of this process of transformation. So, you will see Cologne Cathedral, whose material particles disappeared into the middle point, reappearing from the other side. Nothing, absolutely nothing, is lost of what has been accomplished on a planet; it comes back from the other side.

All that came to us during the earliest phase of earthly development, before Saturn, was thus transferred outside, beyond the zodiac. In primeval wisdom this is called "the Crystal Heaven." It is where the deeds of beings belonging to a previous evolution were deposited.

The Spiritual Hierarchies and the Physical World, lect. 10 (CW 110)

Sun and Michael

When we speak from the standpoint of genuine stellar knowledge we are able to say: in the epoch upon which we entered in the seventies of last century, it is above all the spiritual forces emanating from the Sun that must exercise a major influence in everything in the psychic and physical life, in science, religion and art. In our epoch the influence and activity of the Sun forces must become progressively more widespread.

For those with real knowledge the Sun is not the globe of gas described by modern physics, but an aggregate of spiritual beings. And the most important spiritual beings, who radiate the spiritual, as the sunlight radiates physically and etherically, are grouped round a being who, in accordance with ancient Christian-Pagan or Christian-Judaic terminology, may be designated as the Michael being. Michael works from the Sun. The spiritual influences from the Sun can also be called the influences of Michael and his hosts.

In the epoch preceding our own it was not the Sun forces, but the Moon forces that were the driving forces behind man's life, activity and search for knowledge. The Moon forces were the driving forces behind the epoch that ended in the eighteen-seventies after lasting for three or four centuries.

True and False Paths of Spiritual Research, lect. 7 (CW 243)

PLANETARY SPHERES

Hierarchies and Presence in Planets

This can be understood only when it is connected with another fact. I have told you that the many stars in the heavens are but the outer signs of colonies of gods. Where the stars sparkle in the heavens there are, in reality, colonies of spiritual beings. But you must not imagine that these gods have their consciousness only in Venus, or only in the Sun, or in Mercury, or in Sirius. They have their main habitation, the focal point of their existence in these several spheres, and this is true of all spiritual beings of the cosmos who have anything to do with the Earth. But it is impossible to say of their existence in the cosmos that they have their dwelling-place only in Mars, only in Venus, and so forth. Paradoxical as it will seem, I am nevertheless obliged to say that the divine beings who belong to the Earth and who people Mars, Venus, Jupiter or another of the planets—also the Sun—would be blind if they inhabited only one of these spheres. They would live, they would be active—just as we can walk about and take hold of things even if we have no eyes; but they would not see—I mean, of course, in the way in which divine beings "see"—they would lack a certain faculty for perceiving what is happening in the cosmos. But this, my dear friends, will lead you to ask: Where, then, is the eye of the gods, where is their organ of perception? This organ of perception is provided by the Moon, our neighbor in the cosmos—in addition to all its other functions. All the divine beings belonging to the Sun, to Venus, Mercury, Mars, Jupiter, Saturn, have their eye in the Moon and are at the same time in the Moon.

Karmic Relationships, vol. 2, lect. 8 (CW 236)

Saturn-Jupiter Conjunctions

...when at the cosmic hour of destiny in the life of a human being, a certain relationship is established between Jupiter and Saturn, there flash into human destiny those wonderful moments of illumination when many things concerning the past are revealed through thinking. If we look in history for occasions in the time of the Renaissance [ca. 1400–1600]—particularly during the last period—when there was a great renewal of ancient wisdom impulses, we shall find that this was directly connected with a certain relationship between Jupiter and Saturn.

Initiation Science, lect. 1 (CW 228)

Moon, Mercury, Venus

So you see, we go through the Moon, Mercury, Venus, and Sun spheres. In each sphere we meet, to begin with, what corresponds to the inner forces that we bring with us. Our emotions, urges, passions, sensual love, unite us to the Moon sphere. In the Mercury sphere we meet everything that is due to our moral imperfections; in the Venus sphere all our religious shortcomings; in the Sun sphere, everything that severs us from the purely human.

Life between Death and Rebirth, lect. 5 (CW 140)

Mercury and Venus

We come next to Mercury. In contrast to the other planets, Mercury is not interested in things of a physical, material nature as such, but in whatever is capable of coordination. Mercury is the domain of the Masters of coordinative thinking; Jupiter, the habitation of the Masters of wisdom-filled thinking.

When a human being comes down from pre-earthly life into earthly existence, it is the Moon impulse that provides the forces for his physical existence. Venus provides the forces for the basic qualities of heart and temperament. But Mercury provides the forces for capacities of intellect and reason, especially of intellect. The Masters of the forces of coordinative knowledge and mental activity have their habitation in Mercury.

Initiation Science, lect. 1 (CW 228)

The Human Being in Relation to the Planets

Thus you will realize that man is in fact a microcosm. He is related to those things that he never perceives in normal consciousness. But he would be unable to fashion, or to order his life, if the Moon forces were not active within him from birth to his seventh year. He perceives later on the nature of their influence. He would not be able to re-create his experiences between the ages of seven and fourteen if the Mercury mysteries were not active within him; nor would he be able to re-create this experiences of the years between fourteen and twenty-one—the period when powerful creative forces pour into him, if he is karmically predisposed to receive them—if he were not inwardly related to the Venus sphere. And if he were not united with the Sun sphere, he would not be able to develop ripe understanding and experience of the world between the ages of twenty and forty-two, the period when we pass from early manhood to maturity.

True and False Paths of Spiritual Research, Aug. 1924 (CW 243)

Speech, Walking, Thinking; Mars Jupiter Saturn; Morality in the Etheric Realm

Walking, speaking, and thinking here on the Earth have their correspondences in the spiritual world: in the orientation among the

Hierarchies, in the resounding of the Cosmic Word, and in the inner lighting up of the Cosmic Thoughts.
Man and the World of Stars, Nov. 26, 1922 (CW 219)

Saturn vs. Moon

There, of course, they are something altogether different from the tiny, insignificant, bluish rays of Saturn that can be visible to us here on Earth. There they are spiritual rays, radiating out into the Universe—even ceasing to be spatial; they radiate into a sphere beyond space. They appear to us in such a way that between death and rebirth we look back in gratitude to the outermost planet of our earthly planetary system (for Uranus and Neptune are not actual Earth planets; they were added at a later stage). We are aware that this outermost planet not only shines down upon the Earth but out into the far spaces of the Cosmos. And to the spiritual rays that it radiates out into the Cosmos we owe the fact that we are now divested of earthly gravity, divested of the physical forces of speech, divested of the physical forces of thought. Saturn, as it radiates out into cosmic space is in very truth our greatest benefactor between death and a new birth. Regarded from a spiritual standpoint it constitutes, in this respect, the very antithesis of the Moon-forces.

The spiritual Moon-forces keep us on the Earth. The spiritual Saturn-forces enable us to live in the wide expanse of the Universe.
Man and the World of Stars, Nov. 26, 1922 (CW 219)

Saturn, Jupiter, Mars

Saturn is helped by Jupiter and Mars, which have special functions to perform of which I shall speak on some future occasion—as long, therefore, as man is under the influence of Saturn, Jupiter and Mars, he is a being who does not strive to walk or speak or think in the earthly sense, but to find his orientation among spiritual beings, to experience the Logos resounding within him, to have the Cosmic Thoughts lighting up within him. And with these inner aims and intentions the spirit-seed of the physical organism is, in very truth, dispatched to the Earth.
Man and the World of Stars, Nov. 26, 1922 (CW 219)

Sun, Mercury, Venus in Relation to the Outer Planets and Walking, Thinking, Speech

The human being who is descending from the spiritual worlds to the Earth has not the least inclination to be exposed to earthly gravity, to walk, or to bring the organs of speech into movement so that physical speech may resound, neither has he any inclination to think with a physical brain about physical things. He has none of these faculties. He only acquires them when, as a physical spirit-seed, he is sent down from the sphere of the Saturn-forces to the Earth, passes through the Sun-sphere and then enters the other planetary spheres—the spheres of Mercury, Venus and Moon. The Mercury, Venus, and Moon-spheres transform the cosmic predisposition for spiritual orientation, experience of the Logos and lighting up of Cosmic Thoughts inwardly, into the rudimentary faculties of walking, speaking, and thinking. And the actual change is effected by the Sun, that is to say, the spiritual Sun.

Through the fact that man enters the sphere of the Moon—and the Moon-forces are helped by those of Venus and Mercury—through this, the heavenly predispositions for orientation, for experience of the Logos, and for Cosmic Thought, are transformed into the earthly faculties.

Man and the World of Stars, Nov. 26, 1922 (CW 219)

Sun and Freedom and Destiny

In the midst of all these deeds and impulses of the planetary individualities stands the Sun, creating harmony between the liberating and the destiny-determining planets. The Sun is the individuality in whom the element of necessity in destiny and the element of human freedom interweave in a most wonderful way. And no-one can understand what is contained in the flaming brilliance of the Sun unless he is able to behold this interweaving life of destiny and freedom in the light that spreads out into the universe and concentrates again in the solar warmth.

Nor can we grasp anything essential about the nature of the Sun as long as we take in only what the physicists know of it. We can grasp the nature of the Sun only when we know something of its nature of spirit and soul. In that realm it is the power that imbues with warmth the element of necessity in destiny, resolves destiny into freedom in its flame, and if freedom is misused, condenses it once more into its own active substance. The Sun is as it were the flame in which freedom becomes a luminous reality in the universe; and at the same time the Sun is the substance in which, as condensed ashes, misused freedom is moulded into destiny—until destiny itself can become luminous and pass over into the flame of freedom.

Initiation Science, lect. 1 (see full lecture; CW 228)

Sun Sphere and the Role of Christ

This is followed by the Sun sphere. Only what bridges the differences between the various religious confessions can help us in the Sun sphere.... We must consider that between death and rebirth we also dwell in the Sun sphere where a thorough understanding of the Christ impulse is essential. We must bring this understanding along with us from the Earth, for Christ once did dwell in the Sun but, as we know, He descended from the Sun and united Himself with the Earth. We have to carry Him up to the Sun period, and then we can become sociable beings through the Christ impulse and learn to understand Him in the sphere of the Sun.

We must learn to discriminate between Christ and Lucifer, and in our time this is only possible by means of anthroposophy. The understanding of Christ that we bring with us from the Earth leads us as far as the Sun sphere. There it acts as a guide, so to speak, from man to man, irrespective of creed or confession. But we encounter another being in the Sun sphere who utters words that have virtually the same content. That being is Lucifer. We must have acquired on Earth an understanding of the difference between Christ and Lucifer, for Lucifer is now to accompany us through the further spheres between death and rebirth.

Life between Death and Rebirth, Nov 26, 1912 (CW 140)

Sun Sphere after Death

...where there is space, space alone, there is nothing; but where the Sun is there is less than nothing, there is a lacuna in space—and there dwell the spiritual beings referred to in the book *Outline of Esoteric Science* as the Exousiai, the Dynamis, the Kyriotetes.

There they have their abode, sending their own essence and power through all creation. Among them man spends the greater part of his life between death and a new birth. In association with the Exousiai, Dynamis, Kyriotetes, with human souls karmically connected with him who have also passed through the gate of death, and with yet other beings whose existence is hardly even conjectured, the karma for the next earthly life is worked out and formulated. Conditions in this Sun region are not as they are on Earth. Why do our clever scientists—and clever they certainly are—picture the Sun as a globe of incandescent gas? It is because a certain illusory, materialistic instinct makes them want to detect physical processes in the Sun. But there is nothing physical in the Sun. One may at most speak of physical processes in the Sun's corona, but certainly not in the Sun itself. In the Sun there is nothing like natural law, for it is a world of purest spirit....

In the Sun sphere, man is concerned only with his moral qualities and with those attributes of his being that have remained healthy; the rest has been laid aside. It persists in him as a kind of incompleteness but this is made good in the Sun sphere. During the first half of existence in the Sun sphere we are engaged in making preparation for the appropriate physical organization of the next earthly body. During the second half of the Sun existence, in union with the Exousiai, Dynamis, Kyriotetes, and with human souls karmically connected with us, we are concerned with the preparation of the moral side of karma, the moral qualities that will then be present in the next life. But this moral part and the spiritual part of karma—for example, specific talents in one direction or another—are then further elaborated in the Mars sphere, in the Jupiter sphere and in the Saturn sphere. And in passing through these spheres we come to know what the "physical" stars are in reality.

Karmic Relationships, vol. 7, lect. 2 (CW 237)

Sun Spots and Change in Planetary Conditions

You know that approximately every eleven years we have a period of Sun-spots, when in the shining of the Sun upon the Earth certain places are darkened, covered with spots or blotches. This was not always so. In very ancient times the Sun shone down as a uniform disc of light. There were no Sun-spots. Moreover, after some thousands of years the Sun will have very many more spots than it has today. The Sun is growing ever more spotted. This again is the outer manifestation of the fact that the Michael Power, the Cosmic Power of Intelligence is still decreasing. In the increase of the Sun-spots in the course of Cosmic Evolution is revealed the Sun's decay; the Sun within the cosmos grows increasingly dim and old. And at the appearance of a sufficiently large number of Sun-spots, the other Planetary Intelligences recognized that they would now no longer be ruled by the Sun. They resolved no longer to allow the Earth to be dependent on the Sun, but to make it dependent henceforth on the entire cosmos directly. This took place through the planetary Counsels of the Archangels. Notably under the leadership of Oriphiel, this emancipation of the Planetary Intelligences from the Sun-Intelligence took place. It was a complete separation of Cosmic Powers that had hitherto belonged together. The Sun-Intelligence of Michael and the Planetary Intelligences gradually came into cosmic opposition one with another.

Karmic Relationships, vol. 3, lect. 11 (CW 237)

Mercury Sphere

Mercury Sphere after Death and in Relation to Illness

When man enters the Mercury sphere, he undergoes further purification. Even when he has laid aside in the Moon sphere those moral attributes that are unfit for the Cosmos, the spiritual counterparts of his physical weaknesses, of his physical infirmities, still remain with him, as do the tendencies to illness and the effects of the illnesses from which he suffered here on Earth. Surprising as it may seem, it is the case that in the life between death and a new birth, man lays aside his moral failings first and his physical infirmities only later, when he enters the Mercury sphere. In the Mercury sphere his soul is purged of the inner effects of those morbid processes that came to expression in illness during his life on Earth and in his soul he becomes completely healthy. You must remember that man is a single whole. From the occult standpoint it is erroneous to speak of him as a compound of spirit, soul and body. He is not a compound of these three constituents, but when we observe him he is revealed on the one side as body, on the other as spirit, and between body and spirit, as soul. In reality, man is one whole, a self-contained unity. The soul and the spirit too are involved in the conditions that prevail in illness. And when man has laid aside the physical body at death, the effects of the experiences resulting from the disease-processes are, to begin with, still present in his soul. But in the Mercury sphere these effects are obliterated under the influences of the beings we know as the Archangeloi.

Karmic Relationships. vol. 7, lect. 2 (CW 239)

These Genii are, however, also to be met with on the path of another kind of research to which I have alluded and the results of which appear in the book that Dr. Ita Wegman and myself have worked out together in the sphere of medicine. [Fundamentals of Therapy: an Extension of the Art of Healing through Spiritual Knowledge. Rudolf Steiner Press, 1967.] When one seeks in this way for an Initiate-knowledge of nature, one comes in a similar way to Mercury Genii; these Mercury Genii approach one because they play a special part in the karma of human beings. When man is passing through the life between death and a new birth, he is first of all purged in respect of his moral qualities; this takes place under the influence of the Moon beings. Through the Mercury beings his illnesses are transformed into spiritual qualities. In the Mercury sphere the illnesses a man undergoes in life are transformed by the Mercury Genii into spiritual energies, spiritual qualities. That is an exceedingly important fact and one that leads further, namely to the investigation of questions of karma in matters that are in any way connected with disease.

Karmic Relationships. vol. 8, lect. 5 (CW 240)

Mars, Mercury, Venus Example in Life after Death

On Herbert Heine karma: Having absorbed the influences operating in the Mercury sphere and the Venus sphere, this individuality passed into the Mars sphere, where a certain strain of aggressiveness developed for the next earthly life; the experiences of an earlier life were transformed into a faculty in which there was a certain vein of aggressiveness. In the Mercury sphere the soul acquired the tendency to flit from one experience to another, one concept to another, and in the Venus sphere an element of eroticism—eroticism in the spiritual sense—crept into the imaginative, conceptual faculties.

Karmic Relationships, vol. 7, lect. 3 (CW 239)

VENUS SPHERE

Therefore when we arrive in the Venus sphere, we have been mutilated in a certain respect. In the Venus sphere the element of purest Love prevails—purest Love in the spiritual sense; and it is this Cosmic Love that bears what now remains of the human being from the Venus sphere into the Sun existence.

Karmic Relationships, vol. 7, lect. 2 (CW 239)

The next sphere after death is the so-called Venus sphere In this sphere we become hermits if on Earth we have had an irreligious disposition. We become sociable spirits if we bring a religious inclination with us. Inasmuch as in the physical world we are able to feel our devotion to the Holy Spirit, so in the Venus sphere shall we find all those of a like inclination toward the divine spiritual. Men are grouped according to religious and philosophic trends in the Venus sphere. On Earth it is so that both religious striving and religious experience still play a dominant part. In the Venus sphere the grouping is purely according to religious confession and philosophic outlook. Those who share the same world-conception are together in large, powerful communities in the Venus sphere. They are not hermits. Only those are hermits who have not been able to develop any religious feeling and experience.... In general we can say that we come together with those of the same world-conception, of the same faith as ourselves. Other confessions are hard to understand in the Venus sphere.

Life between Death and Rebirth, lect. 7 (CW 141)

Venus and Buddha

You must here call to mind the description in *An Outline of Esoteric Science* of the beginning of Earth evolution,—how, after the interval between Moon and Earth, the Sun was reunited with Earth and the other planets, and how they all then separated again, being shed, as it were, like a husk or shell one after the other. (See also my lecture cycle on the Spiritual Hierarchies.) There was, therefore, at one time the condition in which the Earth was united with the Sun. Then Earth and Sun separated, and you know that after that came the separation also of the Moon, and the strengthening of the Earth through souls coming from other planets. Let us now fix our attention on the point of time when the Sun has just separated from the Earth. When this separation took place, the two planets Venus and Mercury—I am giving them their astronomical names—were still within the Sun. The Earth alone separated off, Venus and Mercury remaining within the Sun. We have therefore now Sun and Earth. On Earth, evolution continues. Only a small number of human beings remain behind; others go up to the planets, to return again later on. With the Sun went also beings; for the world does not consist just of external matter, but of beings. Beings went with the Sun when it separated from the Earth. And their Leader is the Christ. For at the time in Earth evolution when the Sun separated from the Earth, what one may call the taking precedence by the Christ over Lucifer and the other planetary Spirits had already come to fulfillment. Then later on, Venus separated, and Mercury. Let us consider for a moment the exit of Venus from the Sun. Together with Venus are beings who had also at first gone with the Sun but were not able to remain there. These break away and inhabit Venus. Among them is the being who stands behind the later Buddha. He went as a messenger from the Christ to the dwellers on Venus. The Christ sent him to Venus, and here on Venus Buddha passed through all manner of stages of evolution. Later on, souls came back from Venus to Earth. The ordinary human souls were of course but little developed. Buddha, however, who also descended to Earth with the Venus souls, was a highly evolved being—so highly evolved that he could at once become a Bodhisattva and afterward early a Buddha. Thus we have in Buddha one who had long ago been sent out by Christ and had the task of preparing the work of Christ on Earth. For his mission to the Venus men had this meaning,—that he should go to Earth beforehand, as a forerunner of the Sun. And now you will be able to understand that Buddha, having been with Christ for a longer time than the other Earth men—for the Earth separated off earlier—needed only that portion of the Christ Impulse that he still had in him from the Sun, to enable him to follow the Christ Event from the spiritual world. For Buddha that sufficed. Other human beings had to await the Christ Event on Earth. But because Buddha had this special relationship to the Christ, because he had been sent out by the Christ as a forerunner, he did not need to await on Earth the Christ Event. He took with him from Earth the capacity of remembering—even without the help of the Christ, which other men need—what the I means on Earth. Hence he was able also to look down and behold the Christ Event from higher worlds. Thus was preparation made long beforehand in the World All for the remarkable mission that Buddha had undertaken at the behest of Christ. For he was first sent to the Venus men—and compare what I am now telling you with the lectures I gave at Helsingfors—and afterward to the Earth; then he made his way back to the Mars men, and there has to continue working, carrying out on Mars the mission for which he had so long been preparing.

Man in the Light of Occultism, Theosophy, Philosophy,
lect. 10 (CW 137)

Mars Sphere

Mars the Speaker

Mars is the planetary individuality who in the course of the evolution of humanity instigates human beings in manifold ways to make statements about the mysteries of the cosmos. Mars has his good and his less good sides—he has his Genius and his Demon. His Genius works in such a way that men receive from the universe the impulses for speech; the influence of his Demon results in speech being misused in many and various ways. In a certain sense Mars may be called the Agitator in our universe. He is always out to persuade, whereas Jupiter wants only to convince.

Initiation Science, lect. 1 (see full lecture; CW 228)

Mars Sphere Nature and Deed of Buddha

When a man passes from the Sun sphere into the Mars sphere, the conditions of existence into which he enters are quite different in our present age from what they were a comparatively short time ago. To the eyes of the seer it is quite evident that there was good reason for the statements, originating from the clairvoyance once possessed by humanity, about the several bodies composing the planetary system. It was entirely in keeping with the facts that Mars was considered to be the member of our planetary system connected with all warlike, aggressive elements in the evolution of humanity....

Then, in the seventeenth century, the Buddha withdrew from earthly existence and accomplished for Mars a deed that, although not of the magnitude of the Mystery of Golgotha, nevertheless resembled it and corresponded on Mars to the Mystery of Golgotha on Earth. At the beginning of the seventeenth century the Buddha became the redeemer, the savior of Mars. He was the individuality whose mission it was to inculcate peace and harmony into the aggressive nature of Mars. Since then the Buddha impulse is to be found on Mars, as the Christ impulse is to be found on the Earth since the Mystery of Golgotha.

Life between Death and Rebirth, lect. 7 (see full lecture; CW 140)

On Mars it is so, that the men who have remained there stand in great peril, even as the Earth men were in peril, from which Christ set them free. The danger for the Mars men is, that their astral body—they have, as you know, not an I to develop as we—their astral body, and thereby indirectly also their ether body, may suffer a very serious diminution of force and become dried up. The whole nature of the Mars men has proved to be of a kind that leads to terrible wars. The men of Mars tend to settle permanently on a certain spot. Men on the Earth are cosmopolitanly inclined; Mars men are wedded to the soil, there are very few cosmopolitans among them. And there is, or rather was, on Mars constant war and strife, due to the astral bodies that are very strong and not tempered and made gentle by an I. If you will think it over you will understand that among men who develop in this way there must inevitably be a terrible amount of strife and conflict. Mars is nothing else than a kind of re-incarnated Moon; what the astral body holds is not tempered with the softening influence of the I, with the result that the men of Mars have quite an exceptional lust for war. The Greeks acted on a true knowledge when they made Mars the God of War. One is indeed filled with wonder and amazement when one finds in the world of legend these echoes of the truth. Unforgettable is the impression one receives when, having discovered that terrible wars took place there, one finds that this occult knowledge is present in the names that were given out of the knowledge contained in the ancient Mysteries.

Think of the continuation of the life of Buddha, this Master of Compassion and Love, this Master in the overcoming of caste-distinctions, and you will understand the mission that Buddha had on Mars—to introduce something to that the Mars men could never come unaided, something that would seem to them like an exaggerated piety, a kind of monastic attitude to life. For it was the mission of Buddha by means of a conspicuous example of exceeding humility and poverty to quicken the Mars men to life in this direction. I can only just begin to draw for you the picture of Buddha's influence upon Mars. The meaning of his work there for the Mars men who live without the I, is in point of fact entirely similar to the influence of a redeemer and a Saviour, one who liberates men to a higher worldview. And while upon Earth universal brotherhood and love of one's neighbor are connected in their deepest impulse with the Christ, cosmopolitanism in its essential character is connected with the Deed of Salvation that Buddha has to fulfill on Mars.

Man in the Light of Occultism, Theosophy and Philosophy,
lect. 10 (CW 137)

Mars Sphere and Possibilities for Karma Depending on Human Being

When a soul passed through the Mars sphere in times before the Buddha Mystery, it was endowed primarily with forces of aggressiveness. Since the Buddha Mystery a soul undergoes essentially different experiences if it is fitted by nature to gain something from the Mars forces...for a certain period between death and a new birth, during the passage through the Mars sphere, every human soul has the opportunity of being a Franciscan or a Buddhist and of receiving all the forces that can flow from feeling and experience of this kind. The passage through the Mars sphere can therefore be of great importance for the human soul. Man, however, inscribes his perfections and imperfections into whatever sphere he enters according to their affinity with the characteristic qualities of that sphere.

Life between Death and Rebirth, lect. 7 (CW 140)

Mars Influence Described in Voltaire and Ignatius Loyola, Founder of Jesuits

He acquired thereby a strongly aggressive nature, but on the other hand also a wonderful gift of speech; for Mars beings prepare from out of the cosmos all that belongs to speech and language and place it into the karma of human beings. Wherever artistic skill and fluency in speech show themselves in the karma of a human being, these are to be traced to the fact that his karmic experiences have brought him into the vicinity of Mars beings.

Karmic Relationships, vol. 8, lect. 5 (CW 240)

Jupiter Sphere

Jupiter or Kyriotetes

Jupiter is the Thinker in our planetary system, and thinking is the activity cultivated by all the beings in his cosmic domain. Creative thoughts received from the universe radiate to us from Jupiter. Jupiter contains, in the form of thoughts, all the formative forces for the different orders of cosmic beings. Whereas Saturn tells of the past, Jupiter gives a living portrayal of what is connected with him in the cosmic present. But what Jupiter reveals to the eye of spirit must be grasped with thoughtful intelligence. If a man does not himself make efforts to develop his capacities of thinking, he cannot, even if he is clairvoyant, approach the mysteries of Jupiter, for they are revealed in the form of thoughts and can be approached only through a genuine activity of thinking. Jupiter is the Thinker in our universe.

Initiation Science, lect. 1 (see full lecture; CW 228)

Spirits of Wisdom, Kyriotetes

How then does such (clairvoyant) knowledge reveal itself? How is what comes to us revealed when we have prepared ourselves sufficiently? It reveals itself as the feeling of being endowed with grace through the gifts that come to meet us from the spiritual world. If we wish to describe what thus approaches us, bringing us grace and pouring knowledge into us, we can only make use of the expression; it is what comes to meet us, an active inspiring with grace; a bestowing, a giving. Let us grasp the nature of a being chiefly characterized by what I have just described, so as to say of him: he is a bestower, a giver, an offerer of gifts. Such a being whose chief characteristic is the showering of grace around him, the shedding forth of grace from himself. Let our conception of this being show us that in order to attain this possibility of giving forth grace there must be the vision of the sacrifice made by the Thrones to the Cherubim; let us suppose that he was present when the sacrifice was being offered. Let us clearly imagine a being such as this, who through having had this vision is stimulated to shower the gifts of his grace around him. Suppose we were to see a rose and were charmed by it, experiencing the feeling of one enraptured by what we call "beautiful." Suppose another being through the vision of what we have described as the sacrifice by the Thrones to the Cherubim, were inspired to pour forth into the world, to offer to the world as a gift, everything ho possessed—we should thus be describing those beings spoken of in *An Outline of Esoteric Science* as Spirits of Wisdom who on the Sun were added to the beings with whom we become acquainted on ancient Saturn. If now we were to put the question, what is the character of these Spirits who appeared on the Sun in addition to the Saturn Spirits? We must reply: The principal characteristic of these spirits is the virtue of giving, of pouring forth grace. If we wish to find a title for them, we must say: These are the Spirits of Wisdom, the great Bestowers, the great Givers of the Universe. Just as we have called the Thrones "The great Sacrificers," so we must say of the Spirits of Wisdom, they are "the great Givers" who so devote their gift that it weaves and lives in the universe, flowing out into it and first bringing about its order.

Inner Aspects of Evolution, lect. 2 (CW 132)

Jupiter and Cherubim Work with Wisdom; Goethe as Jupiter Soul

And the same applies to the Jupiter sphere. The Jupiter sphere and its beings are experienced when in the process of self-observation one looks back with the insight of Initiation over the period between the forty-ninth and fifty-sixth years of life—and then obliterates the pictures. The vista of the Jupiter sphere may be a shattering experience, for the beings of Jupiter are utterly different from human beings. Think of a quality that is sometimes more and sometimes less in evidence, namely the quality of wisdom. Men insist that they are wise...but what a struggle it is for them to acquire wisdom! The tiniest fragment of wisdom in any field is difficult to attain and demands inner effort. Nothing of the kind is necessary for the Jupiter beings. Wisdom is an integral part of their very nature—I cannot say it is "born" in them, for the Jupiter beings do not come into existence through an embryo as men do on Earth. You must picture to yourselves that there is something around Jupiter like the cloud-masses around the Earth. If you were now to imagine bodies of men forming out of the clouds and flying down to the Earth, that would be a picture of how the new beings come forth from a kind of cloud-mass on Jupiter; but these beings have wisdom as an original, intrinsic characteristic. Just as we have circulating blood, so they have wisdom. But their wisdom is not a merited reward, nor has it been acquired by effort; they have it by nature. Therefore their thinking, too, is utterly different from the thinking of men. The experience is shattering, overwhelming, but we must gradually get accustomed to the idea. Just as we on Earth are pervaded by air, so everything on Jupiter is pervaded by wisdom. Wisdom there has substance, streams in the atmosphere, discharges itself like rain on Jupiter, rises like mist to the heights. But beings are there—beings who ascend in a cloud, a mist of wisdom. Herein live the Cherubim, who in this realm of existence gather up and give shape to the karma of human beings. Other impulses too are in operation, but what holds good unconditionally is that the experiences of an earlier incarnation are gathered together and molded into shape by the forces of the self-subsisting wisdom of the Jupiter sphere. Then, when the individuality comes down again to incarnation on the Earth, he bears the stamp arising from the reshaping of his earlier experiences by wisdom that ultimately takes effect in very diverse forms....

There is an individuality who leads us back to ancient Greece, into a milieu of Platonism, and also of sculpture. This individuality had a very significant incarnation as a sculptor in Greece. What he there experienced was carried over into intermediate incarnations of less importance. This is an individuality whose karma for what is at the moment his latest incarnation was elaborated chiefly in the sphere of the Jupiter wisdom.

The other individuality who had lived in Greece also passed through the Jupiter sphere in the way that is possible for one who had been a sculptor and had unfolded the faculty of creative imagination that was still so potent a force in Greece. This was transformed and re-cast in the Jupiter sphere where the wisdom underlying the Greek talent for plastic representation of the human form, for pictorial conceptions of the world, is present in its very essence, and the individuality came down into a body with a strongly Grecian bent of mind that had been elaborated in the Jupiter sphere, being reborn as Goethe.

Karmic Relationships, vol. 7, lect. 3 (CW 239); see also *The Spiritual Hierarchies,* lect. 5 (CW 110)

Indication of Great Conjunctions Impact

And when, at the cosmic hour of destiny in the life of a human being, a certain relationship is established between Jupiter and Saturn, there flash into human destiny those wonderful moments of illumination when many things concerning the past are revealed through thinking.

If we look in history for occasions in the time of the Renaissance—particularly during its last period—when there was a great renewal of ancient impulses, we shall find that this was directly connected with a certain relationship between Jupiter and Saturn.

But, as already said, Jupiter is in a certain respect impenetrable and his revelations remain in the unconscious if a man does not bring to them clear and active light-filled thoughts of his own. And that is why in ancient times, when active thinking was still at a very early state of development, the progress of humanity was in truth always dependent upon the relation between Jupiter and Saturn. When

Jupiter and Saturn together formed a certain constellation, many things were revealed to our ancestors in those days. Modern man has to depend more upon receiving the memory of Saturn and the wisdom of Jupiter separately in the course of his spiritual development.

Initiation Science, lect. 1 (CW 228)

Saturn Sphere

Saturn presents himself to us as the heavenly individuality who has steadfastly participated in whatever has come to pass in our planetary system and has faithfully preserved it in his cosmic memory. He is silent about the cosmic Present. He receives the things of the cosmic Present into himself and works upon them in his life of spirit and soul. True, the hosts of beings indwelling Saturn lend their attention to the outer universe, but mutely and silently they receive the happenings in the universe into the realm of soul, and they speak only of past cosmic events. That is why Saturn is like a kaleidoscopic memory of our planetary system. As a faithful informant concerning what has come to pass in the planetary system, he holds its secrets of this kind within himself.

Whereas in endeavoring to fathom the mysteries of the universe we should turn to the Moon in vain, whereas we must win the confidence of the Moon beings if we are to learn anything from them about cosmic mysteries, this is not necessary with Saturn. With Saturn, all that is necessary is to be open to receive the spiritual. And then, to the eyes of spirit and soul, Saturn becomes a living historian of the planetary system. Nor does he withhold the stories he can tell of what has come to pass in the planetary system. In this respect Saturn is the exact opposite of the Moon. Saturn speaks unceasingly of the past of the planetary system with such inner warmth and zest that intimate acquaintance with what he says can be dangerous. For the devotion with which he tells of past happenings in the universe arouses in us an overwhelming love for the cosmic past. Saturn is the constant tempter of those who listen to his secrets; he tempts them to give little heed to earthly affairs of today and to immerse themselves in what the Earth once was. Above all, Saturn speaks graphically about what the Earth was before it became Earth, and for this reason he is the planet who makes the past unendingly dear to us. Those who have a particular inclination toward Saturn in earthly existence are people who like to be gazing always into the past, who are opposed to progress, who ever and again want to bring back the past. These indications give some idea of the individuality, the individual character, of Saturn.

Initiation Science, lect. 1 (CW 228)

Saturn Sphere after Death and Relation to Karma

Let us consider the Saturn sphere in particular. If during his present Earth life a man has made efforts to master the concepts of spiritual science, the passage through the Saturn sphere is of special significance for his next life. It is in this sphere that the conditions are created that enable him to transmute the forces acquired through the knowledge of spiritual science or anthroposophy into forces that elaborate his bodily constitution in such a way that in his coming life he has a natural inclination toward the spiritual. A human being may grow up today and be educated as a materialist, Protestant or Catholic. Spiritual science approaches him. He is receptive to it and does not reject it. He inwardly accepts it. He now passes through the gate of death. He enters the Saturn sphere. In passing through it, he absorbs the forces that make him in his next life a spiritual man, who shows even as a child an inclination to the spiritual.

Life between Death and Rebirth, lect. 8 (CW 141)

An Example of Saturn Influence on a Person

He witnessed the cruel persecutions of the Christians, the brutalities of Roman Imperialism, the unjust treatment meted out to the better types of men. Filled with profound indignation by these happenings, he passed through the gate of death in a mood of despair and resignation, questioning whether there is any hope of progress for a world...the experiences of the Greco-Roman incarnation had engraved deep furrows in the life of soul and it was these experiences that, as the eighteenth century approached, were elaborated and wrought out in the Saturn sphere into the subsequent karma of this individuality. The Saturn sphere has a deep and incisive effect upon the shaping of karma. Whenever it is a case of laying hold of the human soul in its very depths and of developing radical, potent

forces from these depths, the Saturn sphere works in such a way that the forces will penetrate deeply, very deeply into the physical organization. Everything that happens in the Saturn sphere is intrinsically and essentially spiritual but also takes far deeper effect when the human being descends to earthly embodiment. The result is a physical organization that strives for a balancing-out of the experiences undergone by the soul in an earlier earthly life. The element of retrospection is always strongly at work. When a man's karma is being wrought out in the Saturn sphere he looks backward, to remembrances, to the past. Then, when he comes down to the earthly realm, the negative image as it were of what he has lived through in the Saturn sphere discloses itself. The intense concentration upon the past is transformed into a resolute striving for ideals that lead forward, toward the future. Human beings who bring down their karma from the Saturn sphere are fired with enthusiasm for the future, for ideals that point to the future, precisely because in a purely spiritual life in the Saturn sphere their gaze was directed mainly toward the past. The individuality of whom I am speaking appeared again in the second half of the eighteenth century as Friedrich Schiller....think of the deep seriousness, the profound melancholy that weighed upon his soul. See how everything in Schiller, especially the pathos of his early destiny, emanates from the vein of melancholy that is so deeply rooted in his soul... then see how these experiences are deepened and wrought out into new karma by the forces of the Saturn sphere. Schiller is through and through a Saturn man in respect of his karma.
Karmic Relationships, vol. 7, lect. 4 (CW 239)

How to Read Stars and on Saturn

These things are not rightly experienced if they are regarded as so many theories. They can be truly grasped only by one who with all the forces of his heart and mind steeps himself in the realities of this spiritual life and being in the starry worlds—in this case, the Saturn sphere—and having acquired a deeper understanding of an individual earthly destiny, observes them in manifestation there.

Saturn-karma—Saturn-karma above all—works in deep, very deep regions of the soul. I want now to direct your attention to an individuality who in an earlier incarnation was actually an Initiate.
Karmic Relationships, vol. 7, lect. 4 (CW 238)

An Initiate into Hibernian Mysteries; Strong Saturn Experience after Death

But the modern age held in store for this individuality a body and a kind of education by which the most significant elements were obscured—yet for all that came to a certain expression in keeping with the civilisation of the nineteenth century. In this case too, what had been retained of the great cosmic retrospect was transformed when the soul came down into a physical body and underwent a kind of education neither of which in truth were suited to experiences lived through in an Hibernian Initiation and wrought out in the Saturn sphere. When the soul descended, this was all transformed into ideals reaching out to the future. But because the body was that of a Frenchman of the nineteenth century and therefore altogether different from the remarkable bodies of the old Irish Initiates, a very great deal receded into the background, transforming itself into sublime but fantastic pictures that, however have a certain power, a certain grandeur about them. This individuality reincarnated as Victor Hugo.

Karmic Relationships, vol. 7, lect. 4 (CW 239)

Saturn and Grail/Parsival

What sort of time was it when Parsifal entered the Castle, where Amfortas lay wounded and on Parsifal's arrival suffered unceasing pain from his wound? What was this time? The saga itself tells us—it was a Saturn time [i.e., a period when the forces of Saturn work with particular strength]. Saturn and the Sun stood together in Cancer, approaching culmination.

Christ and the Spiritual World, lect. 6 (CW 149)

Saturn and Sacrificed Substance

Occult observation reveals that in the beginning, when ancient Saturn began to be formed, certain spiritual beings poured forth the fundamental substance of Saturn—warmth—from their own substance as a sacrifice. They had matured so far that they did not need to absorb anything as nourishment, they were even in a position to sacrifice themselves to pour out their own substance. These beings are the Thrones. It is they who through their sacrifice formed the foundations of the human physical body. One who can occultly observe the physical body on Saturn can say: It has flowed forth from the substance of the Thrones. The physical body changes from stage to stage, it develops ever higher, but what we bear within us is always the transformed substance of the Thrones.

Universe, Earth and Man, lect. 5 (CW 105)

URANUS, NEPTUNE, PLUTO

Now the ancients rightly considered Saturn the most distant planet of our solar system; it is the farthest away. From the standpoint of materialistic astronomy it is quite justified to add Uranus and Neptune to our system; but they have a different origin and do not belong to the solar system; so that we may speak of Saturn as the outermost planet of our system.

They appear to us in such a way that between death and rebirth we look back in gratitude to the outermost planet of our earthly planetary system (for Uranus and Neptune are not Earth planets; they were added at a later stage).

Man and the World of Stars, lect. 1 (CW 219)

Moon and Saturn, therefore, are the heavenly bodies that stand nearest to and farthest from us in the planetary system. The planetary system as it is today is really an inorganic structure because as far as Saturn* it came out of what was once a single cosmic body, whereas Uranus and Neptune came from beyond and joined themselves to it. As antiquity did not discover Uranus and Neptune, Saturn was taken to be the outermost planet and it is still justifiable today to go as far as Saturn. Astrologers still have an inkling of these things for they connect Uranus and Neptune only with those human qualities that transcend the personal, make a man a genius, go beyond the individual personal element—where he is concerned with things that no longer have to do with his personal development. All astrological statements are to this effect. Uranus and Neptune only come into play when a man becomes a genius or strives to transcend the human element, when his organization has the tendency to expand or decay too strongly. Uranus and Neptune are planets who have behaved like

---

* TRANSLATOR'S NOTE: In the German, the text gives *Jupiter*, but the sense appears to indicate *Saturn*.

tramps in the universe and were then held captive by the planetary system belonging to our Earth. The near and the far heavenly bodies regulate what is in the human being—the Moon regulates his form, Saturn—working from the Earth—the formless spiritual, inasmuch as Saturn breaks down form, dissolves it inwardly all the time. And the Sun brings about rhythm between the two.

Course for Young Doctors, lect. 3 (CW 316)

Steiner on Three Levels of Adversaries

We have the physical world, the astral world, the Lower Devachan and the Higher Devachan. If the body is thrust down lower even than the physical world, it comes into the sub-physical world, the lower astral world, the lower or evil Lower Devachan, and the lower or evil Higher Devachan. The evil astral world is the province of Lucifer, the evil Lower Devachan the province of Ahriman, and the evil Higher Devachan the province of the Asuras. When chemical action is driven down beneath the physical plane—into the evil Devachanic world—magnetism arises. When light is thrust down into the sub-material—that is to say, a stage deeper than the material world—electricity arises. If what lives in the Harmony of the Spheres is thrust down farther still, into the province of the Asuras, an even more terrible force—which it will not be possible to keep hidden very much longer—is generated. It can only be hoped that when this force comes to be known—a force we must conceive as being far, far stronger than the most violent electrical discharge—it can only be hoped that before some discoverer gives this force into the hands of humankind, men will no longer have anything un-moral left in them.

Reflected as sub-physical world:

Astral World	the province of Lucifer
Lower Devachan	the province of Ahriman
Higher Devachan	the province of the Asuras*

Etherization of the Blood, Q&A session (CW 130)

---

* See diagram on page 59.

Human Biography: Charts[*]

Moon before Birth.
Good on Sun Sphere and Negative Space

When man is descending to earthly life from the existence he spends in worlds of soul and spirit between death and a new birth, he passes through the different cosmic regions, the last being the Moon-sphere. As he passes through the Moon-sphere he encounters those beings of whom I spoke yesterday, saying that they were once the primeval Teachers of humanity. He meets these beings out yonder in the Universe, before he comes down to the Earth, and it is they who inscribe everything that has happened in life between one human being and another, into that delicate substance that, as opposed to earthly substances, the oriental sages have called Akasha. It is really the case that whatever happens in life, whatever experiences come to men, everything is observed by those beings who, as spirit beings not incarnate in the flesh, once peopled the Earth together with men. Everything is observed and inscribed into the Akasha substance as living reality, not in the form of an abstract script. These spiritual Moon beings who were the great Teachers during the age of primeval cosmic wisdom, are the recorders of the experiences of mankind. And when in his life between death and a new birth a man is once again drawing near the Earth in order to unite with the seed provided by the parents, he passes through the region where the Moon beings have recorded what he had experienced on the Earth in earlier incarnations. Whereas these Moon beings, when they were living on the Earth, brought men a wisdom relating especially to the past of the Universe, in their present cosmic existence they preserve the past. And as man descends to earthly existence, everything they have preserved is engraved into his astral body. It is so easy to say that man consists of an Ego organization, an astral body, an etheric body, and so forth. The Ego organization is most akin to the Earth; it comprises what we learn and experience in earthly existence; the more deeply lying members of man's being are of a different character. Even the astral body is quite different; it is full of inscriptions, full of pictures. What is known simply as the "unconscious" discloses a wealth of content when it is illumined by real knowledge. And Initiation makes

---

[*]   See *Karmic Relationships,* vol. 6, entire lectures 1, 3, and 6.

it possible to penetrate into the astral body and to bring within the range of vision all that the Moon beings have inscribed into it as, for example, the experiences shared with other human beings. Initiation science enables us to fathom the secret of how the whole past rests within man and how "destiny" is shaped through the fact that in the Moon-existence there are beings who preserve the past so that it lies within us when we again set foot upon the Earth.

And now another case. When the Initiate meets a man in connection with whom the ordinary consciousness simply receives an aesthetic or mental impression unaccompanied by dreams, no picture rises up in him, to begin with. In this case the gaze of the Initiate is directed to the Sun, not to the Moon. I have told you of the beings who are connected with the Moon—in the same way, the Sun is not merely the gaseous body of which modern physicists speak. The physicists would be highly astonished if they were able to make an expedition to the region that they surmise to be full of incandescent gases and that they take to be the Sun; at the place where they have conjectured the presence of incandescent gases, they would find a condition that is not even space, that is less than a void—a vacuum in cosmic space. What is space? Men do not really know, least of all the philosophers who give a great deal of thought to it. Just think: if there is a chair here and I walk toward it without noticing its presence, I hit against it—it is solid, impenetrable. If there is no chair I walk through space unhindered.

But there is a third possibility. I might go to the spot without being held up or knocked, but I might be sucked up and disappear: here there is no space, but the antithesis of space. And this antithesis of space is the condition in the Sun, The Sun is negative space.* And just because of this, the Sun is the abode, the habitual abode, of the beings who rank immediately above man: Angeloi, Archangeloi, Archai. In the case of which I am speaking, the gaze of the Initiate is directed toward these beings in the Sun, the spiritual beings of the Sun. In other words: a meeting of this kind that is not part of a karmic past, but is quite new, is for the Initiate a means of coming into connection with these beings. And the presence is revealed of certain beings with some of whom man has a close connection, whereas with others the connection is more remote.

---

* Negative space: see George Adams, *Physical and Ethereal Spaces*; also George Adams and Olive Whicher, *The Plant between Sun and Earth*.

The way in which these beings approach the Initiate reveals to him—not in detail but in broad outline—what kind of karma is about to take shape; in this case it is not old karma but karma that is coming to him for the first time. He perceives that these beings who are connected with the Sun have to do with the future, just as the Moon beings have to do with the past.

Karmic Relationships, vol. 5, lect. 2 (CW 239)

Destiny and Holy Awe

If we make the attempt with the kind of knowledge I have described, we begin to gaze upon the destiny of a single human being with holy awe. For what is it that works in the destiny of each human being? In very truth it is star wisdom—all-embracing star wisdom! Nothing can enable us to behold the working of the Gods in the universe with deeper or truer feelings than to behold it in the destiny of a human being. A world-justice flows through Eternity in the existence, the deeds, the thinking, of the Gods weaving behind the human being [definition of cosmic intelligence].

Karmic Relationships, vol. 6, lect. 6 (CW 240)

Michael and Understanding Karma from Stars

And this elaboration of karma can only be understood if we can look to the world of stars beyond the Earth. For we know that the realm of the stars as it appears to physical sight, reveals only its external aspect....

The only true description of the Earth would be to describe it as the colony of the souls of man in cosmic space.

Thus are all the stars colonies of spiritual beings in cosmic space, colonies that we can learn to know as such. And having passed through the gate of death, our own soul lives and moves among these starry colonies. It goes on its further journey, evolving toward a new birth in community with other human souls that are there, and with the beings of higher or even of lower Hierarchies. And when a man's karma is elaborated and he is ripe to take on an earthly body once again, his soul starts on the returning journey....

To understand karma, therefore, we must return once more to a wisdom of the stars. We must discover spiritually the paths of man between death and a new birth in connection with the beings of the stars.

Now until the beginning of the age of Michael there have been the greatest difficulties for the men of modern time to approach a real wisdom of the stars. And Anthroposophy, having nevertheless found its way to such a wisdom, must be deeply thankful for the fact that the dominion of Michael really did enter the life of Earth-humanity with the last third of the 19th century. For among many things that we owe to the dominion of Michael there is this too: we have gained once more unhindered access to discover what must be investigated in the worlds of the stars if we would understand karma and the forming of karma in the sphere of humanity.

Karmic Relationships, vol. 4, lect. 7 (CW 240)

In the book *How to Know Higher Worlds,* indications are given that, if they are followed, can make us independent of the cosmic forces, although none the less these cosmic forces continue to work in our being. What does this mean to be free of these cosmic forces but that they continue to work in our being?

Man is born on Earth into conditions determined by a constellation in the heavens, but he must equip himself with forces that make him independent of this constellation. It is to this kind of knowledge—a knowledge of man's connection with the Cosmos beyond the Earth—that our civilization must attain.

Materialism and the Task of Anthroposophy, lect. 13 (CW 204)

Right Way to Read and Know Karma

For it is not in external similarities that we must seek for evidence of the working of karma; rather must we be observant of those things that, in the deep foundations of a man's being, are carried over through karma from one earthly life into another. Perception of the karma of an individual human being, or even of one's own karma, requires the right attitude, the right mood-of soul. The whole study of karma is profaned if this study is pursued in the attitude of mind arising from our modern education and civilization. The mood in which all teachings about karma should be received is one of piety, of reverence. Whenever man approaches a truth relating to karma, his soul should feel as though part of the veil of Isis were being lifted. For in truth it is karma that reveals, in a way most intimately connected with human life, what Isis was—the being designated outwardly as: "I am that which was, is, and will be." This must still be the attitude of soul in all study of human karma. In truth, only when we study karma in the way we have now been doing and having observed how it takes effect in the process of world evolution acquire the reverence befitting such study, then and only then can we gaze with the right attitude of soul at what may be our own karma, perceiving how from earlier earthly lives it has unfolded and taken shape as a result of experiences in the spiritual worlds of the stars between death and a new birth. With our whole being we gaze at supersensible worlds when we "read" karma with the right mood of soul. For the study of karma acquaints us with laws that are in utter contrast with the laws of external Nature. In the external world, Nature-relationships hold sway, but these must be discarded entirely and we must be able to gaze at spirit-relationships if we are to discern the law operating in the working of karma.

Karmic Relationships, vol. 7, lect. 4 (CW 239)

One must never speculate about the spiritual world in research, never invent anything, but only make the preparations for enabling something to reveal itself from the spiritual world. Anyone who believes he can force the spiritual world to reveal this or that to him will be very greatly mistaken; nothing but errors will come of it. Preparation must be made for what one may hope to receive out of the spiritual world more or less by grace.

Karmic Relationships, vol. 7, lect. 7 (CW 239)

The Epoch and Spirit Seed

What, then, is our outer world in that spiritual existence? It is what is now our inner nature. We fashion what is then our outer world into a kind of spirit-seed from which our future physical body on Earth is to spring into existence. Together with the beings of the Higher Hierarchies we elaborate this spirit-seed, and at a certain point of time in our life between death and a new birth, it is there as a spirit-entity, bearing within it the forces that then build up the physical body, just as the seed of the plant bears within it the forces that will eventually produce the plant. But whereas we picture the seed of the plant to be minute and the plant itself large in comparison, the spirit-seed of the human physical body is, so to speak, a universe of vast magnitude—although in the strict sense it is not quite accurate to speak of "magnitude" in this connection. [prenatal Epoch] I have also said that at a certain point this spirit-seed falls away from us. From a certain point of time onward we feel: in association with other beings of the Universe, with beings of the Higher Hierarchies, we have brought the spirit-seed of our physical organism to a definite stage of development; now it falls away from us and descends into the physical forces of the Earth, with which it is related and come from the father and the mother. It unites with the human element in the stream of heredity and goes down to the Earth before we, as beings of spirit-and-soul, ourselves descend. Thus we still spend a certain period—although a short one—in the spiritual world when the nexus of forces of our physical organism has already gone down to the Earth and is shaping the embryo in the body of the mother.

It is during this period that we gather together from the cosmic ether its own forces and substances and so build up our etheric body to be added to our astral body and ego. Then, as a being of ego, astral body and etheric body, we ourselves come down to the Earth and unite with what the physical body—the seed of which was sent down earlier—has now become.

Man and World of the Stars, lect. 1 (see full lecture; CW 219)

Spirit Germ Fall to Earth

While we are going through these pictures, the spiritual seed of the physical body that we were preparing falls ever farther from us and disappears. We are obliged to witness this: the spiritual seed has fallen from us; it has gone down into a physical mother and father, entering into the forces of generation, into the stream of generation upon the physical Earth. So it is in all reality. The physical body we were also preparing shrinks and contracts and falls into the streams of generation—into a physical father and mother upon Earth—while we ourselves as soul and spiritual being are left behind, feeling that we belong to what has fallen from us, yet cannot unite with it directly. In this condition—it is our only means of reuniting with it—we now begin to draw to ourselves the forces of the Ether that are there throughout the Cosmos; we begin to form our ether body. We do this when the spirit-seed of our physical body has already fallen from us and is down there on Earth, preparing the physical body in the mother's womb, while we are gathering the forces with which we form our ether-body. With this etheric body we then unite ourselves, when the human seed has already been for a time in the mother's womb.

Spirit as Sculptor of the Human Organism, lect. 7 (CW 218)

Inscription in Moon Sphere

In this backward journey after death that lasts for a third of the time of the earthly life, karma is prepared. For the Moon beings mingle with these "negatives" of a man's deeds, also of his deeds in the life of thought. The Moon beings have a good memory and they inscribe into the cosmic ether every experience they share with the human being.

We pass through the life between death and a new birth and then, on the return journey when we come back once more into the Moon sphere we find everything inscribed there. And we bear it all with us into our life in order to bring it to fulfillment by means of our earthly will.

Karmic Relationships, vol. 2, lect. 9 (CW 236)

Materialistic Thinkers Cannot Approach Stars after Death

It was as though the Spirits, the primeval Teachers of mankind who had once brought to humanity the original and spiritual wisdom, called out again and again to this human being, the archetype of Strader: "Thou canst not come to us, for owing to thy special qualities as man thou mayst not know anything as yet about the stars. Thou must wait, and first repeat and recapitulate many things that thou didst undergo not only in thy last, but in thy former incarnations. Thou mayst not know anything at all of the stars and their real being, till thou hast thus prepared thyself." It was a strange scene. One had before one an individuality who simply could not grow out toward the spiritual of the world of stars—or could only do so with the greatest difficulty. And in this case I made the strange discovery that these modern individualities of the rationalistic, intellectualistic mind, find the great hindrance in the shaping of their karma, inasmuch as they cannot approach the spiritual being of the stars unhindered.

Karmic Relationships, vol. 4, lect. 7 (CW 238)

Seven-year Cycles in Biography and Relation to Planets (for Moon Graph)

We see right through our life; when the consciousness has been emptied of all pictorial impressions and we have achieved Inspiration, we behold the living, weaving activity of the Moon sphere in place of the tableau of early childhood from birth until the seventh year. We behold this living, weaving activity. And so Initiation in the form that is normal and right for this present age brings us knowledge of the secrets of the Moon sphere, when the pictures of our own life up to the seventh year are obliterated in the consciousness of Inspiration and we perceive what now flashes up in their place.

Then, if we observe the tableau of life between the seventh and fourteenth years and again obliterate the pictures in the consciousness of Inspiration, we gaze into the Mercury sphere. Everything has to do with the being of man, for man is an integral part of the whole Universe. If he learns to know himself as he really is, in the innermost core of his being, he learns to know the whole Universe. And now I would ask you to pay attention to the following. Deepest respect arises in us for the old, instinctive Initiation Science that gave things that have remained in existence to this day, their true and proper names. Designations that are coined nowadays result in nothing but confusion, for modern scholarship is incapable of naming things in accordance with reality. An unprejudiced observation of life will fill us with reverence for the achievements of ancient Initiation Science. Ancient Initiation Science knew by instinct something that is confirmed today by statistics, namely, that the illnesses of childhood occur most frequently in the first period of life; it is then that the human being is most prone to illness, and even to death; after puberty this tendency abates, but the healthiest period of all, the period when mortality is at its lowest, is between the ages of seven and fourteen. The wise men of old knew that this is due to the influences of the Mercury sphere and again today we may make the same discovery when through modern Initiation Science we penetrate the secrets of existence. Such things fill us with reverence for these sacred traditions of humanity.

By looking back into our experiences from the fourteenth to the twenty-first years and obliterating the pictures in the consciousness of Inspiration, we are led to the secrets of the Venus sphere. Here again the wonderful wisdom of ancient Initiation Science comes into evidence. The human being reaches puberty; love is born. When the pictures of this period of life are illumined by Initiation Science, the secrets of the Venus sphere are disclosed. Everything I am now describing is part of the true self-knowledge that unfolds in this way.

When the pictures of experiences occurring between the twenty-first and forty-second years of life are eliminated in the consciousness of Inspiration, we are led to the Sun sphere. Through deepened self-knowledge the secrets of the Sun sphere can be experienced in this retrospective contemplation of the events of our life between the twenty-first and forty-second years. To acquire knowledge of the Sun existence our vision must cover a period three times longer than that of the periods connected with the other planetary bodies.

I told you that the karma of a certain well-known personality in history had taken shape mainly in the spheres of Mercury and Venus, and you will now understand how such things are investigated. We look back, firstly, into the period of our own life between the seventh and fourteenth years, and then into the period between the fourteenth and twenty-first years; when the pictures have been eliminated in the consciousness of Inspiration, light is shed upon the secrets of the Mercury sphere and the Venus sphere. Through this illumination we perceive how such an individuality worked together with the beings of the higher Hierarchies and with other human souls, and how his subsequent earthly incarnation in the nineteenth century took shape.

Now if the elaboration of karma has taken place mainly in the Mars sphere, investigation is more difficult. For if a man attains Initiation before the age of 49, it is not possible for him to look back into the period of life that here comes into question, namely, the period between the forty-second and forty-ninth years. He must have passed his forty-ninth year if he is to be able to eliminate the pictures of this particular set of experiences and penetrate the secrets of the Mars sphere. If Initiation is attained after the age of fifty-six it is possible to look back into the period between the forty-ninth and fifty-sixth years of life, when karma that is connected with the Jupiter sphere takes shape. And now we are at the point where the various sets of events come together in one connected whole.

It is not until the period between the fifty-sixth and sixty-third years can be included in this retrospective vision that we are able to survey the whole range of experiences and to speak out of our own inner knowledge. For then we can gaze into the profoundly significant secrets of the Saturn sphere. Karmas that were wrought out mainly in the Saturn sphere operate in mysterious ways to bring men together again in the world. In order to perceive all these connections in the light of Initiation Science itself—they can of course be explained and so become intelligible—but in order to perceive with independent vision and be able to judge them, we must ourselves have reached the age of sixty-three. A human being appears in some earthly life—thus for example there is a certain great poet of whom I shall speak later—and we find that through his faculties, through his literary creations, he was giving expression to that in his karma that could have been wrought out only in the Saturn sphere.

Karmic Relationships, vol. 7, lect. 2 (CW 239)

Thrones in Mars, Cherubim in Jupiter, Seraphim in Saturn

When we look up to the Sun, to the planetary system—and the same applies to the rest of the starry heavens for they are connected in a very real way with the being of man—we can witness how human karma takes shape in the Cosmos. The Moon, the planets Venus, Jupiter—verily these heavenly bodies are not as physical astronomy describes them. In their constellations, in their mutual relationships, in their radiance, in their whole existence, they are the builders and shapers of human destinies, they are the cosmic timepiece according to which we live out our karma. As they shine downward from the heavens their influences have real power. This was known in the days of the ancient Mystery-wisdom but the old Astrology—which was a purely spiritual science, concerned with the spiritual foundations of existence—has come down to posterity in a degraded, amateurish form. Anthroposophy alone can contribute something that will enable us to perceive the spiritual connections as they truly are and to understand how through the great timepiece of destiny, human life on Earth is shaped according to law.

From this point of view let us think of the human being and his karma. Those who with the help of Anthroposophy evolve a healthy conception of the world as against the unsound views prevailing today, will unfold not only quite different concepts and ideas but also quite different feelings and perceptions. For you see, if we really understand the destiny of a man, we also learn to understand the secrets of the world of stars, the secrets of the Cosmos. But nowadays people write biographies without the faintest inkling that something is really being profaned by the way in which they write. In times when knowledge was held to be sacred because it issued from the Mysteries, nobody would have written biographies in the way that is customary today. Every ancient "biography" contained indications of the influences and secrets of the world of stars. In human destiny we can perceive, firstly, the working of the Angeloi, Archangeloi, Archai; then of still loftier Sun beings, Exousiai, Dynamis, Kyriotetes; then of the Thrones who are concerned mainly with the elaboration of karma in the Mars sphere; then of the Cherubim who elaborate the karma belonging to the Jupiter sphere; and then of the Seraphim who work together with man at the elaboration of karma in the Saturn sphere—Saturn karma. In a man's destiny, in his karma, we behold the working of the higher Hierarchies. This karma, at first, is like a veil, a curtain. If we look behind this veil we gaze at the weaving deeds and influences of Angeloi, Archangeloi, Archai, Exousiai, Dynamis, Kyriotetes, Thrones, Cherubim, Seraphim. Every human destiny is like script on a sheet of paper.

Karmic Relationships, vol. 7, lect. 2 (CW 239)

Becoming a Man or a Woman

> Due preparation has to be made. If the soul desires to be a woman, it will approach the Earth at the time of Full Moon. When we, looking from the Earth, see the Moon full, the soul that is approaching from the spiritual world will see it dark. Now what the soul sees is of course, the spiritual aspect of the Moon. Seeing it dark, the soul sees it "peopled," as it were, with certain beings. And these beings it is who will prepare the soul, so that, when it comes on Earth, it shall be attracted to a female body. On the other hand, when we, looking from the Earth, see New Moon—which means, we cannot see it at all—then the soul that is descending and sees the Moon from the other side, will see it lit up, will see the light that rays forth from it out into cosmic space—that is, of course, the spiritual in the light. In this case, the soul can become a man. Whether it receives the forces that bring it to a male or to a female incarnation depends, you see, on the manner of the soul's journey through the spheres of the stars.
>
> *Planetary Spheres and Their Influence on Man's Life on Earth and in the Spiritual Worlds*, lect. 4 (CW 218)

Birth and Epoch

> Then we begin to draw together again, pass through the different spheres down to the Venus sphere, contract and become ever smaller until the time comes when we can again unite with an earthly human germ.
>
> What kind of a being are we when we unite with this germ? We are the being we have described, but we have received into us the forces from the whole cosmos. What we receive during the outward journey depends on the extent to which we have prepared ourselves for it, and our karma is formed according to the way we have lived together with the human beings we have met during life on Earth. The forces by means of which an adjustment takes place in a new Earth life are built up as a result of having been together with those human beings after death. That we appear as a human being, that we are inwardly able to have karma imbued with cosmic forces, depends on the fact that we

received forces from the whole cosmos during a certain period between death and a new birth. At birth a being who has contracted to the minutest dimensions, but has drawn into itself the forces of the wide expanse of the whole cosmos unites itself with the physical human germ. We bear the whole cosmos within us when we incarnate again on Earth. It may be said that we bear this cosmos within us in the way in which it can unite with the attitude that we, in accordance with our earlier Earth existence, had brought with us in our souls on the outward journey when we were expanding into the spheres.

Life between Death and Rebirth, lect. 5 (CW 140)

Knowing Being in Sun Sphere

Between death and rebirth everything depends upon knowledge of the being. In the Sun sphere the greatest danger is to take Lucifer for the Christ because both use the same language, as it were, give the same teaching, and from them both the same words resound forth. Everything depends on the being. The fact that this being or that being is speaking—that is the point, not the doctrinal content because it is the real forces pulsing through the world that matter. In the higher worlds, and above all in what plays into the earthly spheres, we only understand the words aright when we know from which being they proceed. We can never recognize the rank of a being merely by the word, but only by knowledge of the whole connection in which a being stands. The example of the words that men are like the Gods is an absolute confirmation of this.

Life between Death and Rebirth, lect. 5 (CW 140)

Death Stars

When a person passes through the gate of death he dies under a certain constellation of stars. This constellation is significant for his further life of soul because it remains there as an imprint. In his soul there remains the endeavor to enter into this same constellation at a new birth, to do justice once again to the forces received at the moment of death. It is an interesting point that if one works out the constellation at death and compares it with the constellation of the later birth, one finds that it coincides to a high degree with the constellation at the former death. It must be remembered that the person is born at another spot on the Earth that corresponds with this constellation. In fact, he is adapted to the cosmos, members himself into the cosmos, and thus a balance is established in the soul between the individual and the cosmic life.

Life between Death and Rebirth, lect. 5 (CW 140)

Importance of Receiving the Mystery of Golgotha for after Death and Next Life

At a certain stage of the period between death and a new birth we behold as an outer cosmic painting what we are in our innermost being. There is no better painter than these forces, and the firmament after death is filled with what we truly are in heart and mind. We behold this innermost tableau just as here on Earth we behold the firmament of the heavens. Thus we have a firmament between death and a new birth, and it remains with us. It is conditioned by whether we have received the Mystery of Golgotha into the innermost depths of our soul in the sense referred to previously as expressed in the words of St. Paul, "Not I but the Christ in me." If we experience the Christ within us, then we have the possibility during our Sun existence to experience in the surrounding Akasha picture-world the Christ in His most wondrous form, in His manifested glory, as the element in which we live and dwell. This thought need not merely have an egotistical significance. It may also be of objective significance because in our further existence this outspread picture is again taken into the soul and is brought down into our next incarnation. As a result, we do not only make ourselves into better human beings, but also into a better force in the evolution of the Earth.

So the efforts we make to transform our heart forces are intimately connected with our faculties in the next life, and we see the technique that is at work in transforming our heart forces into a great cosmic panorama, a cosmic firmament between death and a new birth that is then again incorporated into our being, giving us stronger forces than previously. Thus an all-around strengthening process is the result of the fact that we behold in the period between death and a new birth what has been experienced inwardly in life.

Life between Death and Rebirth, lect. 6 (CW 140)

Significance of Lucifer and Christ

…the spheres of Mars, Jupiter and Saturn. Here Lucifer is our guide and we enter into a realm that bestows new forces upon us.… We grow into the divine-spiritual world, and as we do so we must hold fast in memory what we have brought with us of the Christ impulse. We can only acquire this on Earth and the more deeply we have done so, the farther we can carry it into the cosmos. Now Lucifer draws near to us. He leads us out into a realm we must cross in order to be prepared for a new incarnation. There is one thing we cannot dispense with unless Lucifer is to become a threat to us, and that is the understanding of the Christ impulse, of what we have heard about Christ during our life on Earth. Lucifer approaches us out of his own accord during the period between birth and death, but Christ must be received during earthly life.

Life between Death and Rebirth, lect. 5 (CW 140)

Birth Chart

We have yet another mystery. Man has gathered himself together, incarnated in a physical body to which he comes by way of his parents. He has journeyed so far during his expansion in cosmic space that he has recorded his particular characteristics there. As we gaze from the Earth upward to the heavens, there are not only stars but also our characteristics from previous incarnations. If, for instance, we were ambitious in previous Earth lives, then this ambition is recorded in the starry world. It is recorded in the Akasha Chronicle, and when you are here on the Earth at a particular spot, this ambition comes to you with the corresponding planet in a certain position and makes its influence felt.

That accounts for the fact that astrologers do not merely consider the stars and their motions but will tell you that here is your vanity, there is your ambition, your moral failing, your indolence;

something you have inscribed into the stars is now working out of the starry worlds onto the Earth and determines your destiny.
Life between Death and Rebirth (CW 140)

Moral Law Within/Stars Above

Between death and rebirth we are spread out over the starry realms and receive their forces into ourselves, and during our life in a physical body the forces we have gathered are active within us as moral impulses. Looking up to the starry heavens we may say that we dwell among the forces that are active out there during the period between death and rebirth. This now becomes the guiding principle of our moral life. The starry heavens outside, the moral law within are one and the same reality. They constitute two sides of that reality. We experience the starry realms between death and rebirth, the moral law between birth and death.
Life between Death and Rebirth, lect. 7
(See full lecture; CW 140)

Expansion and Contraction to Birth through Spheres

First it must be emphasized that as the person expands into other spheres, all his imperfections are there inscribed. He expands from the Moon sphere into the Mercury sphere; I am speaking entirely from the aspect of occultism, not from that of ordinary astronomy. Something is inscribed by him in all the spheres, in the Mercury sphere, the Venus sphere, the Sun sphere, the Mars sphere, the Jupiter sphere, the Saturn sphere and even beyond.

Most inscriptions, however, are made within the Sun sphere, for as we heard in the last lecture, outside the Sun sphere a man mainly has to adjust matters that are not just left to his own individual discretion.

Thus after having cast away more or less completely what still draws him to the Earth, man journeys through the planetary spheres and even beyond them. The contact thus established with the corresponding forces provides what he needs in his evolution between death and a new birth. When I spoke in the last lecture of man coming into contact with the higher hierarchies and receiving the gifts they bestow, that was the same as saying that his being expands into the cosmos. When the expansion has been completed he contracts again until he has become minute enough to unite as a spirit-seed with what comes from the parents. This is indeed a wonderful mystery. When the human being passes through the gate of death he himself becomes an ever-expanding sphere. His potentialities of soul and spirit expand. He becomes a gigantic being and then again contracts. What we have within us has in fact contracted from the planetary universe. Quite literally we bear within us what we have lived through in a planetary world.

Life between Death and Rebirth, lect. 8 (CW 140)

Birth Chart and Planetary Aspects/Relations

When in astrology we ascertain the positions of the planets and also their relative positions to those of the fixed stars, this gives some indication of what we ourselves have inscribed. The outer planets are in this case a less important factor. What actually has an effect upon us is what we ourselves have inscribed in the several spheres. Here is the real reason why the planetary constellations have an effect upon man's nature. It is because he actually passes through the several planetary spheres. When the Moon stands in a certain relationship to Mars, and to some fixed star, this constellation works as a whole. That is to say, the Mars quality, Moon and fixed star work in conjunction upon the man and bring about what this combined influence is able to achieve.

So it is really the moral inheritance deposited by us between death and rebirth that appears again in a new life as a stellar constellation in our karma. That is the deeper basis of the connection between the stellar constellation and man's karma. Thus if we study the life of a man between death and a new birth we perceive how significantly he is connected with the whole cosmos.

Life between Death and Rebirth, lect. 13 (CW 140)

Da Vinci (Relation to Willi Sucher Historic Similars)

Leonardo da Vinci. He is a spirit of greatness and universality equaled by few others on Earth, but compared with what he intended, his actual achievements in the external world in many respects remained incomplete. As a matter of fact, no man of similar eminence left as much uncompleted as Leonardo da Vinci. The consequence of this was that a colossal amount was inscribed by him in the Moon sphere, so much indeed that one is often bound to exclaim, "How could all that is inscribed there possibly have reached perfection on the Earth!"... It is then discovered that the inscribed imperfections worked as inspirations into the souls of Leonardo's successors, into the souls of men who lived after him.

The imperfections of an earlier epoch are still more important for the following epoch than its perfections. The perfections are there to be studied, but what has been elaborated to a certain degree of perfection on the Earth has, as it were, reached an end, has come to a conclusion in evolution. What has not been perfected is the seed of the following divine evolutionary process. Here we come to a remarkable, magnificent paradox. The greatest blessing for a subsequent period is the fruitful imperfection, the fruitful, justifiable imperfection of an earlier period. What has been perfected in an earlier epoch is there to be enjoyed. Imperfection, however, imperfection originating in great men whose influences have remained for posterity, helps to promote creative activity in the following period.

Life between Death and Rebirth, lect. 8 (CW 140)

Stars and Ether Body after Death

So does the ether-body expand into the Cosmos after death; after a very few days it is there no more. Initiation wisdom shows that this can last only for few days. For by Initiation we are able—as it were, artificially—to make use of the ether-body even during earthly life. Though it remains in the physical body, we become able to disregard the latter, using the ether-body as such. At once we have the panorama of our earthly life until the given moment. Yet at the same time we see glistening and shining forth in our etheric body a reflection of the great Universe. The entire starry Heavens are there in the etheric body. Indeed you cannot ever see the ether-body apart from the physical without its showing you at once the starry world on every hand—the planets and the fixed stars too. It is the planets and the fixed stars that at long last receive our etheric body.

Planetary Spheres and Their Influence on Man's Life on Earth and in the Spiritual Worlds, lect. 6 (CW 218)

Moon Sphere and Being Who Holds Our Karma

These spiritual forces—at once of death and birth, as we have seen—are forces of the Moon, and into them is mingled all that the dead human being, all along the way from birth till death, accumulated by way of moral powers, moral values. Have you been good in any way—in the sphere of these death-Moon-forces you will find, as it were, a specific being, imbued with inner force deriving from your goodness. Yet the same being is imbued with all that derives from your badness. It is a being we ourselves engender, all the time, while living on the Earth. Unaware of it as we are in our normal consciousness, we bear it in us. We leave it every night when we are sleeping, for in effect this entity remains in the physical body when we but go out of it in sleep. I told you, did I not, that our moral and religious feelings are left behind in sleep in the physical and ether-body? There, too, is left behind this real being that we ourselves give birth to during earthly life—the bearer of our Karma.

This being now remains with us after death so long as we are in the realm of the Moon forces. Indeed, just because this being keeps us amid the Moon-forces, that is, in the near neighborhood of Earth, during the first time after death we are obliged to remain connected with these Lunar forces and with our own Karma, so much so that we live again through all the deeds we did on Earth from birth till death. We have to live them through again in a spiritual form of being, three times as fast as we did on Earth.

Planetary Spheres and Their Influence on Man's Life on Earth and in the Spiritual Worlds, lect. 6 (CW 218)

Spiritual Existence after Life Review

And when at last you have arrived at birth, only the "memory" of it will remain with you. It is as though at this moment you were to lay aside yet another body. We are accustomed to say, we lay aside the astral body. What happens in reality is that the living action in which you were hitherto immersed is now transformed for you into a thought-picture—only it is a consciousness pertaining to the stars that thinks it, while here on Earth an earthly consciousness was thinking.

As you set forth now on your further way within the spiritual world you will be living with the beings of whom the physical refulgence are the Sun and Moon and Stars. With the spiritual beings of the Stars you will now live on. Moreover into this life amid the Stars you bear with you the memory of the Karmic entity you had to lay aside with your astral body. Once more, the "laying aside" means nothing else than that the life we were immersed and actively engaged in is but a memory to us now—a memory that we as cosmic Man take with us. Weighted with this memory—the legacy of our earthly life—we step forth into a purely spiritual world.
Planetary Spheres and Their Influence on Man's Life on Earth and in the Spiritual Worlds, lect. 6 (CW 218)

Future Ability to Give our Body to One We Have Harmed and Take on Their Body as Karmic Deed of Love

Through the present leadership of Michael man will now learn to make a very significant decision at the moment when he has already taken on his Karma—taken it into his new ether-body—but is still only setting out upon the way into the physical. With the increasing spread of spiritual knowledge on the Earth and with man's growing experience within himself of universal human love, the following possibility will arise for mankind in coming time. When at the point of descending into a next earthly life, man will be able to say to himself: "This is the body I have been preparing; yet, having sent it down to Earth and having now received my Karma into the ether body which I have drawn together from the Cosmos, I see how it is with this Karma. Through something that I did in former lives, I see that I have gravely hurt some other human being." For we are always in the danger of hurting others through the things we do. The light of judgment as to what we have done to another man will be particularly vivid at this moment when we are still living only in our ether-body, having not yet put on the physical. Here too in future time the light of Michael will be working, and the love of Christ. And we shall then be enabled to bring about a change in our decision—namely, to give to the other man the body we have been preparing, while we ourselves take on the body he prepared, whom we have injured.

Such is the mighty transition that will be taking place from now onward in the spiritual life of men. It will be possible for us of our own decision to enter into the body prepared perforce by another human soul to whom we once did grievous harm; he on the other hand will be enabled to enter into the body we prepared. What we are able to achieve on Earth will thus bring about Karmic compensation in quite another way than heretofore. We human beings shall be able even to exchange our physical bodies. Indeed, the Earth could never reach her goal if this did not take place; mankind would never grow into a single whole.

Planetary Spheres and Their Influence on Man's Life on Earth and in the Spiritual Worlds, lect. 6 (CW 218)

Etheric Heart and Cosmic Star Forces into Incarnation and after Death

Thus we can truly say (and in so saying we mark a real event in the human inner being): from puberty onward man's whole activity becomes inserted, via the astral body, in his etheric heart—and in what has grown out of the pictures of the stars, out of the images of the cosmos.

This is a phenomenon of untold importance. For, my dear friends, we have here a joining together with the cosmos of what man does in this world. In the heart, as far as the etheric universe is concerned, you have a cosmos gathered up into a center; while at the same time, as far as the astral is concerned, you have a gathering together of all that man does in the world. This is the point where the cosmos—the cosmic process—is joined to the karma of man.

This intimate correspondence of the astral body with the etheric body is to be found nowhere in the human organism except in the region of the heart. But there, in truth, it is. Man has brought with him through birth an image of the universe in his etheric body, and the entire universe, which is there within him as an essence, receives all that he does and permeates itself with it. By this constant coming together—this mutual permeation—the opportunity is given throughout human life for human actions to be instilled into the essence of the images of the cosmos.

Then when man passes through the gate of death, this ethereal-astral structure—wherein the heart is floating, so to speak—contains all that man takes with him into his further life of soul and spirit, when he has laid aside the physical and the etheric forms. Now, as he expands ever more widely in the spirit, he can hand over his entire karma to the cosmos, for the substance of the whole cosmos is contained within him; it is drawn together in his heart, in the etheric body of his heart. It came from the cosmos and changed into this etheric entity, then it was gathered up as an essence in the heart, and now it tends to return into the cosmos once more. The human being expands into the cosmos. He is received into the world of souls. He undergoes what I described in my book *Theosophy* as the passage through the world of souls and then through spirit land.

In truth it is so. When we consider the human organization in its becoming, we can say to ourselves: in the region of the heart there takes place a union of the cosmos with the earthly realm, and in this way the cosmos, with its cosmic configuration, is taken into our etheric body. There it makes ready to receive all our actions, all that we do in life. Then we go outward again, together with everything that has formed itself within us through this intimate permeation of the cosmic ethereal with our own human actions. So do we enter again into a new cosmic existence, having passed through the gate of death.

Thus we have now described in a quite concrete form how the human being lives his way into his physical body, and how he is able to draw himself out of it again, because his deeds have given him the force to hold together what he had first formed within him as an essence out of the cosmos.

Life of the Human Soul, lect. 6 (CW 212)

The Problem of Faust

One has a quite wrong and materialistically biased notion if one imagines that there lie already formed in the woman all the forces that lead to the physical human embryo. That is not so. A working of the cosmic forces of the spheres takes place; into the woman work cosmic forces. The human embryo is always a result of cosmic activity. What is described in materialistic natural science as the germ-cell is in a certain measure produced out of the mother alone, but it is a counterpart of the great cosmic germ-cell.
  Goethe's Faust in the Light of Anthroposophy, lect. 4 (CW 273)

Heliocentric

Copernicanism

The Copernican world-conception pictures the universe in a way, which if followed to its logical conclusions would tend to drive all spirituality out of the cosmos in man's conception of it. The Copernican world-picture leads at length to a mechanical, machine-like conception of the universe in space. It was after all in view of this Copernican picture of the world that the famous astronomer said to Napoleon: he had searched through all the universe and he could find no God. It is, indeed, an entire elimination of spirituality.
  Karmic Relationships, vol. 4, lect. 6 (CW 238)

Why Sun Took Over Rulership from Earth

...in the fifteenth, in the sixteenth centuries, and even later, there was a Rosicrucian school, isolated, scarcely known to the world, where over and over again a few pupils were educated, and where above all, care was taken that one thing should not be forgotten but be preserved as a holy tradition. And this was the following. I will give it to you in narrative form.

Let us say, a new pupil arrived at this lonely spot to receive preparation. The so-called Ptolemaic system was first set before him, in its true form, as it had been handed down from olden times, not in the trivial way it is explained nowadays as something that

has been long ago supplanted, but in an altogether different way. The pupil was shown how the Earth really and truly bears within herself the forces that are needed to determine her path through the Universe. So that to have a correct picture of the World, it must be drawn in the old Ptolemaic sense: the Earth must be for Man in the center of the Universe, and the other stars in their corresponding revolutions be controlled and directed by the Earth. And the pupil was told: If one really studies what are the best forces in the Earth, then one can arrive at no other conception of the world than this. In actual fact, however, it is not so. It is not so on account of man's sin. Through man's sin, the Earth—so to speak, in an unauthorized, wrongful way—has gone over into the kingdom of the Sun; the Sun has become the regent and ruler of earthly activities. Thus, in contradistinction to a World-System given by the Gods to men with the Earth in the center, could now be set another World-System, that has the Sun in the center, and the Earth revolving round the Sun—it is the system of Copernicus.
Rosicrucianism and Modern Initiation, lect. 4 (CW 233a)

Alanus ab Insulis, Platonic teacher of the School of Chartres, 12th century

We, in our time, regard the Earth as the center of the Cosmos, we speak of the planets circling around the Earth, we describe the whole heaven of stars as it presents itself to the physical eyes as if it revolved around the Earth. But when he who will thus place the Sun at the center of the spatial universe has come, the picture of the world will become arid. Men will only calculate the courses of the planets, will merely indicate the positions of the heavenly bodies, speaking of them as gases or burning luminous physical bodies; they will know the starry heavens only in terms of mathematical and mechanical laws. But this arid picture of the world that will become widespread in the coming times, has after all, one thing...meager, yet it has it none the less.... We look at the universe from the Earth; he who will come will look at the universe from the standpoint of the Sun. He will be like one who indicates a "direction" only—the direction leading toward a path of majestic splendor, fraught with most wonderful happenings and peopled by glorious beings. But he will give the direction through abstract concepts only." (Thereby the Copernican picture of the world was indicated, arid and abstract yet giving the direction...)

Karmic Relationships, vol. 6, lect. 7 (CW 240)

A different physical view of the world prevailed in pre-Copernican times, a view that may be called erroneous today.... This worldview did not yet result in human beings becoming destructive in the earthly sphere after passing through the portal of death.

Secret Brotherhoods, lect. 2 (CW 178)

What is this Copernican picture of the Universe? It is in reality a picture built up purely on the basis of mathematical principles, mathematical-mechanical principles. The rudiments of it began, very gradually, to be unfolded in Greece, where, however, echoes of earlier thought—for example in the Ptolemaic view of the universe—still persisted. And in the course of time this developed into the Copernican system that is taught nowadays to every child.

The Bridge between Universal Spirituality and the Physical Constitution of Man, lect. 2 (CW 202)

The intrinsic character of spiritual life as it is in the present age, arose for the first time when modern natural science came upon the scene with men like Copernicus....

The very ground slipped from under men's feet when Copernicus came forward with the doctrine that the Earth is moving with tremendous speed through the universe! We should not underestimate the effects of such a revolution in thinking, accompanied as it was by a corresponding change in the life of feeling. All the thoughts and ideas of men were suddenly different from what they had been before the days of Copernicus! And now let us ask: What has occultism to say about this revolution in thinking?

One who asks from the standpoint of occultism, what kind of world-conception can be derived from the Copernican tenets, will have to admit that although these ideas can lead to great achievements in the realm of natural science and in external life, they are incapable of promoting any understanding of the spiritual foundations of the world and the things of the world—for truth to tell there has never been a worse instrument for understanding the spiritual foundations of the world than the ideas of Copernicus—never in the evolution of the human mind! The reason for this is that all these Copernican concepts are inspired by Lucifer. Copernicanism is one of the last attacks, one of the last great attacks made by Lucifer upon the evolution of man. In earlier, pre-Copernican thought, the external world was, indeed, maya: but much traditional wisdom, much truth concerning the world and the things of the world still survived. Since Copernicus, however, man has maya around him not only in his material perceptions but his concepts and ideas in themselves are maya. Today men regard it as self-evident that the Sun stands firmly at the center with the planets revolving around it in ellipses. In no far distant future, however, it will be realized that the view of the world of stars held by Copernicus is much less correct than the earlier, Ptolemaic view. The view of the world held by the school of Copernicus and Kepler is, in many respects, convenient, but as an explanation of the macrocosm it is not the truth.

Esoteric Christianity and the Mission of Christian Rosenkreutz,
Dec. 18, 1912 (CW 130)

Julian the Apostate

For the same individuality reappears in the 16th century as Tycho de Brahe, and stands face to face with the Copernican worldview that emerges within Western civilization at that time.

Karmic Relationships, vol. 4, lect. 6 (CW 238)

Ptolemy's map of the heavens is usually placed next to that of Copernicus and then the former is declared false. This, however, is not true. He then explained that Ptolemy's map is of the astral plane where the Earth forms the center and that of Copernicus is of the physical plane with the Sun at the center.

Reading Pictures of the Apocalypse, June 14, 1906
(following discussion of Chaldean astrology; CW 104a)

Only with the abrupt entry of Copernicanism, with its picture that the whole world spread out in space is also subject to the laws of space, with its picture that the Earth circles around the Sun, only with such pictures arising in the Copernican view is the human being chained to physical-sensible existence and prevented from rising appropriately into the spiritual world after death.

Secret Brotherhoods, lect. 2 (CW 178)

Appendix II:
Suggested Reading by Rudolf Steiner

Ancient Myths and the New Isis Mystery, CW 180, 1918, Dornach.
Anthroposophical Leading Thoughts: Anthroposophy as a Path of Knowledge, CW 26 (trans. M. Adams); also, *The Michael Mystery*, CW 26 (trans. M. Spock), Apr. 1924–Apr. 1925.
Between Death and Rebirth, CW 141, 10 lectures 1912–1913, Berlin.
Christ and the Spiritual World: The Quest for the Holy Grail, CW 149, Dec. 28, 1913–Jan. 2, 1914. (lect. 5 and 6, Leipzig.
Cosmogony, Altruism and Freedom, CW 191, Oct. 1919, Dornach.
The Cycle of the Year as Breathing Process of the Earth, CW 223, Mar. 31–Apr. 8, 1923, Dornach.
The Evolution of the Earth and Humanity and the Influence of the Stars, CW 354, 1924, Dornach
Human and Cosmic Thought, CW 151, Jan. 1914, Berlin.
Interdisciplinary Astronomy: Third Scientific Course, CW 323, Jan. 1–18, 1921.
Karmic Relationships: Esoteric Studies (specifically stars and Michael and Christ references): vol. 2, lect. 6, 8, 10-13; vol. 3, lect. 2, 3, 7–11 (on Michaelites); vol. 4, lect. 6, 7; vol. 5, lect. 1–4, 6–7, 8–9 (on Michael and intelligence); vol. 6, lect. 1, 6, vol. 7: lect. 1–4; vol. 8, lect. 3 (Michael), 5.
Life between Death and Rebirth, The Active Connection Between the Living and the Dead, CW 140; collected lectures.
Macrocosm and Microcosm, CW 119, March, 1910, Vienna
Man and the World of the Stars, The Spiritual Communion of Mankind, CW 219, Nov. 26–Dec. 31, 1922, Dornach.
Man in the Light of Occultism, Theosophy and Philosophy, CW 137, June 1912, Oslo.
Mystery Knowledge and Mystery Centres, CW 232, Nov. 23–Dec. 23, 1923, Dornach.
The Mystery of the Trinity; Mission of the Spirit, CW 218
Mystery of the Universe: The Human Being, Image of Creation, CW 201, April/May 1920, Dornach.
An Outline of Esoteric Science (trans. C.E.Creeger), CW 13, written in 1909.
Planetary Spheres and their Influence on Man's Life on Earth and in the Spiritual Worlds, CW 211, 214, 218, London, 1922.
Spiritual Beings in the Heavenly Bodies and the Kingdoms of Nature, CW 136, April 1912, Helsinki
The Spiritual Guidance of Humanity, CW 15, June 6–8 1911,
The Spiritual Hierarchies and their Reflection in the Physical World: Zodiac, Planets & Cosmos, CW 110, Apr. 1909, Düsseldorf.
Spiritual Relationships in the Human Organism; Apr., Aug., Nov. 1922, London

The Sun Mystery, CW 214
Supersensible Man, CW 231, Nov. 1923, The Hague
Theosophy: An Introduction to the Spiritual Processes in Human Life and in the Cosmos (trans. C.E.Creeger), CW 9, written in 1904.
Universal Spirituality and Human Physicality: Bridging the Divide: The Search for the New Isis and the Divine Sophia, CW 202, Dec. 23–26, 1920,

◊

*In addition to the foregoing bibliography, I am grateful to R.S.W. Bobbette (1998) for the following Rudolf Steiner star-knowledge references. Some duplicate the list above. References that give two to five pages of information are italicized, whereas those that give more than five pages of information are in **bold italics**.*

CW 7 Mystics after Modernism: Discovering the Seeds of a New Science in the Renaissance, 2000, Anthroposophic Press.
CW 11 Cosmic Memory: The Story of Atlantis, Lemuria, and the Division of the Sexes, 1987, SteinerBooks.
CW 13 An Outline of Esoteric Science, 1997, Anthroposophic Press.
CW 15 The Spiritual Guidance of the Individual and Humanity, 1992, Anthroposophic Press.
CW 26 The Michael Mystery, 1984, SteinerBooks.
CW 27 Extending Practical Medicine: Fundamental Principles Based on the Science of the Spirit, 1997, Rudolf Steiner Press.
CW 35 "Mathematics and Occultism," in *Anthroposophical Movement,* vol. 5, no. 28, 1928.
CW 40 The Calendar of the Soul, 1988, Anthroposophic Press.
CW 55 "Blood Is a Very Special Fluid," in *Supersensible Knowledge,* 1987, Anthroposophic Press.
CW 58 **Transforming the Soul,** vol. 1, 2005, Rudolf Steiner Press.
CW 60 The Spirit in the Realm of Plants, 1978, Mercury Press.
CW 61 Prophecy: It's Nature and Meaning, 1950, Anthroposophical Publ.
CW 79 Self-consciousness; The Spiritual Human Being, 2010, SteinerBooks.
CW 93a Foundations of Esotericism, 1983, Rudolf Steiner Press.
CW 94 An Esoteric Cosmology: Evolution, Christ & Modern Spirituality, 2008, SteinerBooks.
CW 95 *Founding a Science of the Spirit,* 1999, Rudolf Steiner Press.
CW 99 Rosicrucian Wisdom: An Introduction, 2000, Rudolf Steiner Press.
CW 101 Occult Signs and Symbols, 1972, Anthroposophic Press.
CW 102 **Good and Evil Spirits and their Influence on Humanity,** 2014, Rudolf Steiner Press.
CW 104 The Apocalypse of St. John, 1985, SteinerBooks.
CW 104a Reading the Pictures of the Apocalypse, 1993, Anthroposophic Press.
CW 105 Universe, Earth, Human Being: Their Relationship to Egyptian Myths and Modern Civilization, 2023, Rudolf Steiner Press.
CW 106 Egyptian Myths and Mysteries, 1971, Anthroposophic Press.
CW 107 Disease, Karma, and Healing: Spiritual-Scientific Enquiries into the Nature of the Human Being, 2013, Rudolf Steiner Press.
CW 107 The Disease, Karma, and Healing: Spiritual-Scientific Enquiries into the Nature of the Human Being, 2013 (lect. 16)," Rudolf Steiner Press.

CW 109	*The Principle of Spiritual Economy: In Connection with Questions of Reincarnation: An Aspect of the Spiritual Guidance of Man,* 1986, Anthroposophic Press.
CW 109	*Rosicrucian Esotericism,* 1978, Anthroposophic Press.
CW 110	**The Spiritual Hierarchies and the Physical World: Zodiac, Planets & Cosmos,** 2008, Anthroposophic Press.
CW 112	*The Gospel of St. John and Its Relation to the Other Gospels,* 1994, Anthroposophic Press.
CW 113	**The East in the Light of the West,** 2017, Rudolf Steiner Press.
CW 117	*The Universal Human,* 1990, Anthroposophic Press.
CW 119	**Macrocosm and Microcosm,** 2021, Rudolf Steiner Press.
CW 121	**The Mission of Folk Souls,** 1989, SteinerBooks.
CW 122	*Genesis: Secrets of Creation,* 2003, Rudolf Steiner Press.
CW 123	*The According to Matthew: The Gospel of Christ's Humanity,* 2002, Anthroposophic Press.
CW 124	*Background to the Gospel of St. Mark,* 1968, Rudolf Steiner Press.
CW 128	*An Occult Physiology,* 1997, Rudolf Steiner Press.
CW 129	*Wonders of the World, Trials of the Soul, Revelations of the Spirit,* 2021, Rudolf Steiner Press.
CW 130	*Esoteric Christianity and the Mission of Christian Rosenkreutz,* 2001, Rudolf Steiner Press.
CW 132	*Evolution in the Aspect of Realities,* 1989, Garber.
CW 134	*The World of the Senses and the World of the Spirit,* 1947, Rudolf Steiner Press.
CW 135	*Reincarnation and Karma: Two Fundamental Truths of Human Existence,* 2001, Anthroposophic Press.
CW 136	**Spiritual Beings in the Heavenly Bodies and in the Kingdoms of Nature,** 2011, SteinerBooks.
CW 137	**Man in the Light of Occultism, Theosophy and Philosophy,** 1989, Garber.
CW 140	*Life between Death and Rebirth,* 1997, Anthroposophic Press.
CW 141	**Between Death and Rebirth,** 2022, Rudolf Steiner Press.
CW 144	*The Mysteries of Initiation: From Isis to the Holy Grail,* 2022, Rudolf Steiner Press.
CW 145	**The Effects of Spiritual Development,** 1945, Anthroposophic Press.
CW 149	*Christ and the Spiritual World: The Quest for the Holy Grail,* 2023, Rudolf Steiner Press.
CW 151	**Human and Cosmic Thought,** 2015, Rudolf Steiner Press.
CW 153	*The Inner Nature of Man: And Our Life between Death and Rebirth,* 2013, Rudolf Steiner Press.
CW 156	*Inner Reading and Inner Hearing and How to Achieve Existence in the World of Ideas,* 2008, SteinerBooks.
CW 157	*The Destinies of Individuals and of Nations,* 1987, Rudolf Steiner Press.
CW 158	*Our Connection with the Elemental World: Kalevala–Olaf Åsteson–the Russian People: The World as the Result of Balancing Influences,* 2017, Rudolf Steiner Press.
CW 159	*The Etheric Body as a Reflection of the Universe,* 1940, Anthroposophic News Sheet, nos. 39–42.
CW 163	*Chance, Providence and Necessity,* 1988, Anthroposophic Press.
CW 169	*Toward Imagination,* 1990, Anthroposophic Press.

CW 170   *The Riddle of Humanity*, 1990, Rudolf Steiner Press.
CW 171   *Inner Impulses of Evolution*, 1984, Anthroposophic Press.
CW 173/4 *The Karma of Untruthfulness: Secret Societies, the Media, and Preparations for the Great War*, vol. 1-2, 2005, Rudolf Steiner Press.
CW 175   *Building Stones for an Understanding of the Mystery of Golgotha*, 1972, Rudolf Steiner Press.
CW 176   *The Karma of Materialism*, 1985, Anthroposophic Press.
CW 177   *The Fall of the Spirits of Darkness*, 1993, Rudolf Steiner Press.
CW 178   *Geographic Medicine*, 1986, Mercury Press.
CW 180   **Ancient Myths and the New Isis Mystery**, 2018, SteinerBooks.
CW 181   *Dying Earth and Living Cosmos*, 2015, Rudolf Steiner Press.
CW 184   *Eternal and Transient Elements in Human Life: The Cosmic Past of Humanity and the Mystery of Evil*, 2016, Rudolf Steiner Press.
CW 185   *From Symptom to Reality in Modern History*, 2015, Rudolf Steiner Press.
CW 186   *The Challenge of the Times*, 1979, Anthroposophic Press.
CW 187   *How Can Mankind Find the Christ Again?* 1984, SteinerBooks.
CW 191   *The Influences of Lucifer and Ahriman*, 1976, Anthroposophic Press.
CW 197   *Polarities in the Evolution of Humanity*, 2022, Rudolf Steiner Press.
CW 201   **Mystery of the Universe: The Human Being, Image of Creation**, 2001, Rudolf Steiner Press.
CW 202   *The Bridge between Universal Spirituality and the Physical Constitution of Man*, 1958, Anthroposophic Press.
CW 204   **Materialism and the Task of Anthroposophy**, 1987, Anthroposophic Press.
CW 205   *Therapeutic Insights: Earthly and Cosmic Laws*, 1994, Mercury Press.
CW 206   *Man as a Being of Sense and Perception*, 1981, Steiner Book Centre.
CW 207   *Cosmosophy*, vol. 1, 1985, Anthroposophic Press
CW 210   *Old and New Methods of Initiation*, 1991, Rudolf Steiner Press.
CW 212   *Life of the Human Soul and its Relation to World Evolution*, 2017, Rudolf Steiner Press.
CW 214   *The Mystery of the Trinity: Mission of the Spirit*, 1991, SteinerBooks
CW 219   *Man and the World of Stars*, 1982, Anthroposophic Press.
CW 221   *Earthly Knowledge and Heavenly Wisdom*, 1991, Anthroposophic Press.
CW 223   *The Cycle of the Year*, 1984, Anthroposophic Press.
CW 227   *The Evolution of Consciousness*, 2006, Rudolf Steiner Press.
CW 228   **Initiation Science and the Development of the Human Mind**, 2017, Rudolf Steiner Press.
CW 229   *The Four Seasons and the Archangels*, 1996, Rudolf Steiner Press.
CW 230   **Harmony of the Creative Word**, 2002, Rudolf Steiner Press.
CW 232   *Mystery Knowledge and Mystery Centres*, 2013, Rudolf Steiner Press.
CW 233   *World History and the Mysteries*, 2021, Rudolf Steiner Press.
CW 233a **Rosicrucianism and Modern Initiation**, 2020, Rudolf Steiner Press.
CW 234   *Anthroposophy and the Inner Life: An Esoteric Introduction*, 1994, Rudolf Steiner Press.
CW 235   *Karmic Relationships: Esoteric Studies*, vol. 1, 1972, Rudolf Steiner Press.
CW 236   **Karmic Relationships:** *Esoteric Studies,* **vol. 2**, 1974, Rudolf Steiner Press.

Appendix II: Suggested Reading by Rudolf Steiner

CW 237–240 *Karmic Relationships: Esoteric Studies,* vols. 3–8, 1971–1983, Rudolf Steiner Press.
CW 243 *True and False Paths in Spiritual Research,* 2020, Rudolf Steiner Press.
CW 254 *The Occult Movement in the Nineteenth Century and Its Relation to Modern Culture,* 1973, Rudolf Steiner Press.
CW 257 *Awakening to Community,* 1974, Anthroposophic Press.
CW 275 *Art as Seen in the Light of Mystery Wisdom,* 1996, Rudolf Steiner Press.
CW 283 *The Inner Nature of Music and the Experience of Tone,* 1983, Anthroposophic Press.
CW 291 *Colour,* 1997, Rudolf Steiner Press.
CW 302 *Education for Adolescents,* 1996, Anthroposophic Press.
CW 312 *Introducing Anthroposophical Medicine,* 1989, SteinerBooks.
CW 317 *Education for Special Needs: The Curative Education Course,* 2015, Rudolf Steiner Press.
CW 318 *Broken Vessels: The Spiritual Structure of Human Frailty,* 2002, Anthroposophic Press; formerly *Pastoral Medicine.*
CW 326 *The Origins of Natural Science,* 1985, Anthroposophic Press.
CW 327 **Agriculture,** 1993, Biodynamic Farming & Gardening Association.
CW 347 **From Crystals to Crocodiles... Answers to Questions,** 2004, Rudolf Steiner Press.
CW 348 *From Comets to Cocaine...Answers to Questions,* 2002, Anthroposophic Press.
CW 351 *Bees,* 1998, Anthroposophic Press.
CW 352 *From Elephants to Einstein...Answers to Questions,* 2001, Rudolf Steiner Press.
CW 354 *The Evolution of the Earth and Man,* 1987, Anthroposophic Press.

Collections and unpublished:

The Interior of the Earth: An Esoteric Study of the Subterranean Spheres, 2006, Rudolf Steiner Press.
Planetary Spheres and Their Influence on Man's Life on Earth and in Spiritual Worlds, 1952, Rudolf Steiner Press.
Readings in Goethean Science, 1978, Bio-Dynamic Literature.
Rudolf Steiner Speaks to the British, 1998, Rudolf Steiner Press.
The Reappearance of Christ in the Etheric: A Collection of Lectures on the Second Coming of Christ, 2022, SteinerBooks.
The Relation of the Diverse Branches of Natural Science to Astronomy (typescript).
Myths and Symbols II and IV (typescript).
Planetary and Human Evolution, (typescript).
On Chaos and Cosmos, unpubl. typescript
Comets and Their Significance for Earthly Existence; Male and Female in the Cosmos (typescript).
Perception of the Nature of Thought (typescript).

Appendix III: Willi Sucher's Books Indexed by Subject

INTRODUCTION AND HISTORY OF ASTROSOPHY

Astrosophy.com Website:
    Introduction to Astrosophy
    Biography of Willi Sucher and Dr. Elizabeth Vreede
Isis Sophia III: Part 2, chapter 1:
    Good on astronomy and astrosophy; union of observation with contemplation/meditation. *One of the gravest dangers of the cosmologist, is that he or she gets submerged in calculation.*
Isis Sophia III, Part 4, chapter 1–3:
    General history; Precession of Equinoxes and cultural ages
The Changing Countenance of Cosmology:
    Chapter 2 The Development of Cosmology in History:—history of cosmology and Copernicanism, introduces idea of spiritual heliocentric
    Chapter 3 Roads to a Modern Cosmology and Astrosophy – Good intro new astronomy, change needed for spiritual star wisdom
    Chapter 4 The Archangel Michael and Astrosophy – on role of Michael in connecting us to stars, examples of Beethoven and Raphael
Living Universe, Part One, Thoughts on the Future of Astrology:
    Good on old vs new astrology and significance of death chart for new approach to stars; changing stars
Cosmology Course, Feb. 4, 1955:
    Good on new star wisdom and Klingsor story, good Q&A on decadence of mysteries and star wisdom gone wrong
Practical Approach I, introduction:
    Good on what new astronomy should be
Practical Approach III, Nov., 1970:
    First letter, EXCELLENT, and good intro to why Helio

Zodiac – The World of Duration

Mythologies of Constellations

Drama of the Universe, chapter 1:
    Creates 5 groupings of zodiac with constellations above and below
    Mythology of first group: Ram/Fishes, Andromeda–Perseus complex, Cetus, Eridanus
    Mythology of second group: Twins/Bull/Crab, Auriga, Orion, Sirius
    Mythology of third group: Lion/Virgin, Bootes, Hydra with Cup and Ravn
    Mythology of fourth group: Scales/Scorpion/Archer, Antaries, Ophiucus with Serpent, Hercules, Dragon, Lupus, Centaurus
    Mythology of fifth group: Capricorn/Waterman, Great Sea, Southern Fish w/ Fomalhaut, Lyre, Eagle, Swan, Pegasus

Practical Approach I:
    July 1966 – Aries and Taurus and surrounding constellations
    Aug. 1966 – Gemini, Cancer, Lion
    Sept. 1966 – Leo, Virgo
    Oct. 1966 – Libra, Scorpio
    Nov. 1966 – Archer, Capricorn, Fishes

Zodiac and Human Form

Isis Sophia I:
    End 6th Letter – middle 7th Letter
Isis Sophia II, Part Two:
    The Threefold Human Being
Living Universe, Part Two, Jan. 10, 1956:
    Exploring glyphs/symbols in human form

Zodiac Symbols/Glyphs

The Changing Countenance of Cosmology:
    Chapter 5 – Symbology and Cosmology
Cosmology Course:
    Feb. 11, 1955 – on symbols Aries through Virgo
    Feb. 18, 1955 – on zodiac symbols Ram through Fishes

Cultural Ages and Zodiac

Isis Sophia III, Part Four:
    Chapter 4 – VP Pisces our Age
    Chapter 5 – VP Crab
    Chapter 6 – VP Twins
    Chapter 7 – VP Bull
    Chapter 8 – VP Ram
    Chapter 9 – VP Waterman
    Chapter 10 – VP Goat

Practical Approach I, Jun., 1966:
    Dec. 1970 – VP movement and task of Pisces Age, relation to Per Jupiter
    Jan. 1971 – Per Jupiter 1950 ; Pisces, Andromeda, this century and thinking change, Phoenix

Occult Science, Evolution, and Zodiac

Isis Sophia I: 2nd Letter to end 6th Letter
Isis Sophia II: All Part Two (most comprehensive source)
Cosmology Course: Feb. 11, 1955: First part on sequence of planets and evolutionary cycles

PLANETARY SPHERES—THE WANDERING STARS

The Planetary Rhythms, the Life of the Planets: Sacred Geometry

Cosmic Christianity and The Changing Countenance of Cosmology:
    Chapter 1: The Origin of Occult Symbols on the Basis of Cosmic Rhythmology

The Planetary Spheres: the Cosmic Intelligences

Isis Sophia I:
    8th Letter (general planets)
    9th Letter: Saturn, with historical examples
    10th Letter: Jupiter, with historical examples
    11th Letter: Jupiter cont'd and Mars, with historical examples
    12th Letter: Mars, historical examples
    13th Letter: Sun in the 12 constellations

16th Letter: Moon

17th Letter: Moon in constellations, historical examples

18th Letter: Venus: need to know Ancient Sun evolution

19th Letter: Mercury: rhythms, switch with Venus, evolution

Isis Sopia II:

All Part Three: Saturn – Moon; especially good on Sun and origin of spheres.

Isis Sophia III:

Part 1, chapter 1: Saturn in relation to two World Wars

The Changing Countenance of Cosmology:

Chapter 1: The Origin of Occult Symbols on the Basis of Cosmic Rhythmology – On origins of forms: Venus form, Mercury form, Mars double square; Golden triangle

Chapter 6: The Workings of the Planets and their Spheres – on Cosmic Wave; DaVinci helio chart

Chapter 7: Turning Points in History I – Pluto & Uranus conjunctions

Chapter 8: Turning Points in History II – Saturn Jupiter Great Conjunctions

Cosmic Christianity and The Changing Countenance of Cosmology:

Cosmic Christianity, last chapter Manifestation in History: On Saturn time conversion

Living Universe, Part Two, The Solar Wave:

Lecture 1 – Jan. 9, 1956 – GOOD on nature of Sun and Wave process

Lecture 3 – Jan. 11, 1956 – Wave theory and working through of each planet sphere qualities

Drama of the Universe:

Part 1, chapter 1 – astronomical facts about heliocentric universe and each planet

Part 2, chapter 2 – wave/densification theory and natural disasters, heliocentric

Cosmology Course:

Moon; and Moon Node-1; Moon Node-2: good on Moon and Nodes

Mars: good on Mars

Mars – Conjunctions and Loops: on mars loops, lemniscate and mars geometry

Mars and the Eightfold Path: Mars 16 petals, Buddhist path

Occult Mercury – Astronomical Venus: on switch and about planet Venus and KHW exercises for 10 petaled chakra

Jupiter: GOOD on Jupiter w/ A Sun and future; 2 petaled chakra and lemniscate

Mercury (Occult Venus) in Relationship with Venus (Occult Mercury): explains switch in names, then goes into Mercury geometry, loops, 3 years, chakra

The Planetary Aspects in 1955: example of looking at stars for year

Practical Approach I:

Oct. 1965 – on planets for month with focus on Uranus/Pluto conjunction, also on Moon nodes and Goethe's life

Nov. 1965 – Uranus/Pluto cont'd in history: Goethe Green Snake; Chemical Wedding, Eschenbach Grail story

Dec. 1965 – Wave theory of solar system and connection to Grail

Jan. 1966 – Saturn, Jupiter, Mars intro; focus helio elements with locations; start Saturn

Feb. 1966 – GOOD Saturn, Jupiter, Mars spheres

Mar. 1966 – GOOD Venus and Mercury

Apr. 1966 – Venus cont'd and Moon; Earth and Sun; start outer planets; Mars/Sun conj in commentary

May 1966 – Uranus, Neptune, Pluto; and GOOD summary of all planets

Apr. 1967 – good on occultations of planets by Moon and negative aspects of Saturn and Venus; angular ASPECTS and signs relation to elements and temperaments, diagram

May 1967 – angular aspects continued, Venus angles

Practical Approach III:

May 1972 – Golden Triangle, Kalichakra and Gr Conj's Chart with years

Studies in Historical Events and Stars

Cosmic Christianity:

Last chapter Manifestation in History: Christ events in history, 20th Century

The Changing Countenance of Cosmology:

Chapters 7 & 8: Turning Points in History I and II

I: Christ event at center; Pluto & Uranus conjunctions

II: Saturn Jupiter Great Conjunctions

Living Universe, Part One:

The Zodiac – Evolution of Western consciousness: Aquinas & Scholasticism w/Pisces/Virgin; Templars & Archer; Meister Eckhardt & Mysticism – Gemini

The Zodiac cont'd – 12 constellations and evolution of modern, Western consciousness through examples of biographies; good zodiac table description

Drama of the Universe, Part Two:
> Chapter 3: History and Cosmos – heliocentric view of each planetary realm. Historical charts: Martin Luther, 30 Years War, Fall of Bastille, Napoleon, murder of Ferdinand Archduke (WWI), WWI armistice, Treaty of Versailles, Nazis take power 1933, Lenin, Russian Revolution
>
> Chapter 4: Background of Humanity's Ideas/Discoveries – helio charts of: 1492 Columbus discovery; Steam engine; Electricity and Magnetism events 1600–1831; X-Ray and Radioactivity; Hiroshima; Modern astronomy events 1496–1930; Great Fire of Chicago

Cosmology Course:
> Part One
>> Return of King Arthur – about Tintagel and Arthur and Great Bear
>
> Christmas and the Cosmic Rhythms:
>> Great Conjunctions: Golden Triangle conjunctions and Christianity
>> Shepherds: Gr Conjunction and impulse of Spiritual Freedom
>> Kings: Gr. Conjunction and impulse of Brotherhood
>> St. Paul: Gr Conjunction and impulse of Equality
>
> Individual Lectures
>> The Turn of the Century – Saul/Paul – AD 34 and AD 2000; Etheric Christ return and Saturn conversion, history and Gr Conj; good on how we speak to stars

Practical Approach I:
> Oct. 1965: on planets for month with focus on Uranus/Pluto conjunctions every 253 years in Leo and Aries now, current triple, Oct. 1965, Apr. and Jun., 1966; history and conjunctions; relation to Moon nodes, Grail stream and Goethe's life
>
> Nov. 1965: Uranus/Pluto cont'd in history: Goethe Green Snake; Chemical Wedding, Eschenbach Grail story; cosmic origin of Grail; planets density

Practical Approach II:
> Apr. 1969 – Easter current events and stars; Venus loop; VP movement; CMP's
>
> May 1969 – Great Conj Triangle rotation 1563–1961 image; Gr Conj events; 6 BC
>
> Dec. 1969 – on first of 5 oppositions Saturn/Jupiter conn. to Gr Conj. AD 34 line
>
> Jan. 1970 – Venus pentagram and loops

Feb. 1970 – Helio elements and revolution/wars: French, Russian, Nazis, Hiroshima

Mar. 1970 – Countenance of 20th century: chart of Gr Conj 1901 and 6 BC history

Apr. 1970 – Countenance of 20th century. Cont'd: 6 BC Conj elaborated; also Uranus opp Pluto theme 1901 and Grail stream and Rosenkreuz.

May/Jun. 1970, Countenance of 20th century. Cont'd: 1901 Gr Conj through Moon graph rhythm of 7 years per Moon cycle

Jul. 1970, Countenance of 20th century contd: Gr Conj 1901 and meaning for future century; relate to 6 BC challenge for now; Saturn progression/conversion

Aug. 1970 – Saturn conversion of 1901 cont'd in historical events

Sept. 1970 – Saturn conversion 1901 for Hitler rise and Genghis Kahn

Oct. 1970 – Final *Star Journal* letter; 20th century cont'd: Cathars, Templars, 869 Council, Grail, Rosicrucians

Practical Approach III:

Jul. 1971 – What is Holy GRAIL? Connection to Gr Conjunctions, 6 BC & 747 BC

Aug. 1971 – Time Ratios: Saturn conversion and 747 BC/6 BC

Sept. 1971 – Moon nodes, 6 BC; Holy Grail-Celtic people-Arthur

Oct. 1971 – Celtic Folk Spirit/Grail/Esoteric Christianity-Grail Stream and Gr Conj's and Uranus Pluto; Templars, Rosenkreuz

Nov. 1971 – Rosicrucian stream cont'd; Gr Conj 1444 chart; 1459 Chym Wedding; Moon Nodes in Goethe's life

Feb. 1972 – astrosophy as astrology of Grail; Grail cont'd; Steiner Jan 12 1910 Annunciation of the Second Coming. *The very first of those lectures,…its stellar companionship. Before the lecture, Rudolf Steiner was urged to abstain from delivering it, because there were "dreadful events going on in the heavens." We produce the configuration in the chart in Fig. 16. and bad stars*

Mar. 1972 – Death Raphael cont'd; Sistine Madonna; Saturn conversion for 2nd coming 1935 as world Damascus experience; chart of AD 34 Paul and 1935 Saturn compared; 1901 Steiner work; Geo chart of 3 Years

May 1972 – Golden Triangle, Kalichakra and Gr Conj's Chart with years

Jun. 1972 – Gr Conj in node Mars and deed of Buddha, Buddha and 8-fold path relation to Mars & Venus; diagram Mars/Sun conj's; helio elements and relation to Venus elements; Buddha and Luke Jesus

Jul. 1972 – AD 34 Venus Sun conj; loops of Venus and Damascus impulse in history; helio elements of Venus & Jupiter – historic similars; elements of Mars with Neptune

Christ and the Stars

Isis Sophia I:
> Last Letter: Sun during 3 Years and Imagination of Lamb of God in Zodiac

Cosmic Christianity and The Changing Countenance of Cosmology:
> Part 2: Cosmic Christianity – best source on the Three Years and Stars
> Part 2: Cosmic Christianity, last chapter Manifestation in History: Return of Etheric Christ and history

Cosmology Course:
> Occult Mercury – Astronomical Venus, Mar. 11, 1955 – Venus and 3 Years
> Mercury (Occult Venus) in Relationship with Venus (Occult Mercury)
> Mar 25, 1955 – Mercury and 3 Years
> Cosmology Course, Christmas and the Cosmic Rhythms:
> Great Conjunctions
> Shepherds – Spiritual Freedom – 6 BC conjunction
> Kings – Brotherhood – AD 14 conjunction
> St. Paul – Equality – AD 34 conjunction
> Cosmology Course, Individual Lectures
> The Turn of the Century – Saul/Paul – AD 34 and AD 2000; Etheric Christ return and Saturn conversion, history and Gr Conj
> Christmas Season, Nov. 1957 – Unrevised Lecture – on birth of Jesus and explanation of statement from Steiner about Sun in Virgo on Dec. 24

Practical Approach III:
> Aug. 1971 – Spiritual Nativity of Matthew Jesus Child, 6 BC Gr conj and Moon node
> Sept. 1971 – Moon nodes, 6 BC Jesus children; man sick 38 years, Holy Grail

Charts and Human Biography

Prenatal development – Epoch to Birth

Isis Sophia I:
> 15th Letter: Sun Epoch curve and open space, historic personalities

Isis Sophia III, Part Two:
> Chapter 2 – Embryology and Stars
> Chapter 3 – Physical Deformities and Embryo development (cranial; micro and hydro cephalus; limbs deformed)

Isis Sophia III, Part Three:
> Chapter 1 – Embryology science and Hermetic Rule
> Chapter 2 – 12 Zodiac and prenatal development

Living Universe, Part One:
> Astrology I – Intro to the four charts: Moon (epoch), Sun (spiritual nativity), Saturn, (reincarnation), Death chart; good visual image
> Astrology II – Good on hermetic rule and Birth chart; intro real zodiac; example of Wagner chart
> Astrology III – Moon graph and interpretation of Wagner's chart/moon graph bio

The Prenatal Horoscope cont'd: Epoch and etheric body; the Houses

Practical Approach I:
> Feb. 1967 – Copernicus and Moon Graph in bio

Practical Approach II:
> Jul. 1968 – manual calculation of ASC ; Sidereal Time; ASC meaning
> May 1970 – on time rhythms; Moon graph for 7 years

Articles online, not published

> Constellation of Cosmic Thought, P1-3 Epoch
> Jul. 1937   Astrology I – Prenatal Astrology
> Aug. 1937   Astrology II – Prenatal Astrology
> Sep. 1937   Astrology III – Prenatal Astrology
> Oct. 1937   Astrology III (cont'd) – Prenatal Astrology

Moon Nodes in Spiritual Nativity

Isis Sophia I:
>14th Letter

Living Universe, Part One:
>Gateway of the Moon, 2 chapters – Spiritual Nativity with Wagner and Nietzsche examples

Progressions/Time Conversions

Practical Approach II:
>May 1970 – on time rhythms; Moon graph for 7 years
>
>Jun./Jul. 1970 – Moon graph and Saturn progression/conversion
>
>Aug. 1970 – Saturn conversion cont'd;

Practical Approach III:
>Aug. 1971 – Time Ratios: Saturn conversion and 747 BC/6 BC

Death Chart

Isis Sophia III, Part One:
>Chapters 2–3 – general on stars of death and Tycho Brahe death chart, plus good intro to geo and helio perspectives in explaining Tycho death chart.

Isis Sophia III, Part One:
>Chapter 4 – good on general reason for importance of death chart; then Raphael example of death chart

Living Universe, Part One:
>Horoscope of Death – Ex. of Napoleon, following Saturn
>
>Horoscopes of Birth and Death – Dante death impulse picked up by Michaelangelo and Novalis; how themes are carried over after death ex. Tolstoy birth and death
>
>The Horoscope of Death and the Life After Death – path to birth & path out after death, ex. Raphael, Byron, Schiller, Tolstoy, Saturn for Beethoven; Moon nodes and leaving Moon sphere
>
>Thoughts on the Future of Astrology – good on entire significance of death chart and Wagner ex.

Cosmology Course:
>Eclipses – "take the Moon node at the time when it reaches the place where the Sun was at death" to find entry from kamaloka to spiritland

Historical Personalities Studies: Examples and tools of chart interpretation

Isis Sophia I:
> Letters 20th – 24th: complete chart study Tycho Brahe

Isis Sophia III, Part Two:
> Chapter 4 – Gestation– Lord Byron; Shakespeare; Goethe; Nietzsche

Isis Sophia III, Part Three:
> Chapter 2 – 12 Zodiac and prenatal development goes through each constellation with historical personalities examples

The Changing Countenance of Cosmology:
> Chapter 4 The Archangel Michael and Astrosophy – Beethoven and Raphael
>
> Chapter 6: The Workings of the Planets and their Spheres – DaVinci helio chart

Living Universe, Part One:
> Napoleon's Horoscope of Birth esp. Mars, Uranus, Neptune
>
> The Riddle of Emanuel Swedenborg
>
> Darwin and Haeckel
>
> The Zodiac – Evolution of Western consciousness: Aquinas & Scholasticism w/Pisces/Virgin; Templars & Archer; Meister Eckhardt & Mysticism – Gemini
>
> The Zodiac cont'd – 12 constellations and evolution of modern Western consciousness through examples of biographies; good zodiac table description
>
> Horoscopes of Birth and Death – Dante death impulse picked up by Michaelangelo and Novalis; how themes are carried over after death ex. Tolstoy birth and death
>
> The Horoscope of Death and the Life After Death – path to birth & path out after death, ex. Raphael, Byron, Schiller, Tolstoy, Saturn for Beethoven; Moon nodes and leaving Moon sphere

Drama of the Universe, Part Two:
> Chapter 5, Connection of Individuals with Cosmos – Heliocentric charts: Ben Franklin; Robespierre; Raphael & Michaelangelo and bio events; Goethe and bio events
>
> Chapter 6, Incarnation and the Stars – helio chart and Moon graph bios of Nietzsche and Lord Byron

Chapter 7, Death and the Stars – helio charts of Tycho Brahe, birth, bio events, death; Lord Byron, epoch, bio events, death; Goethe bio events, death

Cosmology Course:
- Saturn I and Saturn II – on Saturn in 1954 in Scales, historical similar of Saturn in Scales at death, Steiner, Mani, Copernicus, Tycho Brahe, Kepler
- Sun-2 – Sun in Scales and on Tycho Brahe (former Julian Apostate, and Herzeleide)

Practical Approach I:
- Dec. 1966 – Willi says letters moving forward will cover current events and historical personalities; starts with Aph Mars and DaVinci, includes following Saturn back through life
- On Copernicus:
- Jan. 1967 – Mars and Pluto focus with Copernicus epoch –birth geo and helio
- Feb. 1967 – good on why helio, Copernicus Moon graph and bio events
- Mar. 1967 – Copernicus Saturn in Twins and Bull, historic similars
- Apr. 1967 – Copernicus Jupiter in Libra to Scorpio conj Uranus, Neptune
- May 1967 – Copernicus Saturn aspects Uranus/Neptune in node Mars
- Jun. 1967 – Copernicus Mars, Venus, Mercury
- Start Historic Similars Saturn in Constellations:
- Jul. 1967 – Saturn in Aries historic similars
- Aug. 1967 – Ex. Saturn, Uranus, Pluto in Aries: Soloviev and Van Gogh
- Sept. 1967 – Saturn Taurus; Saturn Twins; start Saturn Cancer
- Oct. 1967 – Saturn Cancer, with JFK example, and Tolstoy, Beethoven
- Nov. 1967 – Saturn Leo list, with example of Emerson
- Dec. 1967 – Emerson cont'd and other Saturn Leo
- Jan. 1968 – Saturn Libra: Tycho Brahe, Steiner, Goethe, Kepler, Darwin, Lincoln
- Feb. 1968 – Saturn Scorpio similar, example of Lenin
- Mar. 1968 – Lenin Scorpio cont'd; Saturn in Archer similar
- Apr. 1968 – Saturn in Archer cont'd; Saturn in Capricorn
- May 1968 – Saturn in Aquarius; Saturn in Pisces

Practical Approach II:
- Jun. 1968 – Jupiter in Constellations: Aries, ex. Ulysses Grant & Gr. Conj; other similar; Nodes of Mars and generals

Jul. 1968 – Jupiter in Taurus ex. Lord Byron; manual calculation of ASC using Sidereal time and tables; ASC meaning

Aug. 1968 – ASC using signs; historical similar ASC in Cancer; Byron cont'd with Saturn, Pluto, Venus at MC; open sector of Sun curve as head; Jupiter in Taurus cont'd similars; Byron Mars geo and helio with similar

Sept. 1968 – Byron cont'd Moon graph in biography

Oct. 1968 – Jupiter in Gemini, example of Nostradamus and similars; Mars of Nostradamus in Gemini and similar with Mars Gemini. Steiner at death ex.

Nov. 1968 – Jupiter in Cancer, ex. Wagner and similar; Wagner Mars and similar

Dec. 1968 – Wagner Venus and Mars and Mercury with similars; Sun Wagner

Jan. 1969 – Jupiter in Lio example Paracelsus and Hahneman with similars

Feb. 1969 – Jupiter in Virgo ex. Raphael and similars; Jupiter in Libra Tolstoy

Mar. 1969 – Jupiter Libra similars; Jupiter Scorpio Van Gogh, Soloviev, Copernicus and Lenin death. Ex. of resurrection and death perspectives. Jupiter in Archer similars and Steiner death

Jun. 1969 – Jupiter Capricorn similars, Novalis, Tycho Brahe; Jupiter in Aquarius similars; Jupiter in Pisces similars. Start Chart study of Tycho Brahe

Tycho Brahe full study, Jun. – Nov. 1969:

Jul. 1969 – Tycho Brahe: 3 zodiacs; houses explained; epoch explained, geo chart

Aug. 1969 – Tycho Brahe bio and geo chart interpretation, esp Saturn

Sept. 1969 – Tycho Brahe bio and geo chart cont'd

Oct. 1969 – Tycho Brahe Heliocentric chart interpretation

Nov. 1969 – Tycho Brahe cont'd esp. Saturn Jupiter heliocentric

Practical Approach III:

Feb. 1971 – Chart of Shelley, geo and helio, similars

Mar. 1971 – Shelley cont'd; Venus/Damascus; conn to Savonarola and GB Shaw

SOLOVIEV

Apr. 1971 – Start SOLOVIEV charts/bio

May 1971 – Soloviev cont'd chart interpretation and bio

Jun. 1971 – Soloviev cont'd

Dec. 1971 – Chart conversation betw Goethe/Schiller; chart Goethe death; Mars elements & Venus elements; historic similars

Jan. 1972 – Elements Venus and Mars; Historic similars P/A Mars and Goetheanism; Connection of Steiner's work/lectures and P/A Mars

Feb. 1972 – Second Coming; death chart Raphael

Practical Approach III, Part 2:

Comprehensive Chart Interpretation of KEPLER

Chapter 1, Aug.–Oct. 1972: Kepler chart study – complete breakdown of manual construction of Kepler geo chart, with explanation of epoch, and Moon graph in bio; heliocentric complete chart with historic similars

Chapter 2, Nov. 1972–Jan. 1973: Full Kepler Chart interpretation – planets in elements and zodiac; Conn to Taurus; Steiner on Mystic Lamb; Jupiter in Pisces; Mars movement; Sun movement conjunct Mars at Epoch in Archer at Birth; Earth in elements

Chapter 3, Feb.–Apr. 1973: Kepler cont'd inner planets: Sun path and corresponding bio events; Sun-Moon relation at his death; geo Mercury movements and bio; helio Mercury; Venus and bio; Venus and 3 years loops; helio Venus

Chapter 4, May–Jul. 1973: Kepler Moon factors; ASC/DESC; Hermetic rule; Moon nodes and Spir Nativity/Philosophies; then start history of Elements in general

Chapter 8, May–Jul. 1974: Practical Application Concerning the Geocentric and Heliocentric Approach: Ralph Waldo Emerson Geo and Helio Chart

HELIOCENTRIC PERSPECTIVE

Drama of the Universe, Part Two:

Chapter 1 – Heliocentric intro and natural disasters charts

Practical Approach I:

Jan. 1966 – on Helio Elements, with locations

Feb. 1967 – GOOD intro on why helio now

Practical Approach III:

Nov. 1970 – first letter, EXCELLENT on why Helio

Dec. 1970 – Perihelion Jupiter at VP and relation to task of 5th Pisces Age

Practical Approach III, Part Two:

The Elements of the Planetary Spheres Their History and Their Realization in Human Biographies
Chapter 4, May–Jul. 1973:
After Kepler, CHART of ALL ELEMENTS; history of Mercury elements
Chapter 5, Aug.–Oct. 1973:
Historic Examples of Associations with the Nodes of Mercury
Register I: Nodes Mercury
Register II: P/A Mercury
History of the Elements of Venus
Register III: P/A Venus
Historic Examples of Associations with the Elements of Venus
Chapter 6, Nov. 1973–Jan. 1974:
The History of the Elements of Mars
Register IV: P/A Mars
Comments on Historical Examples
History of the Elements of Jupiter
Register V: Nodes of Jupiter
Historic Events in Connection with the Jupiter Nodes
Chapter 7, Feb.–Apr. 1974:
Register VI: P/A Jupiter
Historic Events in Connection with the Perihelion-Aphelion of Jupiter
Elements of the Sphere of Saturn
Register VII: Nodes Saturn
Historic Events in Connection with the Nodes of Saturn
Register VIII: P/A Saturn
Historic Events in Connection with the Perihelion-Aphelion of Saturn
Elements of the Newly Discovered Planets: Uranus, Neptune, Pluto
Chaper 8, May–Jul. 1974:
Ralph Waldo Emerson Geo and Helio Chart Interpretation
Practical Application Concerning the Geocentric and Heliocentric Approach

Lemniscate Perspective

Living Universe, Part Two:
    Lecture Four – 12 Jan. 1956 – entire lecture excellent
Cosmology Course, Part One:
    Sun 1 – includes about 33 yr rhythm

Appendix IV: Willi Sucher's Books Indexed by Title

Isis Sophia I: Introducing Astrosophy
    1st letter: Intro the solar system
    2nd letter to end 6th Letter: Cosmic Evolution/Occult Science
    6th letter end–middle 7th Letter: Human Form
    8th letter: General Planets
    9th letter: Saturn, with historical examples
    10th letter: Jupiter, with historical examples
    11th letter: Jupiter cont'd and Mars, with historical examples
    12th letter: Mars, historical examples
    13th letter: Sun in the 12 constellations
    14th letter Moon Nodes and Spiritual Nativity
    15th letter: Sun Epoch curve and open space, historic personalities
    16th letter: Moon
    17th letter: Moon in constellations, historical examples
    18th letter: Venus: need to know Ancient Sun evolution
    19th letter: Mercury: rhythms, switch with Venus, evolution
    20th–24th letter: complete chart study Tycho Brahe
    Star Events at the Time of Christ: Sun during 3 Years and Imagination of Lamb of God in Zodiac

Isis Sophia II: Outline of A New Star Wisdom
Part One
    Greek Mythologies of Constellations
Part Two
    The Threefold Human Being
    Comprehensive Occult Science evolution: A. Saturn, A. Sun, A. Moon, Earth
Part Three
    Each planetary sphere: Saturn - Moon; especially good on Sun and origin of spheres.

Isis Sophia III: Our Relationship with the Stars

Part One
>Chapter 1: Saturn in relation to two World Wars
>
>Chapters 2-3: general on stars of death and Tycho Brahe death chart, plus good intro to geo and helio perspectives in explaining Tycho death chart.
>
>Chapter 4: good on general reason for importance of death chart; then Raphael example of death chart

Part Two:
>Chapter 1: good on astronomy and astrosophy as bringing together correct observation with contemplation/meditation. One of the gravest dangers of the cosmologist, in the sense of spiritual science, is that he or she gets submerged in calculation.
>
>Chapter 2: Embryology and Stars
>
>Chapter 3: Physical Deformities and Embryo development (cranial; micro and hydrocephalus; limbs deformed)
>
>Chapter 4: Gestation- Lord Byron; Shakespeare; Goethe; Nietsche

Part Three:
>Chapter 1: Embryology science and Hermetic Rule
>
>Chapters 2-12: Zodiac and prenatal development thru each constellation with historical personalities examples

Part Four:
>Chapters 1-3: general history and Precession of Equinoxes/cultural ages
>
>Chapter 4: VP Pisces, current Age
>
>Chapter 5: VP Crab
>
>Chapter 6: VP Twins
>
>Chapter 7: VP Bull
>
>Chapter 8: VP Ram
>
>Chapter 9: VP Waterman
>
>Chapter 10: VP Goat; and on Pegasus/Andromeda myth

Cosmic Christianity and The Changing Countenance of Cosmology

The Changing Countenance of Cosmology:
>Chapter 1: The Origin of Occult Symbols on the Basis of Cosmic Rhythmology - On origins of forms: Venus form, Mercury form, Mars double square; Golden triangle

Chapter 2: The Development of Cosmology in History: - history of cosmology and Copernicanism, introduction of spiritual heliocentric

Chapter 3: Roads to a Modern Cosmology and Astrosophy – Good intro new astrosophy, change needed for spiritual star wisdom

Chapter 4: The Archangel Michael and Astrosophy – on role of Michael in connecting us to stars, examples of Beethoven and Raphael

Chapter 5 - Symbology and Cosmology – explanation of zodiac symbols/glyphs

Chapter 6: The Workings of the Planets and their Spheres – on cosmic wave; Da Vinci helio chart

Chapter 7: Turning Points in History I - Pluto & Uranus conjunctions

Chapter 8: Turning Points in History II - Saturn/Jupiter Great Conjunctions history

Cosmic Christianity

Best source on stars during the Three Years of Christ; through each planet, Saturn - Mercury

Manifestation in History: On Saturn time conversion and historical events; Return of Etheric Christ and history

Living Universe: Studies in Astrosophy

Part I:

Astrology I: Intro to the four charts: Moon (epoch), Sun (spiritual nativity), Saturn, (reincarnation), Death chart; good visual image

Astrology II: Good on hermetic rule and Birth chart; intro real zodiac; example of Wagner chart

Astrology III: Moon graph and interpretation of Wagner's chart/moon graph bio

The Prenatal Horoscope: Epoch and etheric body; the Houses

Gateway of the Moon (2 chapters): Moon Nodes and Spiritual Nativity; examples Wagner and Nietzsche

The Horoscope of Death: Ex. of Napoleon, following Saturn

Napoleon's Horoscope of Birth: focus on Mars relation to Uranus, Neptune

The Riddle of Emanuel Swedenborg: Chart interpretation

Darwin and Haeckel: Chart interpretation

The Zodiac – Evolution of Western consciousness: Aquinas & Scholasticism w/Pisces/Virgin; Templars & Archer; Meister Eckhardt & Mysticism -Gemini

The Zodiac cont'd: 12 constellations and evolution of modern Western consciousness through examples of biographies; good zodiac table description

Horoscopes of Birth and Death – Dante death impulse picked up by Michaelangelo and Novalis; how themes are carried over after death, ex. Tolstoy birth and death

The Horoscope of Death and the Life After Death – path to birth & path out after death, ex. Raphael, Byron, Schiller, Tolstoy, Saturn for Beethoven; Moon nodes and leaving Moon sphere

Thoughts on the Future of Astrology: good on old vs new astrology and significance of death chart for new approach to stars; changing stars

Part II:

Lecture One: January 9, 1956 – good on nature of Sun and Wave process

Lecture Two: January 10, 1956 – exploring glyphs in human form

Lecture Three: January 11, 1956 – wave theory and working through of each planet sphere qualities

Lecture Four: January 12, 1956 – entire lecture excellent on Lemniscate perspective

The Drama of the Universe: A New Interpretation

Part One:

Chapter 1: astronomical facts about heliocentric universe and each planet

Chapters 2–5: groupings of zodiac with constellations above and below

Mythology of first group: Ram/Fishes, Andromeda-Perseus complex, Cetus, Eridanus

Mythology of second group: Twins/Bull/Crab, Auriga, Orion, Sirius

Mythology of third group: Lion/Virgin, Bootes, Hydra with Cup and Ravn

Mythology of fourth group: Scales/Scorpion/Archer, Antaries, Ophiucus w/ Serpent, Hercules, Dragon, Lupus, Centaurus

Mythology of fifth group: Capricorn/Waterman, Great Sea, Southern Fish w/ Fomalhaut, Lyre, Eagle, Swan, Pegasus

Part Two:

Chapter 1, Events in Nature: Heliocentric intro and natural disasters charts

Chapter 2, Interplay Between Cosmos and Earth: cosmic wave/densification theory; natural disasters from heliocentric view

Chapter 3, History and Cosmos: heliocentric view of each planetary realm. Historical charts: Martin Luther, 30 Years War, Fall of Bastille,

Napoleon, murder of Ferdinand Archduke (WWI), WWI armistice, Treaty of Versailles, Nazis 1933, Lenin, Russian Revolution

Chapter 4, Background of Humanity's Ideas/Discoveries: helio charts of: 1492 Columbus discovery; Steam engine; Electricity and Magnetism events 1600–1831; X-Ray and Radioactivity; Hiroshima; Modern astronomy events 1496-1930; Great Fire of Chicago

Chapter 5, Connection of Individuals with Cosmos: Heliocentric charts: Ben Franklin; Robespierre; Raphael & Michaelangelo and bio events; Goethe and bio events

Chapter 6, Incarnation and the Stars: helio chart and Moon graph bios of Nietzsche and Lord Byron

Chapter 7, Death and the Stars: helio charts of Tycho Brahe, birth, bio events, death; Lord Byron, epoch, bio events, death; Goethe bio events, death

Cosmology Course I (series of short lectures with Q&A after)

Return of King Arthur: on Tintagel and Arthur and Great Bear

Saturn I and Saturn II: on Saturn, 1954 in Scales, historical similars of Saturn in Scales at death, Steiner, Mani, Copernicus, Tycho Brahe, Kepler, Faust Prologue

Sun 1: about 33 year rhythm

Sun-2: Sun in Scales and on Tycho Brahe (former Julian Apostate and Herzeleide)

Moon, Moon Node-1 and Moon Node: 3 lectures general about Moon sphere and nodes

Eclipses: about "take the Moon node at the time when it reaches the place where the Sun was at death" to find entry from kamaloka to spiritland"

Cosmology: good on new star wisdom and Klingsor story, good Q&A on decadence of mysteries and star wisdom gone wrong

Mars: on sequence of planets and evolutionary cycles, cosmic evolution; two halves of Earth evolution- Mars & Mercury, Mars movement; on zodiac symbols Aries through Virgo

Mars – Conjunctions and Loops: on zodiac symbols Aries through Fishes; on mars loops, lemniscate and mars geometry

Mars and the Eightfold Path: Mars 16 petals, Buddhist path

Occult Mercury - Astronomical Venus: on switch and about planet Venus and KHW exercises for 10 petaled chakra; Venus and 3 Years

Jupiter: Good on Jupiter w A Sun and future; 2 petaled chakra and lemniscate

Mercury (Occult Venus) in Relationship with Venus (Occult Mercury): explains switch in names, Mercury geometry, chakra; Mercury and 3 Years

The Planetary Aspects in 1955: example of how to look at stars for the year

Christmas and the Cosmic Rhythms:

Great Conjunctions: Golden Triangle conjunctions and Christianity

Shepherds: Gr Conjunction and impulse of Spiritual Freedom

Kings: Gr. Conjunction and impulse of Brotherhood

St. Paul: Gr Conjunction and impulse of Equality

Individual Lectures

The Turn of the Century – Saul/Paul: on AD 34 and AD 2000; Etheric Christ return and Saturn conversion, history and Gr Conj; good on how we speak to stars

Christmas Season: on the Magi vision; explanation of Steiner stating Sun in Virgo at first Christmas (?); the Christmas Star

Essay on Freedom: Steiner lecture from Mysticism at the Dawn of the Modern Age

Practical Approach I, Star Journals One, Toward A New Astrosophy: Aug. 1965 – May 1968

Introduction: good on what new astrosophy should be

Oct. 1965: on planets for month with focus on Uranus/Pluto conjunctions every 253 years in Leo and Aries now, current triple, Oct. 1965, April and June. 1966; history and conjunctions; relation to Moon nodes, Grail stream and Goethe's life

Nov. 1965: Uranus/Pluto cont'd in history: Goethe Green Snake; Chemical Wedding, Eschenbach Grail story; cosmic origin of Grail; planets density

Dec. 1965 – Wave theory of solar system and connection to Grail; planets distances

Jan. 1966 – Saturn, Jupiter, Mars intro; focus on helio elements with locations; start Saturn

Feb. 1966 – Good Saturn, Jupiter, Mars spheres, in Theosophy, rhythms, in body, etc.

Mar. 1966 – Good Venus and Mercury, in Theosophy, rhythms, in body, etc.

Apr. 1966 – Venus cont'd; about Moon and meaning at birth; meaning Earth and Sun, helio & geo; start outer planets; start Uranus & Neptune; Mars/Sun conj in commentary

May 1966 – Uranus, Neptune, Pluto Theosophy and in chart and historically; Good summary of all planets

Jun. 1966 – general on precession of VP; and start Zodiac in Persia, Zaruna Akarana

Jul. 1966 – Aries and Taurus and surrounding constellations, (same as Isis Sophia III)

Aug. 1966 – Gemini, Cancer, Lion

Sept. 1966 – Leo, Virgo

Oct. 1966 – Libra, Scorpio

Nov. 1966 – Archer, Capricorn, Fishes

Dec. 1966 – Willi says letters moving forward will cover current events and historical personalities; starts with Aph Mars and death of Da Vinci, Saturn back through life

[Jan. – Jun. 1967: On Copernicus]

Jan. 1967 – good on stars at birth, quote from Michael Mystery; good for understanding how chart conn. to person; Mars and Pluto focus with Copernicus epoch-birth geo and helio; epoch as ground plan/intentions for coming life; birth positions more about past life continuing in karma of present, star brother

Feb. 1967 – good on why helio now, Copernicanism denuded univers of notions of divine, giant mechanism; distinction betw. Copernicanism and spiritual helio world view; Copernicus Moon graph and bio events; hermetic as triplicity of Sun, Moon, Earth

Mar. 1967 – on Mercury 20 year cycle of double triangle and meaning in life; Copernicus interpretation cont'd Saturn in Twins and Bull, historic similars

Apr. 1967 – Copernicus Jupiter in Libra (Scales of Osiris) to Scorpio conj Uranus, Neptune; good on occultations of planets by Moon and negative aspects re Saturn and Venus; angular aspects and signs relation to elements and temperaments, diagram

May 1967 – Copernicus Saturn aspects Uranus/Neptune in node Mars, historic similar; angular aspects continued, Venus angles; Steiner on Copernicus (Life Betw. Death and New Birth, lecture V); decline of Mars in middle ages, souls with scientific inclinations picked up materialistic impulses then in Mars sphere, i.e. Copernicus; Mars and Arabism; Henry Navigator and Templar impulse in relation to exploration and inventive impulses of present age

Jun. 1967 – Copernicus: Mars, Venus, Mercury; Andromeda/Pegasus myth;

[Start Historic Similars Saturn in Constellations]

Jul. 1967 – Saturn in Aries meaning and historic similars, ex. Dante, Savanarola, Durer

Aug. 1967 – Ex. Saturn, Uranus, Pluto in Aries: Soloviev and Van Gogh

Sept. 1967 - Saturn Taurus – practical realization of ideals; Saturn Twins – experience duality, divisions, contradictions of human condition; start Saturn Cancer – live in earthly house, painful separation from divine, need for conscious understanding of this.

Oct. 1967 – Geo needs Imagination; Helio needs Inspiration; Saturn Cancer cont'd, JFK, and Tolstoy, Beethoven

Nov. 1967 – on Eclipse life cycles; Saturn Leo list, with example of Emerson

Dec. 1967 – Emerson cont'd and other Saturn Leo; Saturn Virgo (Schiller quote, "every individual bears within a second ideal man and it is the noblest task of existence to grow more and more into his likeness")

Jan. 1968 – in helio chart constellations not as important as activity of planets in elements; Saturn Libra: Tycho Brahe, Steiner, Goethe, Kepler, Darwin, Lincoln

Feb. 1968 – Mercury loops on realization of will impulses, Mercury conn. to life of will spiritually hidden in limbs which receives constant impacts from thought realm therefore spiritual handling of Mercury depends on harmonious, disciplined relation of will to thinking; on P & A of spheres; Saturn Scorpio relation to mysteries of death and impulse for resurrection; example of Lenin as failure of potential; good statement on general interpretation and chart as ocean of facts and can be drowned in it.

Mar. 1968 – interpretation of Elements of Mercury; Lenin Scorpio cont'd; Lenin past life and Venus loop; Moon as hieroglyph of descent of soul and direction of incarnation; ASC birth conn of Moon, etheric element and Earth incarnation; ASC of Epoch line of entry from spirit world to Moon sphere; Lenin ASC at Epoch Cancer, materialism to bolshevism; ASC of Epoch and themes in Lenin life; Nodes of Mercury meaning;

[Saturn in Archer similars]

Apr. 1968 – Saturn in Archer cont'd – expect wide range of centaurian potentials; Saturn in Capricorn similars, Hahneman good example of realization of potential of Saturn Capricorn; Marie Antoinette, Henry VIII, Louis XIV as fallen examples of Saturn Capricorn, spiritual potential becomes materialistic extravagance/arrogance

May 1968 – Saturn in Aquarius conn with periphery, universal, ex. Cayce; Saturn in Pisces, good on interpretation, persons of this age who work with mastery of Earth forces, ex. Ben Franklin, James Watt, Marconi, Rutherford

(1st nuclear reaction), Newton, Einstein; good on 2 fishes and conflict of past mode of thinking (Aries age) applied to new ways to transform Earth realm. Ghosts of romanism perpetuate in present as block to new.

Practical Approach II, Star Journals Two, Toward A New Astrosophy: Jun. 1968 – Oct. 1970

Jun. 1968 – Jupiter in Constellations: Aries, ex. Ulysses Grant & Gr. Conj; Grant past life; other similars Gandhi, JFK, Charlemagne; Nodes of Mars relation to military generals

Jul. 1968 - Jupiter in Taurus ex. Lord Byron; dramatic birth image Venus, Saturn, Pluto conjunct at MC; good on manual calculation of ASC and Sidereal time and tables; ASC meaning;

Good description of Epoch and descent of spirit germ

Aug. 1968 – with ASC use signs (later writings not this) historical similar ASC in Cancer; Byron cont'd with Saturn, Pluto, Venus at MC; open sector of Sun curve as head; Jupiter in Taurus cont'd similars; Byron Mars geo and helio with similar

Sept. 1968 – Byron cont'd Moon graph in biography; on early death and ether substance sacrificed for later generation to draw from

Oct. 1968 - Jupiter in Gemini, example of Nostradamus and similars; Mars of Nostradamus in Gemini and similar with Mars Gemini. Steiner at death ex.

Nov. 1968 – Jupiter in Cancer, ex. Wagner and similar; Wagner Mars and similar

Dec. 1968 – Wagner Venus and Mars and Mercury with similars; Sun Wagner

Jan. 1969 – Jupiter in Leo example Paracelsus and Hahneman with similars

Feb. 1969 – Jupiter in Virgo ex. Raphael and similars; Jupiter in Libra Tolstoy

Mar. 1969 – Jupiter Libra similars; Jupiter Scorpio Van Gogh, Soloviev, Copernicus and Lenin death. Ex. of resurrection and death perspectives. Jupiter in Archer similars and Steiner death

Apr. 1969 – Easter current events and stars; Venus loop; VP movement; CMP's

May 1969 – Great Conj Triangle rotation 1563-1961 image; Gr Conj events; 6 BC

Jun. 1969 – Jupiter Capricorn similars, Novalis, Tycho Brahe; Jupiter in Aquarius similars; Jupiter in Pisces similars. Start Chart study of Tycho Brahe

[Tycho Brahe full study, June - November 1969]

Jul. 1969 – Tycho Brahe: 3 zodiacs; houses explained; epoch explained, geo chart

Aug. 1969 – Tycho Brahe bio and geo chart interpretation, esp Saturn

Sept. 1969 – Tycho Brahe bio and geo chart cont'd

Oct. 1969 – Tycho Brahe Heliocentric chart interpretation

Nov. 1969 – Tycho Brahe cont'd esp. Saturn Jupiter heliocentric
Dec. 1969 - on first of 5 oppositions Saturn/Jupiter; more on Gr Conj. In history
Jan. 1970 – Venus pentagram and loops
Feb. 1970 – Helio elements and revolution/wars: French, Russian, Nazis, Hiroshima
Mar. 1970 – Countenance of 20th century: chart of Gr Conj 1901 and 6 BC history
Apr. 1970 – Countenance of 20th cent. Cont'd: 6 BC Conj elaborated; also Uranus opp Pluto theme 1901 and Grail stream and Rosenkreuz.
May 1970 – on time rhythms; Moon graph for 7 years
Jun. 1970 – Countenance of 20th cent. Cont'd: 1901 Gr Conj through Moon graph rhythm of 7 years per Moon cycle
July 1970 – Countenance of 20th cent contd: Gr Conj 1901 and meaning for future century; relate to 6 challenge for now; Saturn progression/conversion
Aug. 1970 – Saturn conversion of 1901 cont'd in historical events
Sept. 1970 – Saturn conversion 1901 for Hitler rise and Genghis Kahn
Oct. 1970 – Final *Star Journal* letter; 20th century cont'd: Cathars, Templars, 869 Council, Grail, Rosicrucians

Practical Approach III, Star Journals Three, Toward A New Astrosophy: Nov. 1970- Jul. 1974

Nov. 1970 – first letter, good intro to why Helio
Dec. 1970 – Perihelion Jupiter at VP and relation to task of 5th Pisces Age
Jan. 1971 – Per Jupiter 1950 ; Pisces, Andromeda, this century and thinking change, Phoenix
Feb. 1971 – Chart of Shelley, geo and helio, similars
Mar. 1971 – Shelley cont'd; Venus/Damascus; conn to Savonarola and GB Shaw
Apr. 1971 – Start Soloviev charts/bio
May 1971 – Soloviev cont'd chart interpretation and bio
Jun. 1971 – Soloviev cont'd
Jul. 1971 – What is Holy Grail? Connection to Gr Conjunctions, 6 & 747 BC
Aug. 1971 – Spiritual Nativity of Matthew Jesus Child, 6 BC Gr conj and Moon node; Time Ratios: Saturn conversion and 747 BC/6 BC
Sept. 1971 – Moon nodes, 6 BC Jesus children; man sick 38 years, Holy Grail
Oct. 1971 – Celtic Folk Spirit/Grail/Esoteric Christianity-Grail Stream and Gr Conj's and Uranus Pluto; Templars, Rosenkreuz
Nov. 1971 – Rosicrucian stream cont'd; Gr Conj 1444 chart; 1459 Chym Wedding; Moon Nodes in Goethe's life

Dec. 1971 – Chart conversation betw Goethe/Schiller; chart Goethe death; Mars elements & Venus elements; historic similars

Jan. 1972 – Elements Venus and Mars; Historic similars P/A Mars and Goetheanism; Connection of Steiner's work/lectures and P/A Mars

Feb. 1972 – Second Coming; death chart Raphael ; astrosophy as astrology of Grail; Grail cont'd; Steiner Jan 12 1910 Annunciation of the Second Coming. *The very first of those lectures,…its stellar companionship. Before the lecture, Rudolf Steiner was urged to abstain from delivering it, because there were "dreadful events going on in the heavens." We produce the configuration in the chart in Fig. 16 and bad stars*

Mar. 1972 – Death Raphael cont'd; Sistine Madonna; Saturn conversion for 2nd coming 1935 as world Damascus experience; chart of AD 34 Paul and 1935 Saturn compared; 1901 Steiner work; Geo chart of 3 Years

Apr. 1972 – Second Coming – Etheric body of Christ envelope around Earth as New Grail; 1917 and 1935 and relation to etheric Christ stars; Planets during 3 Years and relation to 1935 years

May 1972 – Golden Triangle, Kalichakra and Gr Conj's Chart with years

Jun. 1972 – Gr Conj in node Mars and deed of Buddha, Buddha and 8-fold path relation to Mars & Venus; diagram Mars/Sun conj's; helio elements and relation to Venus elements; Buddha and Luke Jesus

Jul. 1972 – AD 34 Venus Sun conj; loops of Venus and Damascus impulse in history; helio elements of Venus & Jupiter- historic similars; elements of Mars with Neptune

Practical Approach III, Part Two

Elements of the planetary spheres and their realization in human biographies
[chapters 1–4: Comprehensive Chart Interpretation of Kepler]

Chapter 1, Aug. –Oct. 1972: Kepler chart study – complete breakdown of manual construction of Kepler geo chart, with explanation of epoch, and Moon graph in bio; heliocentric complete chart with historic similars

Chapter 2, Nov. 1972–Jan. 1973: Full Kepler Chart interpretation – planets in elements and zodiac; Conn to Taurus; Steiner on Mystic Lamb; Jupiter in Pisces; Mars movement; Sun movement conjunct Mars at Epoch in Archer at Birth; Earth in elements

Chapter 3, Feb.–Apr. 1973: Kepler cont'd inner planets: Sun path and corresponding bio events; Sun-Moon relation at his death; geo Mercury movements and bio; helio Mercury; Venus and bio; Venus and 3 years loops; helio Venus

Chapter 4, May–July 1973: Kepler Moon factors; ASC/DESC; Hermetic rule; Moon nodes and Spir Nativity/Philosophies; after Kepler, CHART of ALL ELEMENTS; history of Mercury elements

Chapter 5, August-September-October 1973: Historic Examples of Associations with the Nodes of Mercury; Register I: Nodes Mercury; Register II: P/A Mercury; History of the Elements of Venus; Register III: P/A Venus; Historic Examples of Associations With the Elements of Venus

Chapter 6, Nov. 1973–Jan. 1974: The History of the Elements of Mars; Register IV: P/A Mars; Comments on Historical Examples; History of the Elements of Jupiter; Register V: Nodes of Jupiter; Historic Events in Connection with the Jupiter Nodes

Chapter 7, Feb.–Apr. 1974: Register VI: P/A Jupiter; Historic Events in Connection with the Perihelion-Aphelion of Jupiter; Elements of the Sphere of Saturn; Register VII: Nodes Saturn; Historic Events in Connection with the Nodes of Saturn; Register VIII: P/A Saturn; Historic Events in Connection with the Perihelion-Aphelion of Saturn

Elements of the Newly Discovered Planets: Uranus, Neptune, Pluto

Chapter 8, May–July 1974: Ralph Waldo Emerson Geo and Helio Chart Interpretation; Practical Application Concerning the Geocentric and Heliocentric Approach

Appendix V: Books by Willi Sucher

All available as PDFs at astrosophy.com or paperback can be requested by emailing info@astrosophy.com (not included are misc lectures/articles available on the website)

Isis Sophia I: Introducing Astrosophy (originally published as monthly astronomical letters from April 1944 to March 1946)

Isis Sophia II: Outline of A New Star Wisdom (originally published in manuscript form in 1951)

Isis Sophia III: Our Relationship with the Stars (first published in 1952 in manuscript form as *Man and the Stars*)

Cosmic Christianity and The Changing Countenance of Cosmology
Two courses in same dates, originally published separately as *The Changing Countenance of Cosmology*: Eight lectures at Hawkwood College, Stroud, England, Aug. 24–31, 1969. First published in 1970 as a booklet.

Cosmic Christianity The Stars during the Three Years of Christ's Ministry and Practical Viewpoints with Regard to Evolution: Eight lectures at Hawkwood College, England, Aug. 24–31, 1969. First published in 1971 as a booklet.

Living Universe: Studies in Astrosophy (Part I, articles originally published in *The Modern Mystic and Science Review,* from Jan., 1937 to Jan., 1940 and Part II, lectures given at Peredur, Sussex, England–Jan. 1956, first published as *The Living Universe and the New Millennium*)

Cosmology Course (Lecture Series to Members at Rudolf Steiner House, London: Oct. 1–Apr. 1, 1955; plus three unrevised notes from lectures Christmas, 1954, London; plus two unrevised lectures from 1957 and 1969)

Practical Approach I, Star Journals One, toward A New Astrosophy: Aug. 1965–May, 1968, (first of a three volume study series from monthly journals and letters mailed to subscribers over nine years, all start with stars of the month)

Practical Approach II, Star Journals Two, toward A New Astrosophy: June, 1968–Oct. 1970, (second of a three volume study series from monthly journals and letters mailed to subscribers over nine years, all start with stars of the month)

Practical Approach III, Star Journals Three, toward A New Astrosophy: Nov. 1970–Jul. 1974 (third of a three volume study series from monthly journals and letters mailed to subscribers over nine years, all start with stars of the month)

www.ingramcontent.com/pod-product-compliance
Lightning Source LLC
Chambersburg PA
CBHW060111170426
43198CB00010B/853